The Final Fli‹  W

and other stories told by VHPA pilots

Published by

VIETNAM HELICOPTER PILOTS ASSOCIATION

©2016

Cover design by Kay Taylor http://www.kaysphotography.net

"A UH-1D helicopter prepares to land near a Viet Cong cave complex to pick up rice, bananas, and clothing found by Bravo troop Blues."

Public domain photograph by Sp/4 Richard Durrance,
US Army, 28 July 1967.
National Archive cc111-41869.

Compiled by Michael Lazares/Tom Hirschler
Published & edited by the staff of VHPA

All profits from the sales of this book go to the VHPA Scholarship Fund.

All VHPA Scholarships are administered for the VHPA by the AAAA (Army Aviation Association of America). The VHPA Memorial Scholarships are open only to the children and grandchildren of VHPA members in good standing currently or at their death. The only exception is if the father or grandfather flew helicopters in Vietnam and was killed in action in Vietnam.

Foreword

Michael Lazares approached the VHPA late in 2015 with an idea to publish a collection of stories (or "War Stories") which had been submitted to the VHPA and thereafter placed on our website. Because he is an accomplished author with several books to his credit, his idea was welcomed. He suggested all profits support the VHPA scholarship fund. *The proceeds of each of his books have been and still are, routed to various veterans' organizations.*

CW4 (Ret.) Tom Hirschler (Editor of the VHPA *Aviator*), and Michael read these narratives, made their choices, sought permission to use them in this book, and finally edited those candidates. One of those steps revealed an unfortunate statistic. With one exception, all submissions from Air Force, Navy and Marine pilots were unavailable for use, due to the passing of the various authors. The average age of a VHPA member is seventy-one. Except for the Army, no pilots in the armed services flew helicopters until completing college and often a fixed wing qualification first. Thus the vast majority of those who flew in the other services, have attained or exceeded seventy-six years, the average US male life expectancy for the current year.

Despite the lack of input from those services, the stories reflect a time when EVERY helicopter pilot faced extremely demanding tasks and had little or no history to guide him. The "Helicopter War", and the myriad uses of the machine during same is a "book" written by those who performed the type of feats described herein. The thirty narratives, written by twenty-eight authors, contain humor, frustration, fear, excitement, and of course, sorrow. We hope this treatment will enhance the legacy and preserve the history of the young men who went to Southeast Asia to fly helicopters. It is dedicated to the senior citizens who were those young men and especially **to the young men frozen in time.**

Thomas Kirk, Managing Editor VHPA *Aviator.*

April 2016

In Memoriam

On March 21, 2016, not long before completion of this book, we lost Michael Lazares to cancer. Without his encouragement and publishing knowledge, the book would not have been possible.

In a June 9, 2015 *Green Valley News* article, Michael said: Like those who fought in World War II, veterans of the Vietnam War are dying off. "I'm 70, and a lot of these guys are older than I am. It's really necessary to get stories out of these guys before they're gone."

That's what this book is about.

Fortunately for us, Michael's stories have been told.

Thanks, Michael!

Table of Contents

To return to TOC: Control + Click on Author's name.

Shootout on the Cambodian Border

Phil Courts

SAIGON, South Viet Nam (AP).....″ Headquarters also announced that three American helicopters were shot down Friday while supporting ground operations near the Plei Djereng Special Forces camp in the highlands close to the Cambodian border.″

11 November 1966 was a busy and dangerous time for US Forces in Vietnam. It's not surprising the AP made only brief mention to what I'm calling "The Shootout on the Cambodian Border". That same day, five U.S. planes were lost over North Vietnam; Viet Cong infiltrators inflicted heavy casualties on a platoon of American Marines near Da Nang; an ammunition dump near Saigon was blown up and the 45th Surgical Hospital was mortared. Add to this at least five other helicopters, two of them medevac flights, and an F-100 were shot down in the south and a CV-2 Caribou crashed in a rainstorm. This War Story looks in detail at the bravery, sacrifice and skill of the three crews shot down some forty- eight years ago at LZ Red Warrior.

Forty-eight years is a long time to remember an event that lasted no more than ten minutes, but for those who participated in the Shootout on the Cambodian Border or the "Pail Wail Doodle" as noted military historian S.L.A. Marshall called it, it was only yesterday.

On 11 November 1966, I was serving as the platoon leader of the gunship platoon, call sign "Croc 6", of the 119th AHC. We were assigned to the 52nd CAB located at Camp Holloway in the Central

Highlands. At the time, we were providing general aviation support during Operation Paul Revere IV to American and Vietnamese units.

As the day progressed on 10 Nov 1966, the command became increasingly concerned that a CIDG company and their Special Forces advisors were in danger of being overrun. The company, located on a dry lake bed called Pali Wali, was in contact with a large NVA unit. During the day they had suffered 40% casualties while killing some 58 NVA attackers. The location of the battle was close enough to the border that the NVA could bring observed indirect fire on the defenders from Cambodia.

That afternoon, the commander of the 119th, MAJ Bill Edwards, received a warning order to provide 18 slicks and 6 guns to support the insertion of the 1/12th Infantry into LZs approximately 15 miles west of Plei Djereng and very near the Cambodian border. Later that afternoon, I conducted an aerial reconnaissance of the area and reported to MAJ Edwards that although I did not receive any ground fire, there must be a large NVA unit in the area because of the many recently dug, but not occupied, foxholes I had observed.

Early on the morning of 11 November, the 119th AHC departed Holloway Army Airfield for Plei Djereng where we would stand-by while the necessary coordination was made with the ground commanders. As we shut down, I noticed a very confusing and dangerous rearm and refuel operation underway. It was dusty, space was limited and at least 20 helicopters were all jockeying for refueling before getting in position for the first lift. It didn't help any that we were sharing the space with an artillery battery of 175 mm guns firing continuously. These conditions would have tragic results later in the day.

Because my gun platoon was in the process of exchanging our old, tired B Models for new C Models, the 119th could put up only two gunships. The 117th AHC and D Troop 1/10th CAV would each provide two additional gunships. The plan that evolved was for D Troop and 117th guns to escort the initial lift and I would relieve one of the fire teams so we would always have two teams on station. With hindsight, this was not a very good plan. Having three gun teams, one on their first combat assault, who had never worked together before, was asking for trouble. Because of the urgency of the mission, all coordination had been by radio. As it turned out, the situation at Pali Wali became less critical and the ground commander changed the LZ. The new LZ was three KM from the battle at the dry lake bed. For the initial assault landing, suppressive fires were put down, there was no return fire and for subsequent lifts the LZ was considered cold. The first lift landed in LZ Red Warrior around 13:05, much later than originally planned.

Meanwhile back at Plei Djereng I was standing by with my crew: WO1 George W. Williams (on one of his first RVN missions), CE SGT Johnny F. Tompkins and G (gunner) PFC Bohannon. My wingman in 8600 was: AC CPT Walter R. Speare, P 1LT Dee W. Stone, CE SP4 Edmond D. Schoenig, and G SP4 Salvatore C. Gennardo.

At about 13:15, I received a radio call from MAJ Edwards to bring a fire team to the LZ at YA 590570 (Red Warrior LZ). I departed Plei Djereng with my wingman CPT Speare a few minutes later. I received a second radio call reminding me there were friendly troops on the ground, and to consider the LZ "cold". We approached the area at tree top level over pretty dense triple canopy. This put us at a dangerous altitude as we transitioned from dense vegetation to a fairly open grassy plain with elephant grass and small islands of taller trees in the LZ area.

Arriving at Red Warrior at approximately 13:30, I saw friendly troops in the LZ and a team of gunships to the north. WO Williams had the controls while I attempted to make radio contact with the unit on the ground. Almost immediately, CPT Speare called, "Croc 6, break right, you are receiving fire." As I looked up from my map, directly to my front I saw a large straw mat lift up, exposing a 12.7 machine gun on a tripod with four or more NVA crew in khaki uniforms. Their first burst of fire was high, passing above us. I grabbed the controls and dove for the ground while sharply turning right to put some triple canopy trees between us and the fire. SGT Tompkins dropped red smoke and told me he thought CPT Speare had been hit and crashed. Looking back as I completed my turn I saw his gunship on the ground burning, but with the fuselage intact. It looked like a survivable crash. After putting some distance from the NVA positions and not being able to make radio contact with CPT Speare, I maneuvered to setup a firing run from a new direction. Using the red smoke as a target reference point I made one run, firing all 24 rockets at the gun position that had initially fired on me before shifting their fire to my wingman. As I completed the run, I realized there were several more NVA gun positions in the area.* With no rockets and not wanting to engage 12.7s with my 40mm grenade launcher, it was time to think about an exit strategy.

CPT Speare and crew crashed in the middle of at least two NVA battalions. A battle raged for the next 24 hours in and around the area where they crashed. There were airstrikes and artillery barrages from both sides. It was late the next day after 1/12 Infantry had secured the area that we learned CPT Speare, LT Stone, and SP4 Schoenig were KIA and SP4 Gennardo was MIA. Later that night, Gennardo was found alive but in critical condition with burns over 75% of his body. He had tried to pull the crew out of the burning aircraft. When he discovered they were dead, he crawled nearly 1000 meters through artillery barrages and airstrikes back to the LZ.

I owe my life and the life of my crew to the brave and selfless actions of CPT Speare and his crew. As my wingman, they were in the perfect position to warn me I was about to over fly an enemy position and then instantly put effective fire on that position causing the fire to be shifted from my aircraft to theirs.

*It was later determined two companies (12 to 16 guns) of 12.7mm anti-aircraft machineguns were in the immediate vicinity of the original landing zone. One of the first two helicopters shot down crashed directly on an enemy gun *position, destroying the 12.7 anti-aircraft gun and killing three NVA soldiers.*

As I started a turn to the southeast to get back to the relative safety of the triple canopy, I heard a Mayday radio call from an unidentified helicopter that was on fire and going down. I learned later this call was from 08663, one of the 117th AHC gunships I had seen on the north side of the LZ as I approached the area. They were apparently making a gun run on the same NVA 12.7 anti-aircraft positions that had shot down my wingman, and I had just completed a rocket run on.

A witness on the ground described it this way: "08663 had just completed a gun run when they received 12.7 anti-aircraft fire. The aircraft was seen to slow down, settle in a level position toward the ground then disintegrate in the air and crash." The aircraft was burning in the air. The crew members were: CPT John Livingston AC, WO1 Terrence Rooney P, SGT Maynard Humes CE and SP4 Loren Reeves G. All were KIA.**

**A fifth body was found in the wreckage. I was not aware of this until reading a statement by Pruett Helm. It seems that while we were shut down in the PZ at Plei Djereng, LT Hess, a young Special Forces officer was trying to get a ride to the LZ to show us where the "big guns" were located. Tragically, he found a ride on 08663. There was some confusion about which helicopter LT Hess was on. He may have been on 8600.

Within seconds, I received a call from Shamrock 544 on guard that "he had lost his wingman*** and was joining on me." As I completed my turn, Shamrock 544 called again saying I was being fired on from my 4 o'clock position, and he was engaging. As I was breaking left, I looked back to my right and saw a C Model gunship less than 300 feet from me and between me and the enemy gun positions. Within seconds, the gunship was hit by a long burst of 12.7 tracer fire causing the fuel cell to explode and the tail boom to become partially separated. I saw Shamrock 544 not more than 100 feet above the trees, engulfed in flames, starting to go inverted and with both door gunners still firing. It was a sight you never forget. Only later did I learn their helicopter had already taken several hits and had smoke in the cockpit before coming to my assistance.

***08663 was not Shamrock 544's wingman. Their wingman received combat damage earlier and made a successful emergency landing at Plei Djereng.*

Once clear of the immediate area, I contacted MAJ Edwards, the air mission commander, to give him a status report. I reported CPT Speare's crash may have survivors but there was no way we could get in there until the area was secured. I also told him the gunship I had just seen go into the trees on fire did not look survivable. Edwards informed me he was pulling all gunships out of the area until TAC AIR and artillery could be brought in. I turned east and headed for Plei Djereng to rearm and standby. It had been a long day but the excitement wasn't over yet.

After landing back at Plei Djereng to rearm and refuel I was told to stand-by with the returning 119th slicks. It was a long afternoon waiting for some word on the status of the three downed helicopters. Around sunset, the standby was extended. It looked like we would be spending the night. About 30 minutes after sunset, I heard a Huey on approach to the field. As I mentioned earlier, we were staging out of an unlighted, dusty and over-crowded strip. The landing Huey was just coming to a hover when I heard a loud bang followed by the turbine running at a very high RPM. My crew chief came running to tell me the landing helicopter had crashed.

When I got to the helicopter it was running without a rotor or transmission. The crew chief and gunner were still strapped in and as far as I could tell uninjured. As I opened the pilot's door, I realized what had happened. They must have landed hard because of the dust, causing the transmission to break from its mountings. The rotor came forward thru the cockpit, killing both pilots instantly. I knew both pilots; they were due to rotate home in less than a week. They had to borrow flight helmets when flight operations asked for volunteers to make an emergency supply run. A bad day just got worse and it still wasn't over.

For CPT Lawrence Beyer AC, WO Pruett Helm P, PFC John Fish G and SP4 David Pacer CE the crew of 09544, the UH-1C gunship from D Troop 1/10 CAV, the challenge of their life was just beginning. Somehow, the flight crew managed to maintain enough aircraft control to get the nose up and skids level, so as they crashed through the trees, some control was maintained. In other words, "a controlled crash." Considering the helicopter was engulfed in flames, the loss of all torque control and change of CG when the tail boom was blown off, this was a true demonstration of skill and airmanship.

This is how PFC John Fish, the door gunner, described the last few seconds before the crash: "There was a lot of talking on the radio. We went over an area of tall grass and it was full of NVA regulars with grass and branches in their hats, all carrying rifles. I shot into them for a few seconds then we were past them. The helicopter was taking some hits. I could hear them and feel them but they didn't seem to be having much effect except there was an electrical fire. White smoke was coming back between the pilots and it smelled really strong of electrical wiring on fire. Bullets were coming through the helicopter and pieces of metal were flying around inside. The pieces of metal seemed to be just floating in slow motion. Something came up through my left leg and tore it open. Something else came up and went through the side of my face, eye and helmet. The radio still worked. The helicopter was on fire and was spinning around and flames were coming in the door. I was shooting at some smoke in the trees. Someone was calling 'Mayday, Mayday, this is Shamrock 544, we're going down.' We went into the trees and there was dirt and leaves everywhere, even in my mouth. Helm was just sitting there and I couldn't figure out why he didn't get out. I thought he was shot in the chest or stomach but he wasn't bleeding. We couldn't get him out because his legs were sort of tangled around the pedals and things in the nose of the helicopter. I was really stupid not realizing his back was hurt. When he came loose, we all just sort of fell back a little ways. The helicopter was sizzling so we put him down by a log or hump of dirt. Then the helicopter either blew up or just burned really hot and fast."

WO Helm, the pilot, describes the minutes just after the crash: "The aircraft did not explode until approximately two minutes after impact; however, it was a blazing inferno. My back was broken in three places, and I was immediately paralyzed. CPT Beyer's back was also broken, but he didn't sustain any nerve damage. Both Fish, the door gunner and Pacer, the crew chief, were severely burned. Fish also had a shattered femur. On impact, I was momentarily knocked unconscious. I came to with the crew chief and door gunner yelling at me to get out. I tried moving my legs, but they didn't respond. I don't know exactly what I said, but they didn't hesitate to grab me and pull me out with seconds to spare. Injured as they were, they still managed to drag me a short distance away from the burning aircraft. A few moments later the aircraft exploded, leaving only the tail rotor intact. To this day I cannot express strongly enough how I feel about my crew. With the fire raging and ammo starting to cook-off they had every right to leave me in the cockpit. I would not be alive today had it not been for their actions and bravery."

Things did not look good for the crew of Shamrock 544. They had crashed less than 500 meters from the guns that had shot them down and in the middle of two NVA battalions. They were alive, but with injuries which seriously limited their ability to move from the crash site. Only CPT Beyer could move any distance. PFC Fish remembers "right after we got Helm out of the helicopter it burned completely up. We tore the white Kevlar pieces out of my flack vest and laid them out flat on the ground to make an SOS of sorts. We hoped it would be visible from the air and not noticeable from the ground. The bombing and shelling was starting, so we knew the NVA must be pretty close. So we crawled into the brush and waited."

WO Helm describes the next few hours: "Even though my back was broken, I was not in very much pain, but I definitely was in shock. Both the crew chief and door gunner were badly burned and in a great deal of pain. We had no idea as to our exact location and were extremely worried who would find us first. With only one .38 revolver and one M-16 rifle with 20 rounds, we weren't capable of putting up much resistance in our condition. I remember hearing the attacking jets overhead, and having expended brass dropping down on us. Later in the afternoon and throughout the night artillery fire landed in and around our position. It was terrifying, to say the least, to hear the distant whump when the guns were fired then the familiar whistle and explosion. The worst sound was the thunk when the shrapnel embedded into the tree trunks and limbs near us. Our main objective was to stay as quiet as possible, hoping not to attract the NVA's attention."

Artillery and mortar fire from both NVA and friendly units continued throughout the night. There is no evidence anyone, friend or foe, knew exactly where the crew of Shamrock 544 was. Late the next morning, LTC Foy Rice, the Commander of the 52nd CAB, was airborne in his command and control Huey looking for survivors. Concurrently, A Company 1/12th INF was conducting a ground search for the downed crew. LTC Rice spotted the wreckage first. When he realized there were survivors he arranged for a CH-47 Chinook to land and pick him up at the near-by artillery firebase. He needed an aircraft with a hoist and the Chinook had one.

PFC John Fish describes the long night and morning rescue: "There were a lot of artillery explosions, especially when it got dark. A C-47 gunship (Puff the Magic Dragon) orbited overhead at a very high altitude. When he fired, a lot of 20mm brass came down through the trees. I either slept or passed out during most of the night. In the morning I wasn't doing real well. There were a lot of ants in my leg wound and I was getting terribly thirsty. I couldn't use my hands much by then. Some fingers were broken and my partly burned gloves had shrunk up so I couldn't move my fingers or get my gloves off. Probably just as well."

"Then there was a big helicopter hovering over us. They were shooting out of their doors and side windows. A guy came down on a basket sort of standing on it and hanging onto the cable. I remember him as a smallish guy with white hair, a fatigue cap, no rifle, just a .45 pistol and he was a Lieutenant Colonel. I don't remember who went up first, but going up was the only time I was sure I was going to get shot."

WO Pruett Helm: "By morning we were extremely thirsty. Not knowing when we were going to be rescued, CPT Beyer decided to go look for water. He thought he had seen some in some bomb craters not too far away as we went down. Armed with his .38 revolver, he departed on his search. We never saw him again…several hours later a CH-47 Chinook pulled to a hover over our site and LTC Rice came down in the basket and loaded the three of us up, one at a time. Rice wanted me to go first as I was the most seriously injured, but I refused. He was not real happy with me, but he took the others before me. I was the third one to go up. He just rolled me into the basket. He came up last. I told LTC Rice that CPT Beyer was still out there looking for water. I don't know how long the extraction took, maybe eight-to-ten minutes... I bet, to the pilots driving the CH-47 it seemed like a life time. I was told that toward the end of the rescue we began to receive enemy fire."

CPT Beyer was found and picked-up later the same day by LTC Rice, who was slated to give up his command of the 52nd CAB in a few weeks. I've always been impressed with his bravery in finding and rescuing the crew of Shamrock 544. Especially when you know the crew was not part of his battalion.

The CH-47 rescue took place during a brief lull in the battle, but the NVA were still in the area and would launch a major attack against the 1/12th Infantry that night with two battalions and supporting fires from Cambodia. The NVA attack would eventually fail with the help of over 100 sorties from the U.S. Air Force and massive artillery and mortar fire to help brunt the attack.

Finally, in my opinion, what made the "Shootout" different and so deadly for the aviation units was for the first time, at least in the Central Highlands, the NVA set up a deadly trap by placing twelve to sixteen 12.7mm antiaircraft weapons in the middle of the LZ rather than in the tree line around the perimeter of the LZ. They must have known with no concealed route of withdrawal their chances of survival were slim. Each gun was on a tripod, manned by a crew of four to six men, well dug in and camouflaged with large straw mats. This tactic gave the gunners the ability to place deadly, unmasked fire in a 360 degree circle. After the battle, intelligence reports confirmed the 88th NVA Regiment had been given the mission of destroying an American landing zone. By the NVA's own admission, they failed but it could have gone the other way. Had the slicks landed where the NVA thought we would, we could have suffered the greatest single loss of helicopters in the war. The trap was set up in the best, largest LZ in the area. They even took the prevailing winds into consideration. I don't know why the first sortie of slicks chose to land short of the better LZ, but thank God they did. The LZ chosen was smaller, on uneven ground with elephant grass resulting in some slicks having to unload from a 10 foot hover. No slicks were lost. However, this put the gunships directly over the NVA positions. When the NVA realized the slicks were not going to use the LZ where their trap was set-up, they opened up on the gunships with deadly results.

In the "RED WARRIORS BATTLE REPORT," quoted in part… "The Red Warriors had five men killed in action and 40 wounded over the course of this battle, while the aviation support unit lost three helicopters and at least eight personnel. Because of the heroism of the three helicopter crews, many Red Warriors' lives were saved that day. These helicopter crews "took the bullet" for the Red Warriors."

Epilogue

• This "War Story" is based on my participation in the events on 11 November 1966. I have not attempted to tell the story of the ground combat experienced by COL Lay's 1st Battalion 12th Infantry "RED WARRIORS". There is excellent coverage of this in S.L.A. Marshall's book "WEST TO CAMBODIA" and Roger A. Hill's outstanding "RED WARRIORS" BATTLE REPORT 11-13 November 1966. I have tried to use the terms, language, and acronyms familiar to readers who were there to avoid cluttering up the narrative with footnotes.

• Up until 2002, the events of 11 November 1966 were pretty well buried on my hard drive. That year, I received an email from Gary Rogers, a former Croc in the 119th AHC. Gary was responding to a request from Jerry Ewen (VHPA Family Contact Committee) to make contact with Rick Speare's sister Stephanie Peterson. We corresponded and talked over a period of several months. This turned out to be a good experience for me and I believe also for Stephanie. It certainly reinforced my feelings about the value of the VHPA. I mention this because before corresponding with Stephanie I had to do some research on the 119th AHC and this started a background file that has been my reference for much of this war story.

• In the spring of 2011, I received an email from Pruett Helm asking if I had any knowledge of the events of 11 November 1966. I told him I did and a few days later, we talked. When he told me he had been the pilot in Shamrock 544 my first comment was "you are lucky to be alive." Later, when I learned about his long road to recovery I had to wonder if maybe lucky was a poor choice of words.

.• Following my conversation with Pruett Helm, I talked to COL (Ret) Tom Shaughnessy, the former commander of D Troop 1/10th CAV during the 11 November 1966 mission. Tom asked if I would be willing to write a witness statement that would support upgrading the awards given to the crew of Shamrock 544. Trying to upgrade an award 48 years after the event and with only one witness has been frustrating to say the least. After two submissions to DA Awards Branch, it doesn't look hopeful. However, with the endorsement of General Wallace Nutting, the former Commander of 1/10th CAV, maybe there is still hope. I told Pruett that regardless of the outcome on the upgrade, I wanted to tell this story. I am probably the only living person who knows the bravery and skill the crew of Shamrock 544 displayed on 11 November. They had extensive battle damage before coming to my rescue. They had every reason to be heading back to Plei Djereng, but they didn't.

• CPT Walter (Rick) Speare, Aircraft Commander of 08600, Rick was one of the two section leaders in the 119th gun platoon. Like all members of the platoon he volunteered to fly guns. His quiet, steady, no-nonsense style of leadership was just what the Crocs needed during those demanding days in the fall of 1966 when the NVA was making a major move in the central highlands. Rick had a dry sense of humor and a fierce loyalty to those he cared about. The morning before he was killed we spent several hours on standby in the PZ at Plei Djereng. I noticed he was very quiet. I thought he may have had some premonition. Years later, I came across a note from Fred Ferlito, a former 119th pilot, to Rick's sister, Stephanie. In the note he said when Rick's locker was opened to send his belongings home, an envelope had been propped up so it would fall out when the door was opened. The envelope read "I'm going to be killed today" with instructions inside. As someone said about the British pilots during the Battle of Britain: Where Do We Find These Brave Men?

• 1LT Dee W. Stone, Jr., Pilot of 8600- After graduation from West Point in 1964, Dee attended flight school before joining the 119th in July of 1966. As I recall, he made it known the day he arrived he wanted to fly guns. As the 119th SIP I gave him his initial in-country checkout. Unit policy was for new pilots to fly slicks for several months before considering them for the guns. For a new pilot just out of flight training he was good enough to be assigned directly to the gun platoon. By the time of this mission, Dee was ready to be an Aircraft Commander.

• SP4 Sal Gennardo, was the gunner on 8600.He was the only survivor and although severely burned, managed to crawl nearly 1000 meters through an airstrike and artillery barrage to the landing zone. Millie Gennardo, Sal's sister wrote this about his survival: "Sal had managed to escape the aircraft and, though burned over 75% of his body, tried to drag the crew out. When he discovered they had all perished he grabbed Dee Stone's .45 and tried to kill himself before the enemy captured him." *The pistol jammed and in a desperate attempt to get away, he crawled through the elephant grass to a stream where he tore off his shirt and sent it downstream, while he went upstream. He heard shooting downstream but was able to come upon the Special Forces. (These facts were verified in "West to Cambodia") When asked how the rest of the crew was, he became hysterical and passed out. Sal returned home physically and emotionally wounded, leaving his "mind in Vietnam". He was under psychiatric care, and then disappeared for years until his sister found him on a ranch in Wyoming. Convincing him to come home, he eventually married her sister-in-law and had a lot of support and assistance from the family. He had a son whom he named Walter and lived a relatively good life for several years. He was finally overwhelmed at the age of 36 at which time he did take his own life. His son later died in a motorcycle accident and all of Sal's pictures and medals were buried with him."

*Author's note: when Dee Stone's body was recovered his .45 pistol was found several feet away with a jammed round in the chamber. Speculation at the time was that Dee had survived the crash and been involved in a fire fight on the ground. Sal's story makes more sense.

• CPT Larry Beyer, Aircraft Commander of Shamrock 544 was not your typical Army Aviator. He spent 5 years in the US Air Force flying B-47s and B-52s with SAC before transferring to the Army. When asked why he transferred to the Army he jokingly responded, "Air Force flying was boring, he wanted something more exciting." I doubt if those were his feelings after 11 November. He suffered serious back injuries in the crash. CPT Beyer did a hell of job maintaining control of the helicopter. I was positive no one could have survived. For his actions in the air and on the ground he was awarded the Silver Star. He would return to RVN for a second tour and retired as a LTC with 21 years' service. After retirement, he started a second career as an attorney in Florida. At age 65, he lost a courageous battle with cancer.

• WO Pruett Helm, Pilot of Shamrock 544 suffered a compression dislocation of the T12, L1 & 2 vertebrae, resulting in paralysis from the waist down. He spent 13 months undergoing rehabilitation, including 60 days on an artificial kidney machine in the 3rd field hospital in Saigon. In 1972, he married his wife Sherrie; they have been married for 42 years, and have 2 children and 7 grandchildren. One year after completion of rehabilitation, Mr. Helm became the first Air Traffic Controller in a wheelchair, and in 1976, he was the FAA's outstanding Handicapped Employee of the year. In 1982, Mr. Helm retired from the FAA due to health problems associated with his injury. He and his family then relocated from Parker, CO to Polson, MT where they continue to live. After moving to Montana, Mr. Helm designed and began marketing "Equalizer Exercise Machines", which is weight training equipment equally accessible to both the able bodied and disabled users. This equipment is now found in most major rehabilitation facilities in the United States and Canada.

Pruett Helm and John Fish have maintained contact with each other and remain close friends.

• PFC John Fish, Door Gunner of Shamrock 544 spent about four months in various hospitals. Most of that time was in the burn ward in Japan. After his discharge from the army, he and his wife Susan moved to Alaska and have lived there since. They primarily made their living commercial fishing. Now retired, they still actively hunt fish, hike and generally enjoy the outdoors.

• If you are still reading this rather long story you have probably noticed there are many names mentioned only briefly or not at all. If you have anything that would make this story more accurate and complete, my email address is courtship@comcast.net. I am more than willing to update both the story and especially the epilogue.

• The "Shootout" participants each saw the events of 11 November from a different perspective. I believe it's fitting to end this "War Story" by looking at how the North Vietnamese viewed the battle. By pure luck, I had lunch a few weeks ago with Mr. Merle Pribbenow, a retired CIA employee with extensive in-country experience to include speaking fluent Vietnamese. Merle was one of the last to leave our embassy in Saigon, flying out on a USMC CH-46. After retirement, he has been involved in the translation of North Vietnamese documents.

I've included parts of several documents he recently provided to make my argument that as bad as they were, our aircraft losses could have been much worse. It's interesting to note the NVA had their own "body count" problems.

History of the 66th Regiment – the Plei Me Group – 1947-2007

[Lịch sử Trung Đoàn 66 – Đoàn Plei Me 1947-2007]

Published by the People's Army Publishing House, Hanoi

History of the 66th Regiment Page 57:

• Engineers and signal personnel from Front Headquarters worked with the 95th Regiment to build two hanging bridges [suspension bridges] across the Poco River as a diversion, and they ran a phony field telephone line along the western bank of the river. Taking the bait, the enemy used B-52s to carpet-bomb the area of the suspension bridges and sent in commandos [CIDG] to search the area. The U.S. 4th Division then launched Operation Paul Revere 4, attacking the areas east and west of the Sa Thay River.

• On 10 November, the soldiers of 9th Battalion/66th Regiment conducted a maneuver attack that completely annihilated two commando [CIDG] companies on the western side of the Sa Thay River. Our soldiers learned three lessons from this battle: First, when fighting the Americans, you have to gain a grasp on your enemy quickly; Second, you have to surround the enemy quickly; and Third, you have to quickly eliminate the enemy's command element and his communications. The more we attacked the enemy, the deeper he sent his forces into our area to "search for and destroy" our units.

• On 11 November, the U.S. 2nd Battalion/2nd Brigade/4th Division, reinforced by one 105mm howitzer battery and one battery of 106.7mm mortars, landed by helicopter at Landing Zone C1. The Americans had landed right in the center of our pre-planned battle area, where we had deployed the 32nd Artillery Battalion, armed with 120mm mortars, to await the enemy. At 1657 hours on 12 November, 32nd Battalion began a ferocious bombardment of the concentration of American troops on Landing Zone C1. Many of our 120mm mortar rounds landed in the middle of the American artillery position and the American headquarters command post. The American ammunition dump caught fire and burned violently. The 105mm howitzer battery, the 106.7 mortar battery, and the headquarters of the 2nd Battalion were all destroyed, and the enemy infantrymen also suffered heavy casualties.

History of the 66th Regiment, Page 58:

• The 88th Regiment and 7th Battalion/66th Regiment had to cut their way through the jungle and through the thick barbed-wire perimeter, but just before they reached the top of the hill the enemy's 105mm ammunition dump exploded, preventing our troops from advancing further. As a result, we were not able to completely annihilate this American battalion.

• On the 13th, after heavy air strikes, one American company landed to collect the bodies of their dead and then hastily evacuated Landing Zone C1. That same day, in an area south of Landing Zone C1 9th Company/9th Battalion under the command of Deputy Company Political Officer Luu Thanh Tan, supported by the companies of 6th Battalion, completed annihilated one American company. During the days that followed, we continued to conduct ferocious attacks in the area east and west of the headwaters of the Sa Thay River, and these attacks completely disrupted the over-optimistic plans and calculations of the American troops.

• With the victory of the Sa Thay Campaign, the 66th Regiment had helped, along with the rest of the Central Highlands and with our forces throughout South Vietnam, to defeat the second American strategic counteroffensive. The Central Highlands Front's direct rear base and logistics support area expanded into the area east of the Poco River. …

• As the combat period the winter-spring of 1966-1967 began, the armed forces of the Central Highlands were in a good, solid position. We had spent months preparing for the coming battles, and Huu Duc and I, along with a number of our regimental cadre, had reconnoitered the terrain from Plei Djereng all the way to the Vietnamese-Cambodian border, a distance of almost 60 kilometers. We had found locations for fortified blocking positions where we could deploy forces ahead of time, and we had discussed battle tactics on the actual terrain - How, when we lured the enemy to Fortified Position A, Position A would have to lure them on to Position B, and Position B would have to lead them on to Position C, etc., forming a daisy-chain of battles designed to lure the enemy down the path we intended straight into the area where we had decided to fight the decisive battle. The location we selected for the decisive battle was a rather large and fairly flat clearing right next to the border. If the enemy wanted to prevent our forces from escaping across the border, he would have to land a least one battalion of troops in this location. We massed our largest force at this location, and the 88th Regiment sat there, waiting, determined to completely destroy the enemy battalion. We planned that this would be the final battle of the campaign.

Campaign Objectives: Lure American forces out to annihilate them, and at the same time help to shatter the American imperialists' intentions to conduct a dry season counteroffensive. Requirement: Lure one American battalion into *Decisive Battle Point "C1" and completely annihilate that battalion.

*Footnote: "C1" was the designation we gave to an open field cleared for slash-and-burn farming. We would induce enemy helicopters to land at this location so that we could annihilate them).

Chinook Crash FSB Keene

Gary Roush

On 21 November 1968, the 242nd ASHC was resupplying fire support base Keene, south of Cu Chi near the Plain of Reeds. This was in support of the 2nd Battalion, 14th Infantry, 25th Infantry Division. I was the Aircraft Commander of Chinook CH-47A serial number 66-19019, and Captain Roger P. Olney was the pilot. SP5 Alfred T. Calderon was the crew chief in the flight engineer's position for this flight. SP5 Robert W. Jewell was the flight engineer and was in the right door gunner position, and SP4 Bruce A. Knieff was the left door gunner. CPT Olney was new in country.

At the time, which was about six months into my tour in Vietnam, I had accumulated over 700 flight hours in Chinooks with over 400 as an Aircraft Commander. Being one of the few commissioned officers in the company, I was generally assigned to fly with the new higher-ranking officers for in country orientation.

We had an internal load of 16 grunts and several bags of mail plus an external load from Cu Chi. CPT Olney was flying at the time and I was working the radios. We first set down the external load, then hovered over to the resupply pad to unload the internal men and supplies. To hold down dust during the dry season, this Fire Support Base had placed a heavy Neoprene pad on the landing area and held it in place with sand bags. I noticed as we approached the pad had split down the middle exposing the dirt underneath. CPT Olney hovered to the pad and set the back wheels on the ground. I lifted my feet to engage the brakes (the Pilot not flying worked the brakes since the Chinook would roll forward as the front wheels were lowered). Just as the front wheels were touching the ground, I noticed out of the corner of my left eye the left half of the pad was flying up toward the aft rotor.

The Chinook's 110 knot rotor wash was always kicking up poncho liners, empty sandbags, and small tents, so we routinely looked for loose objects. This pad, however, was so big it never occurred to me it would blow up in the blades. I grabbed for the thrust lever to pull pitch but it was too late. The pad hit the aft rotor on the left side. There was an instant severe vibration so I knew we had a serious blade strike which automatically meant a shut down. At the same time, the caution panel lit up so an emergency shut down was in order and I immediately pulled both flight levers to stop.

CPT Olney being new was turning the switches the wrong way so I hit him to keep his hands away from the controls. I was most concerned about the fuel valves, fuel pumps, and generator switches which are on the overhead panel.

The vibration quickly stopped and the front rotor was coasting down normally so I assumed there was no major problem. CPT Olney, however, immediately got out of his seat and quickly left without saying a word, his "chicken plate" (ceramic armor chest protector) crashing to the floor. This was very unusual since both pilots normally stayed in their seats until the rotors stopped. The pilot who flew in the right seat had a rear view mirror so he could see back through the companion way into the cargo compartment. After I completed the shut-down procedure, I looked to see why he left in such a hurry and was shocked to see the Chinook was on fire and it was up to the companion way. *I was trapped!*

As I experienced several times in Vietnam, during periods of pure terror, training takes over and everything fortunately happens in slow motion. I remember being told in flight school about the emergency escape door each pilot had which was operated by a black and yellow striped handle located just above my head on the left. I knew exactly where it was because that is where I always hung my Kodak instant camera. I grabbed for the handle and jerked down. To my horror and surprise the handle broke off in my hand and the door did not pop out like my training said it would. *"Now,"* I said to myself, *"it's time to panic!" "No - wait,"* the voice in my head started again. *"If the emergency handle fails then the door can be kicked out!"* Leave it up to the Army to think of everything. No sweat, just kick out the door. Well, I kicked and kicked but nothing happened. This was not surprising, now that I think about it, because there was not much room to kick.

"Well, this is it, I am trapped," I thought, *"I am going to die!* My training has run out. Not only have I crashed but now I am going to be burned alive!" This gave me a new meaning to the phrase "crash and burn." "Well, I will take one last look at my fate" - Surprise! The fire had backed off just enough for me to get through the companion way and over the right door gun. *"Let's go!"* the

little voice said, ***"Let's get the hell out of here!"*** That is what I did. At the time it seemed like this all took about an hour but in reality it probably lasted about 20 seconds.

I then took inventory. Everyone got out. Thank God! One grunt had scratched his face and the flight engineer had sprained his wrist. He was also soaked in hydraulic fluid and was very lucky not to have caught on fire since he was standing under the aft pylon when it separated and caught on fire. In fact, it all happened so fast his intercom cord was burned in two before he could say anything on the intercom. What a relief and what a fire! The aft rotor and aft pylon had separated from the fuselage with the result of exposing gallons of oil and jet fuel to the hot turbine engine exhaust causing the instant fire. One aft rotor blade was thrown 110 yards.

Fortunately, the pad flew into the left side of the aft rotor that pulled the hub and transmission away from the front rotor and fuselage instead of into them, which a blade strike on the right would have caused. Also, fortunately, because I got the fuel valves off so quickly the fire did not get into the fuel tanks which still had about 2,000 pounds of JP-4 in them and could have caused an explosion or much bigger fire.

As I was trying to figure out what to do next, from out of nowhere a young Lieutenant General appeared with a photographer in tow. Apparently he was flying in the area in his Huey and heard about the accident on the radio. He asked who was in charge of the Chinook and was directed to me. By this time, I was in a nearby bunker because ammunition carried on the Chinook was cooking off and I was afraid the fuel tanks would explode. After I convinced the General I was in charge even though I was a Lieutenant and the pilot was a Captain, he said, "Let's go put that fire out, Lieutenant." I said, "Sir, this thing might explode any minute and, besides, those are M-79 and M-60 rounds cooking off in the fire that you hear." He said to me, as we backed toward a bunker, "don't you have fire extinguishers on that thing?" I said, "Yes sir, but they are little tiny things that last about two seconds and that's a big fire!" All this time, the General's photographer was getting some great pictures of the General with this burning Chinook in the background. I guess I finally convinced him the Chinook was a lost cause because he began directing his energy toward the fire support base commander. He started asking questions about why he did not get resupplied by road instead of by air and other embarrassing questions. This gave me an opportunity to slip away.

I went looking for a radio to call Cu Chi and inform my Company Commander of my predicament and see if we could get something to put out the fire. Shortly, a Huey and a Chinook showed up from Cu Chi. The Chinook brought a large airport-type fire extinguisher from the Muleskinner ramp that was successfully used to put out the fire just as it reached the fuel tanks.

CPT Olney and I climbed into the Huey for the embarrassing ride back to Cu Chi. Surprisingly, I had the emergency handle and my camera with me which confirmed to me that in an emergency you took with you only what was in your hands or attached to your body. My chicken plate was missing, but I had my pistol. As a result, I continued to wear a .45 caliber pistol instead of switching to an M-16 rifle like some of the other pilots did. As the Huey climbed out of the LZ, I tried to take a picture of the wreckage but my camera would not work. It did not matter, however, since the battalion safety officer confiscated all the film from all of the cameras at the fire support base that yielded a full sequence of the action except for the exact instant of the blade strike. I was surprised at the number of pictures. A battalion clerk later gave me 8 x 10 size blow-ups of several of the pictures to add to my emergency handle souvenir.

As I recall, the accident investigation found me partially at fault for not exercising proper care in a hazardous situation and found the ground commander partially at fault for improper maintenance of a landing pad. My guess is the ground commander got more grief than I did because of that General showing up. I was flying the next day and never heard any more about the accident except for a review with the accident investigation officer and a routine check by the flight surgeon. The damage came to $1,290,504.40. I was glad the Army did not make me pay for it.

The good thing was none of the 16 passengers or crew of five were seriously hurt. The bad thing was five or six bags of mail from home were lost in the fire. What was left of the Chinook was hauled to the 539th General support Maintenance Company located at Phu Loi and cannibalized for parts.

Eight days before this accident I was so close to an air strike in an LZ that my Chinook got hit with the debris from the bomb blast. Three days before this accident I called a Mayday because of a complete electrical failure. Two days after this accident I nearly drowned in a swimming pool after my crew threw me in because we got shot up that day. Seven days later I got shot at by an American GI because my Chinook blew dirt in his first hot meal in weeks (turkey dinner for Thanksgiving). Eight days later my Chinook was completely surrounded by enemy tracers at tree top level at a Vietnamese village on the Cambodian border nicknamed Diamond City without taking a single hit. After these events, I decided I was not going to get killed in Vietnam. After living through all of this, I could live through anything!

Flying has been described as hours and hours of boredom interrupted by moments of terror. In Vietnam, flying helicopters in combat was hours and hours of excitement interrupted by intense periods of extreme terror.

The VC Were Predictable Too

Ed Canright

We should all remember from basic training the warnings our instructors preached to us about not becoming predictable.

The warnings from infantry basic and AIT schools went like this: "When patrolling, never use the same trail when going in and out of an area. Mister Charlie will take advantage of your laziness, set up an ambush or booby trap, and really ruin your day."

My Vietnam veteran instructor pilots repeated the same dire prediction in flight school. They lamented "you will pay dearly" if you make the mistake of using the same approach into and out of hot landing zones. During my tour in Vietnam I observed instances when violations of these warnings were made both by our pilots and soldiers, and also by Mr. Charlie. The results were, as you might expect, predictable.

For most of my tour, I was stationed at LZ English with the 61st Assault Helicopter Company (AHC). LZ English was located by the village of Bon Song in Northern Bin Dihn Province. I flew both lift ships and B Model gunships for the unit from September 1969 through September 1970. Our unit's home station was at Lane Army Helipad by An Son, a small village located a few miles northwest of Qui Nhon. Our lift ship call sign was "Lucky Star," and the gunship pilots were known as "Starblazers." Our unit patch contained a design showing two dice with a 6 and a 1 (a good number to roll when gambling) along with a shooting star. The helipad at LZ English was known as the Crap Table.

We flew missions predominantly out of LZ English in support of the 173rd Airborne Brigade, including their LRRP unit known as November Rangers. We also supported the herd at LZs North English, Mahoney, Uplift, Two Bits, Pony and Tape. Our primary area of operations included the An Loa Valley, Happy Valley, Sui Kai Valley, and Crow's Foot Region. The An Loa Valley was a major infiltration route for the NVA during my time in Vietnam. We sometimes ranged west to An Khe and Pleiku in support of the 4th Infantry Division, and also flew in support of the Capitol ROK Infantry Division. The 61st AHC also participated in the excursions into Laos and Cambodia.

I'm not sure about other pilots, but one of the least significant things to me during my Vietnam tour was the day of the week. Aside from payday and major holidays, the day of the week had no significance at all. Sometimes a chaplain would be available and you would think that it was Sunday, but not always. On occasions, such as before large combat assaults, the chaplain would provide services regardless of what day it was.

During my tour, LZ English experienced mortar attacks on a frequent basis. After a period of time, we realized the attacks almost always occurred on Thursdays. The mortar rounds originated from the base of the ridgeline that lay to the west of the LZ. This ridge ran from south to north and separated LZ English from the An Loa Valley. The attacks would begin just a few minutes before sunset. Another significant fact was the mortar rounds always impacted on the helipad and then the shooters began walking rounds from west to east across the LZ. Naturally, anti-mortar artillery and .50-caliber fire would pound the location where the rounds were being fired from.

Unfortunately, we never seemed to be able to eliminate the enemy mortar position. During my tour, numerous patrols and LRRP team missions were inserted into the area in an attempt to locate the exact firing position, but always to no avail. Things became so predictable that on Thursday evenings we would normally have a person sitting on top of our Tactical Operations Center (TOC) bunker to watch and listen for a possible mortar attack. When the first enemy mortar round was fired, we had approximately 22 seconds before the round would impact. This gave us time to sound the attack alarm and head for our bunkers.

One final predictable point eventually became obvious to us. Of the many helicopter revetments we had constructed on the Crap Table, two specific revetments always seemed to take close hits during a mortar attack. It got to the point that if we didn't have many helicopters at the helipad at the end of the day, those two specific revetments would remain empty. But if the helipad was completely full and all revetments had to be used, we would try to park our most expendable ships in those two locations.

Near the end of my tour, probably July or August of 1970, my gunship team was on primary stand-by at LZ English. Shortly after supper, the scramble alarm was sounded and we ran into the TOC to receive our mission. We were being scrambled to cover a dust-off helicopter needed for an emergency medical evacuation mission to the northwest of LZ North English. A platoon from the 173rd had been ambushed and they had two seriously wounded soldiers who required evacuation. At that time, it was normal procedure to cover dust-off missions when enemy fire could be expected.

Our team consisted of two B Model Gunships fitted with rockets and mini-guns. To the best of my memory, on that day my Light Gun Team also included Warrant Officers Frank McFadden, Donald Woods, and Dennis Patterson. We scrambled into the air and awaited the dust-off to lift off from the LZ English medical pad. The flight time to our location was only 10-12 minutes.

As we arrived on the scene and made contact with the friendly unit on the ground, they informed us they had not taken any more enemy fire since initially being hit. They popped smoke, which we immediately identified, and upon receiving verification from the ground it was their smoke, we set up a race track pattern allowing us to provide continuous cover for the dust-off ship while it made its approach for the pick-up. The medevac extraction site was in rice paddies with a small village located about 100 meters to the east. The medevac pick-up went off without any problems, and we escorted the dust-off ship out of the LZ and headed back towards English.

Since the mission had gone off without a hitch, we began talking among ourselves and the fact was brought up this was Thursday evening, and that's when we might expect a mortar attack on LZ

English. We decided against immediately heading back to English and instead headed up the valley behind the ridgeline to the west of English. We checked our watches and decided it was about the time the enemy usually started his mortar attack on our home station.

We gained altitude and climbed over the ridge and LZ English came into view some two to three kilometers to the east. As we looked down the ridgeline, we observed the first flash from the enemy mortar tube. It couldn't have been a more perfect situation. Here we were, a fully loaded gun team, with an enemy mortar position just beginning its attack directly below and in front of us. We immediately opened fire on the target and then set up our race track pattern.

We poured 2.75 inch rockets and 7.62-mm mini-gun rounds into the enemy position. Our rounds hit the target and we were rewarded with two secondary explosions and a lot of smoke and fire. It looked like we completely neutralized the enemy position during our first two passes. At the time we opened up on the enemy we also contacted our operations at LZ English and informed them of the situation. They told us they had witnessed the contact and directed us to stay on station to provide cover for a reaction force that would be inserted. Within 15 minutes we were able to escort the reaction team into the location.

The next morning we received word, as expected, the mortar position had been set up in the draw. The hill to the east of the draw, facing LZ English, protected it from direct fire and almost all anti-mortar fire. The reaction team credited us with two KIAs and two POWs. Our forces recovered the mortar tube, base plate and some mortar rounds. Better yet, we had finally found their launch site. The position was beneath two inches of water in the solid rock streambed. The VC had chipped out locations in the streambed to place the base plate and mortar tube legs, and had etched out a number of holes to allow them to shift the direction of fire. No wonder they were so accurate with their rounds. They literally had our location etched in stone.

The next day a team of demolition specialists from LZ English were taken to the location. They placed explosives in the streambed and destroyed the site. It was never used to attack us again.

As I was warned in basic training and flight school, being predictable will eventually ruin your day.

Milk Run of November 11th

Dave Sebright, Al Gaither

With Jesse Myers - Infantry

Dave: It was a beautiful day to be a newly appointed Aircraft Commander in the 176th Aviation Company. My assigned helicopter was UH-1D, 65-10052 and my new call sign was Minuteman 17. I had been in country since the first of September and had accumulated about 240 combat flying hours. I had been shot at, had my helicopter shot up, and had a few aircraft emergencies under my belt. I felt like I had the world by its gonads. Two months earlier, I had joined up with the unit at Duc Pho and started flying support for the 1st Brigade of the 101st Airborne Division during Operation Cook in the mountains NW of Quang Ngai. On September 11, we airlifted the Screaming Eagles to the mountains NW of Tam Ky and just South of the Que Son Valley. At this time, the 176th also relocated to Ky Ha on the North end of Chu Lai. Life had gotten better with real beds instead of cots, sea huts instead of tents, real food instead of whatever they were feeding us at Duc Pho, and enough Officer Clubs to keep us entertained. Life was good.

Al: I arrived in Cam Ranh Bay, Vietnam reception center on September 24, 1967, with flight school friend and fellow WO-1, Edward A. Fitzsimmons. The next day we were both assigned to Task Force Oregon, I Corps. The following day, September 26, we boarded a UH-1D for a flight to Ky Ha, located at the north end of Chu Lai. We bunked at the 14th AVN BN Hq until the 29th; then we both were assigned to the 176th Assault Helicopter Co. Callsigns for the unit were Minuteman for slicks, Musket for the guns. I was further assigned to the 1st Platoon slicks. As an "FNG", when I drew my flight gear, the only chest protectors left on the shelf were size Short - Small! Seemed about the size of a deck of cards! I made it my business for the next few months to go to the supply room every time I knew someone DEROSed or was evacuated, to see if a bigger one was being turned in. I ended up with an X Long - X Large. Its weight put my legs to sleep, but when the "fit hit the shan" it felt good!

For the next month, I flew missions as a pilot, learning the trade. Most of the assignments were as a C and C, (command and control) where we landed at a field headquarters and picked up the Commander and or staff to fly over their AO, (area of operation), or the second type of mission which was utility. Utility ships had a variety of tasks, including delivery of troop replacements, food, water, medical supplies, ammunition, mail, medevac, and anything else a combat unit might need. These aircraft were also on call for CA, (combat assault) operations, where two or more ships, usually accompanied by UH-1 C gunships, were used to infiltrate or exfiltrate troops into combat areas. On November 11, 1967, I was assigned a mission to fly with AC WO-1 Dave Sebright on a utility mission for the 1st Brigade, 101st ABN Division.

Dave: The relationship between our air crews and the 1st Brigade combat units was very good. The Screaming Eagles were well-trained and led, hard-charging, and battle-tested. There was not much we would not do for these units, even if it meant stretching the safety envelope occasionally. We had seen a lot of battle with the 1st Brigade and they knew how to use their aviation assets.

On November 10th, I was given our mission for the next morning. We were to fly resupply missions for the Brigade S4 to their subordinate units. We would pick up our loads at Chu Lai and Tam Ky and fly them to the various fire bases. This was a milk run mission flying from secure locations to other secure locations. There was not much chance of getting shot up and there should be plenty of flying to keep us busy. W01 Al "Gator" Gaither was my assigned pilot for the mission. Al had been assigned to the 176th since September 29th and was known to be a good pilot. We were both assigned to the 1st Flight Platoon (Slicks). Until this day we had never flown together because before November 8th we were both pilots and had to fly with Aircraft Commanders. We were assigned my aircraft 052. Unfortunately, neither one of us can remember the crew chief or gunner we were assigned that day.

The morning of November 11th we performed our pre-flight inspection on 052, had a short briefing for the crew, then flew to fly to Tam Ky to the forward Brigade resupply pad. We started flying our resupply missions and had flown approximately three hours before we landed on LZ Center. There were Hueys parked all over the LZ, I later learned there was a change of command in progress for B Company 2/327 Inf. and there were two Generals on the firebase. There were gunships shut down on the LZ which was very unusual. It seemed the only open flat space left on the LZ was the "No Slack" resupply pad we had landed on. After we landed, one of the guys working the pad told us they (2 Bn, 327th Inf) had a tactical emergency going on and asked us to shut down. The Bn S3 (Operations Officer) came to the pad and gave us a short operational briefing and asked us if we could conduct an emergency ammunition resupply to Charlie Company. The S3 told us C Company was surrounded by NVA and they were running low on ammunition. The Battalion had requested gunships but none were available at that time (where did the General's gunship escort go?). It was apparent C Company would need ammunition resupply shortly. The Milk Run was going sour.

We loaded up our slick with about 1,000 pounds of 5.56, 7.62, and 40mm. We stacked the ammunition cases along each side of the cargo compartment so they could be pushed out rapidly. We asked for two volunteers to ride along with us to push the ammunition out. This would allow our crew chief and gunner to stay on their M-60s. We quickly had two volunteers to ride along. Unfortunately, we did not know their names, only that they were on the resupply pad. We were now waiting for a lull in the fire fight to deliver the ammunition. The waiting time gave us a chance to evaluate the situation. I knew a high overhead approach was not going to be a good solution since we had no gunships. The best solution seemed to be to fly in low level and try to surprise the enemy on the way in. Coming out of the Company location was not going to be good no matter how we went in since they were surrounded. We had C Company pop smoke while we were still shut down on the resupply pad. We identified the smoke coming from an island of trees on the valley floor. It was several miles away. Al and I stood on the pad trying to pick out a route and identifying landmarks so we could navigate in low level. This was not going to be easy as there were many small islands of trees on the valley floor. Soon someone came running down from the BTOC and told us Charlie Company was out of 7.62 and 40mm and they had redistributed their 5.56. They were down to eleven rounds per man. It was time. I believe we had been on the pad about a half hour but it could have been longer or shorter.

Al fired up the L-11 turbine and brought it up to operating RPM while I tuned the radios. I called C Company and told them we planned to approach low-level from the north asking them to listen for us in case we needed a direction change. I took the controls and we lifted off LZ Center diving down the North mountain side to the valley floor. We could no longer see C Company's position and would not see it for a couple of more minutes. We crossed over a small ridge flying about five feet AGL (above ground level) at 100 knots. The trick then was to go to the correct island of trees. We headed west to a visible check point and turned south directly towards the LZ, I hoped. Al and I were talking while trying to identify that specific island of trees. We were about a mile out traveling over two miles a minute when the RTO heard, then saw us. We were headed directly into the LZ. It was time to flare and decelerate. I stood 052 on its tail and dropped down into a high hover in the tree tops. We were taking fire but the tree tops were helping. I felt Al lightly on the controls. As we were coming to a high hover, the RTO told us to kick the ammo out there.

Al: I could see several NVA scurry back and forth in the underbrush directly to our front not more than 75 to 100 feet away. I could hear rounds hitting the ship and then I saw one of the NVA sit down at the base of the palm tree to our right front. At that moment I thought "He is very close and he is not going to miss!" He began to fire his AK and I felt a burn on my leg and a spray of Plexiglas particles and aluminum hit my chin and lips. I was yelling into the intercom for the gunner on my side to get this guy, not realizing one of his rounds had clipped my commo cord in half, and no one could hear me. It looked to me that he fired several single rounds, and then went "guns-a-go-go" on full auto. Over the noise of the firing and engine, I could hear the ammo pushers and the crew in the back yelling "GO, GO!" Every warning light in the instrument panel still functioning was lit up, and because Dave wasn't answering me on intercom I was sure he was hit. It was time to move out! As I tried to expedite our departure, I felt resistance on the controls and felt the collective come up and the cyclic move forward I realized Dave was OK, or at least was able to fly the ship. It wasn't until we landed at the firebase that I realized why I could not direct the gunner's fire because no one could hear me.

Dave: The two volunteers pushed all of the ammunition out in a few seconds. Our M-60s were laying down fire. The crew chief gave me the all clear and I took 052 to maximum power as I started a left turn directly towards LZ Center. We cleared the trees while making our left turn and the NVA rolled onto their backs and hosed us down with small arms fire. The crew in the back had their M-60s laying down fire and both of the guys from the resupply pad were firing their M-16. The NVA hosed us down good with AKs. Bullets, shrapnel, and Plexiglas were flying all over the cockpit and cargo compartment.

Suddenly, I felt Al coming on the controls. I tried to talk with him on the intercom to get him off them. He was not answering. I yelled at him to get off the controls and he yelled back he thought I was hit since I did not answer him. His helmet communication cord had been shot in half right next to his neck. We were about two minutes out of the LZ and by now climbing out at 80 knots and all of the power 052 could muster. We had engine and transmission gages going wacko, warning lights coming on, and smoke coming from an electrical fire in the nose compartment. The smoke was minor and was soon gone. Some rounds had hit the wiring harnesses. I was communicating with the crew chief and gunner to see if they or the volunteers were injured. It appeared no one had any major wounds. As we were on short final approach to LZ Center, I smelled the distinct odor of hydraulic oil burning on the engine. All was well; we had power and controls. We landed and shut down.

Soldiers from the 2d Bn, 2/327th Inf were all over the pad. Everyone was trying to talk at once. Someone from the BTOC was on the pad and I asked them to call the rear so we could get a ride back to home base. 052 was peppered with bullet holes. Al had his helmet cord shot in half and his baseball cap he had stored in a cubby hole behind his head had a bullet hole through it. One of the volunteers had his steel pot shot off from his head. He had his unread mail tucked in the helmet liner and was pissed he had lost it. Shortly, a slick came in and gave us a ride back to Ky Ha. 052 would need a ride home by a CH-47 Chinook. Back at Ky Ha I headed into operations to file a report and Al caught up with his dad who had arrived in Vietnam the same day. Later, I watched the Chinook bring in 052. At about 10 feet above the ramp 052 started spinning and the hook pilot punched it off. It would be January 1968 before I got 052 out of maintenance. That night, I caught up with Al and his Dad. Al was wearing his hat with the bullet hole in it. Shortly after November 11, 1967, Al went to the Muskets (Gunship Platoon). I don't believe we ever flew slicks together again. If we did, it probably would have only been for a check ride. Maybe once was enough! 052 ended up having 28 bullet holes in her and numerous other holes from shrapnel. During the time 052 was in maintenance for repairs, I flew 054 until Bob Hartley and I flew 054 into a rice paddy, but that is another story, for another time.

Jesse:

Company C, 2nd Battalion, 327th Infantry Airborne November 11, 1967

• The Mission

On November 6, 1967, Company C, 2/327th Infantry, along with the remainder of the Battalion made a helicopter assault into the Hiep Duc Valley, west of Tam Ky, RVN. The Battalion's mission was to block exfiltration routes from the east heading west out of the valley.

• **The Situation**

The next five days passed without major contact with the enemy although there were numerous signs, sightings, and reports of his presence in, or passage through, the area of operations. Late in the morning of November 11, Charlie Company deployed three of its four platoons in patrols using a cloverleaf pattern around the CP location. First, third, and fourth platoons dropped their rucksacks at the CP and second platoon remained with the CP as a reaction force and to secure the rucksacks. Company field strength was around 80 to 85 with nine troops in the CP and 18 to 20 in each platoon. Each platoon had two small rifle squads and two M-60 machine gun teams. Third platoon and fourth platoon both quickly began seeing enemy signs such as a discarded uniform, black pajamas, bulk rice, and a VC ID card.

• **The Battle**

At approximately 1245 hours, the third platoon point man had a meeting engagement with three enemy soldiers. One NVA was killed, one was wounded and captured, and one fled. Third platoon pursued and encountered the main enemy perimeter. They attacked and penetrated the perimeter to what was evidently a command post in a hut. The platoon leader initially estimated there were 15 to 20 NVA soldiers. Subsequently, we determined there were many more, at least a Company. Once third platoon had overrun the CP, the enemy reestablished the perimeter thereby surrounding the platoon. Shortly after penetrating the enemy perimeter, the platoon leader was seriously wounded by an NVA grenade. It was obvious his wounds would impair his ability to direct and adjust artillery, gunships, and TAC air.

Consequently, the CP with a point man borrowed from second platoon, began maneuvering to join up with third platoon to assume control of supporting fires.

As the CP neared third platoon's location, the point man opened fire on three NVA who were positioned to ambush the unit. The point man shot one and the other two fled. Having penetrated the perimeter, the CP maneuvered left to join third platoon. As the CP more closely neared the third platoon location, they came under RPG fire from the left killing the artillery recon sergeant. The CP maneuvered past the RPG and linked up with the third platoon around 1400H.

Meanwhile, the first and fourth platoons were also on the move to link up with the CP and third platoon. First platoon arrived about 45 minutes later, breaking through the western side of the NVA perimeter and linking up with our expanding C Company perimeter. Fourth platoon linked up with the second platoon at the old CP location, policed up their individual rucksacks, and headed to the contact location with the second platoon, minus three men who stayed behind to guard the remaining rucksacks. Fourth and second platoons crashed through the weakening NVA perimeter from the north and joined the rest of the company. Meanwhile, the battalion recon platoon (Hawks) linked up with the three troops from the second platoon to secure the remaining C Company rucksacks.

By this time we had gunships and TAC air, each working in their turn, and we were getting heavy fire from our DS 105 mm battery and a GS 155mm battery. We began running low on M-16 and M-60 ammunition and requested a resupply. We attempted to secure an LZ for the resupply chopper, but even after losing one man killed, we were only able to secure a small area for the landing, leaving the approach unsecured. The resupply chopper was able to get in and kick out a few cases of ammunition, but was shot up coming in and going out. Those few cases of ammunition were vital as third platoon troopers were running low after fighting for about three hours. With those few cases of ammo plus redistribution of ammo from troops from the other platoons, we were able to get everyone up to a level where we could repel a substantial enemy attack. We also tried to get a medevac in, but the pilot aborted because the LZ approach was too hot.

The contact continued sporadically until after midnight. We were tied down with our wounded and KIAs we couldn't evacuate, and the enemy commander was trying to withdraw with his wounded. I have always been convinced the enemy commander probably overestimated our strength. First of all, it was obvious we completely surprised him. He had no idea we were there, consequently, he had not been able to observe us and determine our strength. Second, the way the battle unfolded, with his unit getting attacked initially by third platoon, then from a slightly different direction by the CP group; followed by the first platoon assaulting from a third direction; culminating with an attack from yet another direction by the second and fourth platoons, most certainly appeared to be the work of a much larger force.

• The Aftermath

Around 1800 hrs, A Company made an airmobile assault to set up a blocking position approximately 1500 meters to our west. We continued to employ artillery, helicopter flare ships, and C130 gunships until after midnight and continued to receive sporadic probes and sniper fire. There were, however, no further casualties.

As the morning of the 12th dawned, we were able to evacuate our wounded and dead. As we were preparing to move out, we had gunships hose down the area to our south in case there was any enemy remaining there. Unfortunately, one of the door gunners on the C model Huey gunship became disoriented during a firing pass and hosed down the CP with his M-60 wounding two more troopers. The gunship landed and medevaced the two troopers and C Company headed back to pick up their rucksacks.

Following the conclusion of the contact, information obtained from an A Company POW confirmed the unit we were facing as the 40th battalion of the 1st VC regiment. According to the Brigade S2, the battalion had an estimated strength of 250. Immediate results of the contact were four friendly killed and five wounded plus two more wounded by the gunship. The NVA lost 14 killed by ground fire and one killed by air. One SKS, one RPG, and five AK-47s were captured along with numerous rucksacks. Over the next three days, an additional 11 NVA bodies were discovered in graves and two wounded NVA were captured, as well two additional SKS rifles and two additional AK-47 assault rifles along with ammunition, magazines, rucksacks and grenades. Other information included a FAC report of five NVA dragging a body down to the nearby river just south of the contact. Further, interrogation of a female civilian revealed that after the contact, three NVA with small arms had passed through heading east and the village chief (who was VC) had fled across the river to the south. Finally, interrogation of a civilian in another nearby village said a squad of NVA with small arms had stayed in the village the night of the 12th and left heading west.

• **Larger Implications of the Battle**

The 1st VC Regiment was a battle-hardened outfit. The regimental commander and all three battalion commanders were veterans of Dien Ben Phu. Operation Starlite in August 1965 was the first major offensive regimental size action conducted by a purely U.S. military unit during the Vietnam War. U.S. forces involved included the 2/4th, 3/3rd, 1/7th, and 3/7th Marines. The opponent was the 1st VC Regiment which then consisted of the 60th and 80th VC Battalions. The 1st VC regiment suffered 600 plus killed and had nine prisoners taken. They also lost 109 weapons. The Marines suffered 54 killed and 203 wounded. They lost 22 tanks and APCs and 13 helicopters. The 1st VC regiment was a tough outfit. Later, the 40th battalion which was a local force battalion was added to the 1st VC regiment. Operation Starlite is covered in detail in *The First Battle - Operation Starlite and the Beginning of the Blood Debt in Vietnam* by Otto Lehrack.

Sometime prior to 1967, the 1st VC Regiment, including the 40th VC Battalion, was added to the 2nd NVA Division. During the period April 1967, through early August 1967, the 2nd NVA Division was heavily engaged with the U.S. Marines in the Que Son Valley in I Corps. This battle is chronicled in *Road of 10,000 Pains, The Destruction of the 2nd NVA Division by the U.S. Marines, 1967* also by Otto J. Lehrack. According to Mr. Lehrack, during the battle the U.S. Marines had over 600 men killed while the 2nd NVA Division lost over 6,000. At any rate, the 2nd NVA Division essentially disengaged, refitted, and came back down in August to disrupt the SVN national elections to be held on September 3 and to get control of the rice harvest. Following those actions, the 2nd NVA Division was to head to Da Nang for the Tet Offensive. The Marines reengaged the 2nd NVA Division, disrupting their plans and inflicting more damage.

In August, the U.S. Army began replacing Marine units in the southern part of I Corps and the Marines began redirecting more of their effort to the Northern part of I Corps along the DMZ. Consequently, the Americal Division, including the 1st Brigade of the 101st, began assuming responsibility for the Que Son Valley and the 2nd NVA Division. The 2nd NVA Division had been badly beaten up by the Marines and 1st Brigade S2 put their strength at 4,500. Following the rice harvest, the 2nd NVA division would have been preparing for the Tet Offensive and their objective, the city of Da Nang. The 1st Brigade of the 101st killed 1105 enemy soldiers during engagements with the 2nd NVA Division plus capturing 186 individual weapons and 34 crew served weapons. That damage, combined with other inflicted by the sister brigades in the Americal Division, finished the 2nd NVA Division for the Tet Offensive. Once the Tet Offensive began, only one enemy rifle company was able to make it into the city. Thus Da Nang was saved from the death and destruction suffered by other major cities in South Vietnam and C Company and the 176th Assault Helicopter Company had a hand in it.

Kung Fu Skip

Dorcey Wingo

*Alcohol and Sauerkraut on the Fly

Camp Enari, on the outskirts of Pleiku in the Central Highlands of Vietnam's II Corps area, was where I performed my duties in 1969 for the US Army's Fourth Infantry Division. As a Huey pilot, I was honored to be flying at one time or another for either A Company's Blackjacks or B Company's Gambler Guns. Most of us young Warrant Officers were housed down the hillside in what was referred to as The Ghetto.

Camp Enari had once been an Army of the Republic of Vietnam (ARVN) military compound, and had long rows of barracks lined up four-abreast to house all the pilots. Over time, by scrounging wooden packing crates from thousands of 2.75-inch rocket boxes resourceful helicopter jockeys fabricated themselves custom-made hooches. Nothing fancy, but we were far better off than many others in country who slept in foxholes, or eight to a tent.

There was no such thing as a flush toilet on Post that I recall, unless General Pepke had one. Every other soldier relied on the standard primitive facilities, which were a little farther down the hill from The Ghetto, toward the first row of perimeter barbed wire.

Being an all-male outfit, a concession to practicality was made in that two each "field-type urinals" were located between each row of hooches. These consisted of perforated 55-gallon metal drums, buried until they were almost flush with the ground. The top of the drum was then capped with screen-door wire, perhaps to keep aviators from falling in. A crude wooden shed was then put up, which gave the loitering pilot a little shade with a mere suggestion of privacy.

The Ghetto's hooch maids were local Vietnamese women (civilians, we hoped) who arrived every morning Monday through Friday to "washy clothes," make our bunks tidy, and sweep up a little. Off-duty-and-inebriated Warrant Officers were known to ask for "assistance" from passing hooch maids while standing before the mighty screen, downloading.

This practice was guaranteed to raise a ruckus every time! More than one unit actually fashioned special awards out of these well-used screens to decorate designated debauchers, deserving something beyond standard military pomp and circumstance.

Walking up the inclined boardwalk to the east, one would leave The Ghetto and come upon two rows of Commissioned Officer's hooches. Naturally, the "real" officers' quarters were more presentable, carefully laid-out, and quasi-militarily correct - considering this *was* a combat zone. Being *officers and gentlemen*, a hooch maid was far less likely to see a Real Live Officer (RLO) standing buck-naked before the screen, requesting assistance. RLO is a term warrant officers used for commissioned officers.

One of the more celebrated pilots in The Ghetto was a fellow we called Skip. His real first name was decidedly German. His last name was also from a famous German clan, which we shall keep secret; owing to a dastardly deed - yet to be revealed.

Skip and I arrived in country on virtually the same airplane, so as time passed; it appeared we might just survive to take the freedom flight together, back to the World, a term soldiers used to identify the USA. At around ninety days from DEROS (**D**ate **E**stimated to **R**eturn from **O**ver **S**eas) our next assignment orders suddenly appeared. It was a celebrated time to be able to say "**FIGMO,**" or, **F&$% I**t, **G**ot **M**y **O**rders, to all the guys still breaking in their boots.

Skip was especially elated to have gotten his assignment-of-choice, an Army Aviation Battalion based in West Germany, near his ancestral homeland. Taking a seat at our table in the Officers Club that evening, he was ecstatic! His German accent resurfaced as he laughed about all the great times ahead, "…far away from all these muddy #@!*% rice paddies and slant-eyed people," he laughed, "HA HA HAH!" Which made us laugh too, well aware Skip was rumored to have a secret Vietnamese girlfriend in nearby Pleiku City.

Skip seemed to revel in the fact most of us would get thirty days leave, and then go right back to Fort Wolters, Texas, where we would teach rookie candidates how to fly those old piston-powered training helicopters. Try to envision one thousand little bug-smashers, swarming around at the same time! Practically bent over with joy, Herr Brewmeister stood back up with a fist full of MPC notes; Military Payroll Certificate, used by our troops in Vietnam, and bought a round of beer. Picking up from where he left off, Skip rubbed in the fact that

– after leaving Vietnam - our Huey flying days were probably over. But Skip would be flying armed patrols along the Iron Curtain in the latest version Mike model Huey - flying *über Deutschland!* He celebrated his great fortune with many cans of the diminutive Officers Club's coldest beer, which were usually kind of warm and dented.

As the hour grew late, we slowly wandered outside the O' Club. Skip and several others wobbled around a bit in the dark, adjusting to the darkness or lighting up cancer sticks and/or heading toward the nearest screen. In this case, it was the RLO's brand-spanking new, freshly-buried metal drum. There it stood - practically unscathed - under a sturdy-looking shed of some kind, designed to hide anyone in the process of downloading. A flawless red metal can half full of clean sand hung at arm's reach, a neatly stenciled sign on its side said, "Butts."

The Lieutenants had worked extra hard to get the spiffy new urinal ready before the evening's gathering. It smelled of fresh paint in the dark and while standing in position, one couldn't help but notice the RLOs had come up with some honest, 4-inch-by-4-inch-by-8-foot wood posts, to which were nailed carefully-sawn rocket-box side-partitions. Whereas, down in The Ghetto we possessed nothing so evolved. And to one happy-drunk German, the prissy-hut was a brazen insult to him and The Ghetto - and it must go. He shouted an oath, advising all us would-be down-loaders to **stand aside!**

Always ready for a good laugh, we standers-by raised very few objections as *Skip-turned-Don-Quixote,* challenged the shed with a guttural expletive. He sprang with all the strength his stocky German bod could muster, straight into a near-perfect martial arts flying-side-kick. One had to admire the height and energy a drunken aviator can achieve under these conditions.

Alas, the officers had done a resounding job of packing dirt around the shed's sturdy posts, and the one Skip's GI boot contacted stood its ground, while the Skipper's beefy leg bones suffered under the physics of a *spiral-compound-fracture*. To soften the blow to Skip's *insult to injury,* we declared him an "Honorable Recipient of the Flying Piss Screen Device," in absentia.

And that's the last we saw of ol' Skip, poor guy! He would spend many painful weeks recovering in a drab, stateside military hospital, so he could return to flight duty. And *gone* was that dream tour in Germany. Someone else would upgrade into that slot. *Kung Fu Skip* would be Texas-based, studying the military Method of Instruction manual and mentally preparing for his first flock of grasshoppers.

My First Flight - A Gunship Scramble

Andre Garesche

I arrived at the 134th in July 1970 and was assigned a room. My roommate, whom I hadn't even met yet, Dan Brown, was out on a slick mission. Not knowing where to go or what to do I grabbed the free bunk and took a nap. After a while someone came in and woke me up. A tall lanky guy with a clipboard who told me I was assigned to the gun platoon. He wanted to know what I wanted for a call sign. I said I didn't know and asked him what his was. He said Devil 47, (it was Mark Igoe). I said how about Devil 46. He told me it had to be an odd number so I bumped it down to Devil 45 and that is how I got my call sign. He also told me I had an orientation flight in the morning.

The next morning I was down at operations waiting. Patrick Pavey was the pilot I was going up with and it was in the chunker ship (019). We cranked up and took off north from Phu Hiep and he explained the low-level Vagabond crossing over Tuy Hoa's active runway. Patrick had a wry sense of humor and as we flew along he said, "That's a tree, those are mountains, that's a river, that's the ocean... and you've got it," and with that he gave me the controls.

He said we were going up to Qui Nhon for some lunch. I glanced back and the crew chief and door gunner were asleep. Patrick yawned and stretched and casually reached up to pull the old circuit breaker trick to see if I was watching my gauges. Before he even pulled it I told him I was familiar with the trick but never mentioned I had attended Gunnery I. P. School. He just shrugged, got comfortable and started to doze off.

Now, imagine my first flight time in Vietnam and I'm up there with three guys asleep. Patrick had told me to just follow the coast and that is what I did. I was just about to where the sunken Japanese ship was when the radios lit up. Patrick sat up immediately and took the controls. There were troops in contact and we were getting a mid-air scramble since we were nearest. We did a 180 and headed south toward the river. In a split second, the whole crew had snapped to from what I call "Nam sleep." You are always half awake!

The friendlies were on the north side of the river and the enemy on the south. Patrick asked if I had ever fired a chunker before and I told him I had. I could tell he was nervous about letting me use the weapon because he explained everything twice as to where to fire and that he was turning my radios off and putting me on AFVN. I guess he thought it would keep me calm. So, on my first hot gun run in Vietnam I was listening to Time Won't Let Me by the Outsiders. Some things you never forget.

They taught me a little trick at I.P. school. If you roll the chunker tube up a little and fire six rounds while slowly rolling the tube down, the rounds all land at once. It is sort of like a mini-B-52 strike. The rounds landed exactly where he wanted them. It certainly impressed Patrick because he screamed for me to do that again and again. Even the crew was impressed because they were shouting on the intercom. It's difficult to keep in working-order, but when it's working the chunker is very devastating and unnerving to the enemy. The ground troops even commented on it.

We expended our ordnance and another gun team was nearly there so we headed home. Patrick said he would do the post flight and would meet me at the Officer's Club. On his way to the club he went by Operations and pulled my file which indicated I had been to Gunnery I.P. School. He jokingly gave me a hard time about not telling him. We sat and talked for a long time. Turned out it was his birthday. I had had a pretty full day myself.

Cummings and the Daring Medevac

Lloyd Pool, BG (Ret) USMC

as submitted by
Skip Curtis, COL (Ret) USMC

Glancing around at the clutter in my attic recently, I decided it was time to sort through some of the unpacked boxes associated with my military retirement and move to Pennsylvania.

A fond smile crossed my face as I gingerly pulled out aging flight logbooks. As I randomly scanned the yellowing pages, I was surprised by the vivid and detailed recall the numerous sorties inscribed on those pages evoked.

Aviation seems to have that effect on the mind.

Locked in a trance with my memories, it was the flutter of a small newspaper clipping, surrendering to gravity as it fell from between the pages that snapped the spell of the moment and brought me back to reality. The clipping was a one-line notice from the *Navy Times* announcing the death of my friend, David Cummings, during 1988.

When I first cut out the obituary notice and tucked it away in my logbook, I mentally promised myself one day I would tell the story of his heroics – in another place and time. . .

Vietnam 1969

It was December. Reconnaissance elements from a battalion size Viet Cong force probed the hasty defense perimeter set up by a remote Marine observation team atop Hill 845.

From afar, an OV-10 Bronco aircraft, responding to an urgent call from the outpost for close air support, swept in low from the south. The confines of adjacent mountain ridges, coupled with a rapidly deteriorating cloud base, made the pending interdiction strike especially hazardous.

Monsoon season was well under way and, like the distant thunder, the drone of the Bronco's propellers reverberated off the trees and mountain sides, striking fear in the guerrillas (as wounded VC prisoners would later relate) while providing some semblance of comfort to the beleaguered Marines.

The Bronco pilot, CPT Dennis Herbert, and his rear-seat aerial observer seemed oblivious to the danger. Directed to the attack by a ground-based forward observer (FAC), the Bronco pilot focused his attack on a shallow ravine leading into the outpost encampment.

Squeezing off two Zuni rockets, he visually tracked the missiles (with a little body language) to the ravine where they exploded in a fury of smoke and fire.

Herbert immediately banked his aircraft sharply left to avoid flying debris. Quickly leveling his wings, he simultaneously pulled back hard on the control stick. His Bronco was now pointed straight up. Bleeding off airspeed for rapid altitude gain in an exchange of energy, the Bronco masked itself in the clouds to escape retaliatory ground fire, and to avoid collision with the mountains.

In a matter of seconds, the aircraft punched through the cloud overcast. CPT Herbert leveled off the aircraft, adjusted the throttle, and waited for a radio call to announce the results of his attack. The FAC reported the attack was successful. Further probing by the enemy had ceased. For the time being, a second suppression attack would not be required.

During the siege on the outpost, however, the FAC reported a young Marine had tripped off an enemy booby trap and was seriously injured. Bleeding profusely, he was going into shock. The Bronco pilot was asked to relay a call for an immediate medical evacuation.

Meanwhile, at Landing Zone Baldy, Cobra pilot 1st LT David Cummings and his Aircraft Commander, CPT Roger Henry, were standing by on routine medevac escort alert in their AH-1G helicopter gunship.

The rear cockpit seat of the Cobra, normally flown by the pilot in command, would today be flown by the copilot, LT Cummings, as part of his Aircraft Commander check-ride.

When the call came to escort medevac helicopters, the pilots launched with another Cobra to marry up with two CH-46 Sea Knight transport helicopters as part of a constituted medevac package.

After a smooth join up, the flight headed 40 miles south-west of Da Nang into the Que Son Mountains in Quang Nam Province where they rendezvoused with the Bronco for a mission brief.

Weather at Hill 845 had deteriorated badly. Rain and lowering cloud bases made it virtually impossible for the large Sea Knights to get into the area for the pickup. Despite persistent maneuvering, the rescue flight finally retired to the edge of the weather mass where they loitered to wait for another opportunity to go in and pick up the wounded Marine.

After obtaining approval from the Medevac mission commander, the agile Cobra flown by Henry and Cummings proceeded in to scout the landing zone to facilitate a more expeditious evacuation.

The worsening weather, however, prompted Henry, positioned in the higher visibility front gunner's seat, to assume control of the aircraft's more difficult to use side-console, forward-cockpit flight controls. Visibility was now practically zero.

In those days, there was a variation of a popular song theme that "only mad dogs and Englishmen ventured into noonday monsoons!" Undaunted, Henry and Cummings pressed on despite harrowing weather conditions. The two Marines worked their Cobra up the mountain side amidst severe turbulence generated up and down gnarled mountain slopes.

Scraping tree tops at airspeeds that often dipped below 30 knots, or required holding in perilous zero-visibility hovers, the flyers anxiously waited for a call from the outpost giving them either a visual or sound cue they were above the elusive ill-defined landing zone. After three hours and five different attempts, with refueling runs interjected in-between, the aviators finally found their mark.

Sporadic radio reports confirmed to Henry and Cummings their worst fear; the injured Marine was succumbing to his wounds. Guiding the Cobra down through tall trees, Henry landed the aircraft on the edge of a bomb crater in a skillful display of airmanship. The helicopter settled to the ground amid swirling debris.

The tightness of the landing zone was such that only the front half of the aircraft's skids rested on the rocky outer lip of the bomb crater. While the Cobra rested in this precarious, teeter-totter position, Cummings climbed out of the aircraft to investigate the situation.

Torn and bloody, the wounded Marine was drifting in and out of shock. Having served a previous tour in Vietnam as an infantry officer, Cummings was intimately familiar with the situation now confronting him. He had seen the haunting lurk of death in young men's eyes enough times before to know it was time to get this Marine out immediately. Death, Cummings promised himself, would not visit this Marine today if he had any say in the matter.

With the situation assessed, Cummings ordered the casualty lifted into the Cobra. Strapping the semi-conscious Marine into his rear cockpit seat, Lieutenant Cummings fastened the canopy shut.

As mud-Marines looked on curiously, Lieutenant Cummings climbed atop the starboard stub wing rocket pod. Straddling the pod and facing aft, Cummings banged his fist on the wing to get Henry's attention before giving him thumbs up. With a grim smile, CPT Henry nodded and took off. The cloud base, by now, was less than 100 feet above the outpost.

As the Cobra lifted away, the radio airways snapped to life as radio operators in the vicinity broadcast descriptions of the incredible scene they were witnessing.

Atop the rocket pod, Cummings flashed a V for victory for those remaining in the zone as the Cobra vanished dramatically into the blanket overcast. It was the ultimate stage exit. Marines on the ground stood and cheered. Morale soared.

Leveling off in a cloud mass at 4,000 feet, Henry accelerated the Cobra to 100 knots to improve maneuverability. Once stabilized, he glanced over his shoulder to check on the outrider.

Cummings flashed him back a sheepish grin. Biting rain, extreme cold at altitude, and the deafening shrill and shuffle-vibration of engines and rotors all mixed to fill his senses.

He could hold on only by squeezing his thighs tightly against the rocket pod wing mount. To exacerbate matters, the wind grabbed at the back of Cummings' helmet flexing it forward thereby causing the chin strap to choke him. And all the while, howling winds taunted him. But at their loudest, Cummings merely glanced at the wounded Marine, and howled back.

Herbert, still orbiting on patrol in his Bronco, began his return to home base as fuel began to run low. Enroute, he happened to catch a glimpse of the Cobra darting in and out of the clouds in its tenuous race against time. Zooming down for a closer look he was unprepared for the spectacle of Cummings, hanging outside the aircraft, and the bleeding semi-conscious Marine within.

In mild disbelief, the Bronco pulled up wide abeam the Cobra, gave a thumbs-up and departed. "What a crazy war!" Herbert quipped to his observer while still shaking his head in disbelief. But in his heart, he knew this was the way of the warriors!

After the 25-minute flight through turbulent weather, the gunship descended through the clouds and broke into relatively clear sky at 1,200 feet over a land navigation point called Spider Lake.

The Cobra now headed for a medical facility. Thoroughly exhausted from the strain of the mission, Henry was having trouble discerning the exact location of the medical site when he sensed a series of thumps coming from the starboard wing.

Glancing to his right, he saw Cummings, much like a prize-winning bird dog, with locked pointed finger directing his attention to their destination below.

After landing, the wounded Marine was whisked into a medical triage for stabilization, while Navy Corpsmen, who thought they had seen everything, helped Cummings defrost himself off the rocket pod.

A short time later, a CH-46 arrived to fly the wounded Marine to Marble Mountain for emergency surgery.

Sprinting along through the sky as combat escort for the Sea Knight to the more sophisticated "in-country" medical facility, were Cummings and Henry. The two were weary from fatigue, but nonetheless vested in their interest to culminate the safe arrival of their wounded Marine. The young Marine survived, married, and was last known to be living in Texas.

Despite the long day and fatiguing limits they had endured, Henry continued the training portion of Cummings' check ride on the way back to home base.

Oddly enough, among senior aviators in country, there was talk of censure and a court-martial for the outrider affair. The act, in their opinion, had overtones of grandstanding, regardless of the fact the young Marine would have died had he not received medical attention as soon as he did. When Henry and Cummings, however, were personally invited by the commanding general of the 1st Marine

Division to dine as special guests in his quarters, the issue of court-martial was moot and dead on arrival. For their actions, Henry and Cummings each were awarded the Distinguished Flying Cross.

Years later, when asked about the dining experience with the commanding general, both pilots readily admitted they had a great time. Libations, it appears, were liberally dispensed. And it was reported to the two aviators they were transported horizontally into their hooches and gently tucked into their racks by the grunts.

When Dave Cummings died unexpectedly in 1988, there were the normal expressions of loss, especially for one so young. But none who first attended his lifeless body, and only a few who were present at his hometown funeral, fully realized the magnitude of his life or the legacy he had left with the Corps.

A native of Woburn, MA, Cummings enlisted in the Marine Corps in September 1966. Upon completion of recruit training, he attended Officer Candidate School and the Basic School at Quantico, VA.

Cummings served several months as an infantry platoon leader with the 2nd Battalion, 1st Marine Division in Vietnam. After being seriously wounded in a firefight with Viet Cong forces, he was evacuated to the States.

Cummings had always wanted to fly, so it was a thrill following recuperation, when he was selected for flight training. Earning his

"Wings of Gold," Dave Cummings returned to Vietnam in September 1969 to start his combat flying career.

Nineteen years later, LTC Dave Cummings, enroute to attend a special military course in Albany, GA, stopped in Atlanta for the night. After a routine workout, he returned to his hotel room where the suffered an apparent heart attack and died. He was 42.

Although Dave Cummings' life spanned a relatively short period of time, he managed to walk a worthy journey. Among his awards were four Distinguished Flying Crosses, four single mission Air Medals, the Bronze Star with Combat "V", and a Purple Heart.

In this day and age when the term hero is used so loosely, it is comforting that I can say I actually have known some true heroes in my lifetime. Dave Cummings was a man who set the example. He was a guy who displayed courage all of us who knew him hoped we could muster if the call came.

Dave Cummings was a special piece of the Corps' past, a large measure of its tradition and, maybe more importantly, a sizeable chunk of its soul. He will not be easily forgotten. Semper Fi, Dave.

.

Varsity Standbys

Tom Hirschler

In I Corps, the three 101st Chinook companies rotated all-night flare-ship standby missions. The primary standby Chinook was located at Camp Evans. The other two companies' standby Chinooks remained in their company areas with progressive reaction times if the primary launched from Camp Evans and Basket Ball, an Air Force C-47 flare ship stationed at DaNang, was not available.

The standby Chinooks carried 48 high-intensity flares like eggs in a carton in a large open-top wooden box. When needed, the crew members would remove a flare from the box, set the drop altitude on the flare's bottom, and launch it through a tube mounted in the open cargo-hook hatch. The flare was activated by its lanyard which was attached to a cargo deck tie-down ring. The flare would illuminate and its parachute would deploy when it reached the programmed drop altitude.

On one of those standby nights at Camp Evans, my crew was launched to drop flares over an infantry outfit in contact. Artillery max-ord in the area was around 7,000 feet, so we dropped our flares from 8,000 while maintaining our position with radar vectors from Quang Tri approach control. I was glad to have a flight jacket with me; it was chilly at that altitude with the OAT in the low 30s. The cloud tops were at about 2,000, so the crew set the flares for a 6,000 foot drop, thus starting the illumination at the cloud tops for maximum effect.

With a sky full of stars, we circled for about an hour, watching our dropped flares glow through the clouds. At the end of the hour, we were relieved by Basket Ball which could stay up much longer.

One morning after being released from a quiet, overnight flare-ship standby, we were surprised by what we saw when we returned to Camp Eagle. When we were close enough to see our parking area, the Locker Room, we spotted one of our Chinooks on the ramp, upside-down; lying cross-wise on top of one side of its revetment.

During the evening before, a lone maintenance pilot was doing a test run-up following routine maintenance. The Chinook lifted nose-up and flipped out of control, slinging rotor blade parts around the company area, and sending movie-goers in the maintenance hangar running for cover. The Chinook's only crew member was standing on the ground to the rear, and escaped without injury. The lone pilot twisted an ankle when he dropped from the upside-down aircraft after parts stopped flying.

The cause was unclear; it was either improper maintenance or the pilot's lack of positional awareness allowing the thrust control to creep up.

The following incident occurred a few months into my year with Varsity.

Each morning, when the first mission of the day launched, we had a standby Chinook run-up in case a mission aircraft was not able to get off.

That day I was the standby pilot and Dale Petersen was the Aircraft Commander. The mission launched, and we went back to our hooches and standby-mode with our eyes closed.

Later in the morning, Dale came to tell me we had a mission to the city of Hue, about 8 miles away, and he wanted me to get our aircraft started. A truck had overturned; GIs were trapped and needed our help. Dale went to Operations to be briefed, while I hurried to the flight line and our Chinook.

Our procedure with T-55 L-11 engines was to start the left engine, get it to flight RPM, shut down the APU, and then start the right engine. This was always done with both pilots in their seats. Not waiting for Dale; I was starting the right engine when he arrived. We finished the start and I made the takeoff for Hue, flying while Dale made the radio calls.

Dale gave me the details in the few minutes it took to get to the site. A 5-ton truck had swerved to avoid hitting a Vietnamese civilian on a bicycle who cut the truck off. When the truck swerved, it missed the bridge it was approaching, then rolled upside-down and ended up front first, almost in the river below.

During the short flight, the SP6 Flight Engineer (FE) connected six slings and attached them to the cargo hook. Next to the river were trees some 100 feet tall, so we hovered with the Chinook's nose in the trees while the FE dropped the elongated sling. We were to lift the truck cab, so rescuers could pull out the trapped GIs.

If we lifted the cab too much, the truck would slide into the river. If we let it back down, the truck cab would crush the rescuers. After several minutes hovering at 100 feet with nothing to reference but the limbs of the trees blowing around in our rotor-wash and the FE's instructions over the intercom, the rescuers pulled both GIs from the truck's cab. Unfortunately, one was killed when the truck went off the road.

We found out later it was only eleven minutes from the time of the first call to our operations until we were hovering over the truck.

It was September 1970. T55-L11 engine power turbines were coming apart in flight, so the aircraft with those engines were grounded. Varsity had 12 out of 16 CH-47s parked, and the 196th Flippers came to the rescue with their A models. Flipper and Varsity ACs flew together on Flipper A models and Varsity's four T55-L7C C models. Flipper Dale Tate and I had been friends in the CH-47 course and were able to fly together on his A model on several missions.

On one of those missions, we had an off-shore pickup from hospital ship USS Sanctuary. The 101st Division band had been entertaining wounded soldiers recuperating on the Sanctuary, and needed a ride home. It was late afternoon when we made the pickup, with a 20 minute or so return flight. The first leg of the flight was about 20 miles along the coast, a very short distance from land; we then turned south toward Hue-Phu Bai. Soon after crossing the shore line, we lost a hydraulic system causing us to make a precautionary landing in a sandy area.

After shutting down, the crew found we had blown a hydraulic line in the C box area. This would be difficult to repair even if we had a replacement line. Darkness was not far away; we had the division band armed with their musical instruments. That left us with two M-60s for protection. Dale and I reasoned if we flew low, and not too fast, we could land in the very open area we had yet to fly over should we have another problem. Another 10 minutes of flying saw us on the Hue-Phu Bai ramp without incident. I don't recall our ever reporting to anyone the circumstances of the return flight's precautionary landing.*

*CW4 Dale Tate was killed making an NVG sling-load landing at Ft Campbell, July 24, 1990.

Sometime mid-1970, we were making a routine single-ship sling-load drop off at FSB Rifle. Normally, the pilot flying turned off the radio switches on his intercom/radio control panel when making a sling-load pick up or drop off. This is done to lessen the distractions to the pilot while listening to the directions of the crew-member in the cabin.

This was the last time I followed this practice. While listening to the crew-members directions, I noticed a cloud of dark smoke on the opposite side of the FSB. When I asked the other pilot what was going on, he didn't have a clue. I turned the radio switches back on in time to hear the Pathfinder yelling at us to depart; we were drawing incoming mortar fire.

Another incident occurred around the same time. On a rotating schedule, the exchange system sent a conex to the various FSBs in our area. This was so the FSB soldiers had access to the usual necessities, such as toothpaste, soap, etc. Accompanying the conex was a young soldier to act as its sales clerk. The conex was delivered/retrieved by CH-47, and its accompanying soldier sometimes rode in the Chinook or went by Huey. Someone else delivered the conex that day, and we were given the mission to return it to the Camp Evans log pad. When the mission was passed to us, we were told the soldier would return by Huey; there was no good place for a Chinook to set down to pick him up.

For those not familiar with external load operations, there are three types of loads: high density, low density, and aerodynamic. An example of a high density load would be an artillery piece; a conex is a good example of a low density load; of course, an aerodynamic load would be something such as another aircraft. Each has its flight characteristics, but that day the load of interest was low density.

A low density load has a large surface area relative to its weight. A low-density load has horrible flight characteristics when there is only a single point of attachment between it and the carrying aircraft. This means at airspeeds above 30-40 knots, the load can start swinging. If allowed to swing too much, it can endanger the carrying aircraft to the point where the load would need to be jettisoned, or as was more commonly referred to by Chinook crews "air-mailed."

We picked up the conex, and departed the FSB. Knowing its characteristics, we held our airspeed during the climb to 20 to 30 knots. As it neared the appropriate time to change the radio frequency, I had my hand on the radio frequency selector. Just before I made the frequency change, the Pathfinder made an urgent call telling us there was someone riding on top of the conex.

I immediately asked the Flight Engineer monitoring the load, and he confirmed there was someone on the conex. We slowed to a high hover, and turned to return to the FSB at about 10 knots. After setting the load back on the ground, we hovered down enough for the conex passenger to crawl into the cabin. When asked what in the... was he doing riding on the conex, the sales clerk said he had been told to not let the conex out of his sight. Since his Huey hadn't yet arrived, the only way to follow that order, he thought, was to ride it back to Camp Evans.

The Flight Engineer swore he did not see the soldier on the conex. I found that hard to believe, but had no way to contradict him. It would be difficult to exaggerate how lucky the soldier was, or how lucky we the crew were to return to the FSB without a serious incident to explain.

For the rest of my 18 years and 5,400 hours flying Chinooks, every time a mission included an external load, my preflight crew briefing included the words "and I don't want any passengers riding on the load."

Taking George Home

Dennis Dupuis

1970 April 30

Less drinking at the bar tonight, tomorrow's mission request was ordinary except our report time was 0600 hrs, the time we normally departed. We'd have a 0400 departure. It must be a special mission.

1970 May 1

The Cowboy flight of 10 slicks and 3 guns approached the east side of the Mekong River, about 10 -15 miles south of the Cambodian border. There were hundreds of Hueys in the air, more than I had ever seen. Today we were invading Cambodia. On our approach to the air strip, I saw more Hueys parked on the ground. There were heavy lift Chinook companies, Cavalry units, Cobra Attack companies, and many Assault Helicopter Companies like the 335th AHC Cowboys; all within the perimeter guarded by armored personnel carriers; and there was infantry, a lot of infantry.

We landed in our spot among the helicopters which stretched for as far as I could see. The size of this operation excited and scared me at the same time. The ARVN infantry soldiers filed next to our ships as we shut down the aircraft. Our lead aircraft crewmembers gathered us and repeated their briefing. The ARVN Infantry Division was ordered to secure the Mekong River Ferry Crossing below Phnom Penh, the capital of Cambodia. The 164th Aviation Group mission was to insert, and then support the Infantry Division. The Cowboy's landing zones, (LZs) were planned to secure the ferry crossing's eastern approaches.

We strapped in the aircraft and waited for the lead aircraft to turn on their rotating beacon - the start-engines signal for the flight. The soldiers boarded the aircraft; the gunners double-checked their weapons. The old peasants and young children started to appear. They looked at us; perhaps their father or brother was on board our ship.

Possibilities and consequences of today's mission raced through my mind. The silence was broken by the whistle of a turbine starting in the distance. Lead's rotating beacon was illuminated. I called "Cleeeear," and turned on the battery switch. The copilot announced, "Coming hot," on the intercom and pulled the starter trigger. With every start when the whistle of the starting engine faded; the rotor revolutions increased; the rocking motion of the entire aircraft evolved into small vibrations in the flight controls that told me the aircraft was alive. It was one with me. Wind generated by the rotor system flowed into the cockpit and drove the hot tropical air of the Mekong out of the cabin area. Now she was ready to fly.

The Cowboys departed the staging area. We joined the 164th formation in two Vs of five, escorted by our Falcon gunships. We followed the Mekong River north into Cambodia. We could see the elevated roadway to the ferry crossing in the distance and the smoke that marked the LZ. The gunners manned their weapons. Taking no fire, we landed in the uncontested "cold" LZ. The farmers and children in the PZ (pick-up-zone) had been the only "enemy" we saw.

2- 7 May

There weren't any combat assaults. I remember only routine support missions.

On one of these days, I was flying with Gary "Frenchy" DuMond of Ft Kent, Maine. Gary had a great desire to be a pilot, and wanted to go to flight school when he entered the Army. He really wanted to fly airplanes; the Army really wanted him to fly helicopters. Frenchy was a good aviator but he had to fly "those (expletive deleted) eggbeaters."

Our job was to off-load ammunition from a US Navy ship in the Mekong River, 10 - 15 miles south of the Cambodian border. The majority of ammo was for the helicopter gunships supporting the Cambodian incursion/invasion. We'd pick up a cargo net of ammo as a sling load; then carry the full net to the rearming point. We would take a previously dropped-off net back to the ship where we picked up another load and continued until the ship was unloaded.

A helicopter's total weight is limited primarily by the amount of power available/required to fly; i.e., to lift its total weight into the air. For this mission, we decreased the weight of the helicopter. Working at the airfield, we didn't fill the fuel tank to capacity and saved 1,000 lbs. The Gunner (175 lbs) stayed on the ground to signal us to the rearming point when we delivered the ammo. Less weight equals more power available, which equals more weight in the cargo net.

We started sling loading the ammo to the rearm points. When the gunner moved his arms to look like a big T, we hovered. When he moved both arms down, we descended. When the cargo net touched the ground, the gunner's arms would make an X. He'd disconnect the full net, hook up an empty net and we'd take the empty net out to the ship. We'd off-load another full net; carry the ammo; and bring an empty net to the ship, over and over again. It was a hell of a lot better than going into a hot LZ.

It was hot… I couldn't lift a particular load off the ship; higher air temperatures eat the power available to turbine engines. Some of the ammo would have to be removed to lighten the sling load. I left the ship to recover some of the empty nets. As we entered the destination traffic pattern, our FIRE warning light illuminated. The fire detection system usually was a false alarm. I had the crew chief visually check and he yelled, "We're on fire."

I immediately turned from the traffic pattern and started a very steep descent to the closest part of the field. "Mayday, Mayday, Mayday…Cowboy 21's on fire."

The crew chief ran forward and put his head between Frenchy and me. He looked at me and said, "We're on fire." He looked at Frenchy and said, "We're on fire." He ran to the back, looked outside and said, "Yep, we're on fire."

I had my hands full trying to compensate for his rapid movement inside the chopper. I told the new guy to **sit down**; I briefed Frenchy, "We're landing _**to the ground**_, not to a hover. **Do not** turn the battery switch off when we land." The flight control force trim held the flight controls electrically in a fixed place, no force trim meant the rotors could flex lower than our shoulder height on our way out.

When I pulled pitch to cushion the landing, the Low Rotor RPM warning sounded. I had failed to notice the engine had quit at some time during the descent. The crew chief slapped me on the back on his way out. "Good autorotation, Sir." Frenchy and I were running away from the ship, and I was a close second.

There was no emergency fire equipment at this staging area so close to the border. When we stopped running, we looked back at our aircraft. Black smoke was twisting through the slow turning rotors. We saw the Chinook crews start running into their parked aircraft. I knew they had big fire extinguishers on board. When the crews came out of their aircraft they didn't have extinguishers, they were carrying their cameras. They must have gotten some nice pictures of our bird on fire. They were nice enough to give us a ride home.   "(expletive deleted) eggbeaters."

1970 middle of May

I don't remember the mission, but I remember the Operations jeep was waiting at the revetment when it was over. Before we could shut down the aircraft, the driver signaled me to get out of the aircraft and into the jeep. "What's going on?" I asked the driver. "Just get in, sir." he replied.

Our 335th Operations Officer told me to get enough clothes and shaving gear for three days and to get back ASAP. "A helicopter will take you (an hour and a half flight) to Vinh Long for a briefing."

Fifteen or twenty minutes later I was the only passenger in the helicopter. The guys flying were taking me to 214th battalion HQ in Vinh Long.

I was short, a double-digit midget (less than 99 days left in country). Matter of fact, I had less than 90 days left in country. What's the rush? What was the secret? What could be so important? My wildest thought was "I'd been picked for a POW rescue." The guys went to refuel after landing at our 214th Battalion VIP pad.

I ran to the Headquarters where they were expecting me. A Major handed me a large sealed envelope and asked me to sign a receipt of message. "What's this about?" "The Huey that's landing on the VIP pad is taking you to Saigon. Read your orders on the way. Hurry." It was a little longer than an hour to Saigon. What was so important? I could feel my heart was pounding as I opened the envelope and read the orders. Oh, no! My friend George Mason was KIA (Killed in Action) and his mother had requested me as his Escort.

We landed on the Saigon ramp near the commercial airliner that would take me to Hawaii and then to San Francisco (Oakland Army Depot).

In California, I attended briefings on the responsibilities and conduct of a Body Escort Officer while George was prepared for transportation and burial. I was issued a new Class A uniform and orders for George's return to his hometown for burial in Ringwood, Oklahoma. George and I left San Francisco on a commercial flight to Oklahoma City. I was with the other passengers and George was with the cargo and luggage. The other passengers had no idea George was on board directly under their feet all the way to Oklahoma.

I saluted whenever George's coffin was moving. I rode in the hearse with George for the 2 hour trip to Enid. When he was settled at the funeral home, we went to the Masons' home. I don't remember much about that time before the funeral.

The funeral service was at the high school George had attended. My brother, Bruce, in his Class A uniform, chest full of Medals (from his tour in Vietnam) and spit-shined paratrooper boots, delivered the eulogy. It was very difficult to present the flag to Mrs Mason. I had rehearsed the words but they didn't flow easily when the time came to present George's folded flag to her. I cried, I still cry.

Instead of immediately returning to my unit in Vietnam after the funeral, the Mason family had requested a two week extension to my Body Escort orders. They had told the Survival Assistance officer from Ft Sill they needed me to take care of some personal business for the deceased for them. They hugged me and thanked me for bringing George, their son, home to them; handed a round trip airline ticket to me and told me to go see my mom and dad before I returned to Vietnam.

Bruce had driven from Ft Wolters, TX in his new 1970, 455 cubic inch, Olds 442. We were spotted from the air speeding on a long, flat, two lane highway. We came over a little hill and the cops were waiting at a four way stop sign to give him a ticket. ha ha….

When we got to Texas, we met his flight school class mates at one of the training stage fields. His class mates bought beers that afternoon at the Officers Club Happy Hour. They would be headed to Vietnam next year. They had a lot of questions about the helicopter war and I answered most of their questions.

It was my first time as an officer at a real Officers Club Happy Hour. They said my money wasn't any good. They got me drunk but I had a good time. The next day Bruce took me to the airport and I used the airline ticket from Mr & Mrs. Mason to go home for the remainder of my two weeks.

It was June when I returned to the 335th AHC Cowboys at Camp Bearcat. By the time I returned, I was short and had become the platoon scheduling officer. I didn't know that one of the newer guys, Don Krumrie was also from Enid, OK. As a Blue Star Mom, Don's mother had met and then consoled Mrs. Mason when George died. After Don wrote to his mom, she let Mrs. Mason know Don was in my unit and that we flew together. Don made Aircraft Commander on July 16. That night, I scheduled Don to fly on his first mission as Aircraft Commander the next day. He died that day. My DEROS was 2 weeks later.

George A. Mason - May 5, 1970

Aircraft was shot down at approx. 11:00 hours vicinity of Fire Support Base O'Reilly. Hit by 37 mm anti-aircraft round while flying with sling load. Caught fire and crashed nose down.

11:15 - A Trp 2/17 Air Recon Platoon (ARP) was launched to vicinity 400295 (Varsity AC). The AC was reported as burning.

11:30 - 101st DIV G-2 reported ...that the nearest unit to 'Varsity 295', the downed AC, was A Co. 3rd Bn, 187th, "Rakkasans."

12:05 - Air Recon Platoon on the ground, green LZ. Negative survivors found at AC.

15:15 - A/2/17 ARP extracted 5 bodies from CH-47, ARP extracted at 15:45.

★ ★ ★ ★ ★ ★ ★ ★ ★ ★ ★

The entire Varsity 295 crew together, forever on The Wall:
SP4 Gary W. Brown, SGT Larry D. Buffington,
CW2 George A Mason, PFC Steven E. Wasson,
WO1 Richard L Vandewarker

★ ★ ★ ★ ★ ★ ★ ★ ★ ★ ★

Destiny Joins Fate

J. Bruce Huffman

The sun pushed its way over the horizon of the South China Sea that September morning in 1968. I wandered down to the TOC (Tactical Operations Center) with my map under my arm to get the final briefing for the first-light mission that morning. WO Burns was my "Red Bird" and would drive his UH-1B to always be in a position to rain hell on any foolish NVA unfortunate to find his way into his gun sight reticule and threaten my low bird.

Ernie and I reviewed the final details of the mission and covered the tactical frequencies we'd be operating on, who would monitor the emergency radio channel, and what VHF frequency we'd use to communicate on to stay out of each other's way. The mission was a simple one; check in with a D Troop platoon that had been in an NDP (night defensive position) monitoring trail activity between the *Street Without Joy* and the distant NVA base camps in the mountains west of Camp Evans. I was to be on the alert for military age males without proper ARVN identification; we were to "snatch" them for detailed interrogation at the base camp. Our Blues (Infantry Platoon) were standing by in a lager at Evans, with the Lift (assault helicopters) monitoring the operation from the TOC.

We finished the rest of the coordination briefing and made our way to the revetments to preflight and get cranked up and begin the hunt. My crew was already there and loading up Zero Seven Niner (OH-6A, 67-16079) with the tools of the trade; i.e., fragmentation grenades, white phosphorous, a few thermite and concussion grenades, ammo for the chunker (M-79), clips for the CAR-15 (1 tracer - 3 ball), a half load for the mini-gun, and enough M-60 ammo for Gossages' free gun to give him plenty to work with.

We weren't going on a bear hunt but if we saw a bear; it would be in some serious shit. I loved my crew and was proud of the way we'd come together to fly safe, fight hard, and come back home at the end of the day to yet another cold Balantine beer. My crew chief and gunner was SP4 Douglas Gossage. Doug came from Missouri and could throw a grenade, from any combination of bank and airspeed, through the opening of a bunker with predictable consistency. When his M-60 would talk, six rounds later the target would be down. Doug had just turned 19 years old.

Our observer was SSG John States who had been trained in armor reconnaissance at Ft. Knox. John was from Baltimore and got airsick frequently and had trouble reading the map early on. SSG States had the heart of a lion though, and on those days when we would 'find 'em' he was skilled at sending the bad guys on a very long "dirt nap."

As we began the mission, we flew east over the featureless terrain of the coastal plain toward Quang Tri. The crews had checked their guns and our Pink Team was in the hunt. The mission was a success. We bagged no fewer than 6 guys; they later turned out to be NVA, who had been in the villages the night before and failed to get home before we turned them into "prisoner pumpkins" the following morning.

We had refueled and rearmed at LZ Jane earlier and had completed our last refueling at Camp Evans. All in all, it had been a good morning and I was looking forward to shutting down and pulling out my lawn chair to work on my R&R tan.

I landed to a hover on the nasty, oiled-dirt strip we shared with Bravo Troop and saw WO Wallace running toward my bird. WO John Wallace was relatively new but had shown skill and aggressiveness. I sat the bird down and Wallace leaned in said "Get out! I need your bird and crew. Lobes Echo is in contact and the Snake is cranking." I said, "We've already been up for 3.8 hrs. Give me the damn brief or get your own bird up!" John replied, "We don't have time, it looks like it could be a Prairie Fire!"

I stepped out of the LOH, picked up my "chicken plate" and helmet, and watched as John flew over the concertina wire and turned west headed for the foothills leading to the A Shau. Less than thirty minutes later Cavalier "White" (1LT James G. Ungaro) walked into my hooch to tell me "Wallace is down and they are all dead!"

WO Wallace had checked in with Lobes' Echo and found they felt they were engaged with at least a Battalion of NVA troops. Echo was under canopy on the high ground overlooking a depression held on three sides by the NVA. Echo was a company-sized unit against a much larger enemy force, but they had the high ground and they also had the "great equalizer" on their side: lots and lots of firepower.

John made the initial pass and discovered a 12.7 mm heavy machine gun in a doughnut bunker and had Gossage mark it as they blazed by. The AC of the snake refused to shoot due to the proximity of the friendly positions. He had recently been involved in a "short round" incident that had wounded US troops and he had been badly reprimanded and humiliated by an officer that should have known better. He had done exactly what the US ground commander had requested. While the high bird was fooling around trying to get some artillery cranked up, Wallace decided to take out the gun.

He flew in, and with a combination of M-60 fire and fragmentation grenades got the 12.7 mm. Unfortunately, the other two gun positions protecting the NVA regimental CP got him. The aircraft landed in the wrecked position of the first gun. SSG States stepped over what had once been the front console and canopy, and went head to head with an NVA who got in the first shot. WO Wallace un-strapped and went out the right door, and began a run for his life toward Lobes Echo, who were laying down an intense base of fire to cover him as he ran uphill. With less than 100 meters to go from their downed bird to the ARVN position, Wallace was hit in his legs 40 meters from relative safety. He went down hard and before he could get up, an NVA officer in full view of the US advisor working with the ARVN troops, shot him in the neck with a pistol.

SP4 Gossage had everything he needed; lots of ammo and plenty of targets. The ARVN Rangers said the sound of the M-60 rattled on until finally the NVA fired an RPG-7 into the downed bird and the gun went silent. When our recovery was completed, the bodies of 12 NVA were found in and around the remains of Zero Seven Niner. Gossage had done his duty!

I often reflect on "what if?" about their loss but realize on that day their fate intersected their destiny with terrible consequences. It was my honor to have served with them; warriors to the end!

Street without Joy Bernard B. Fall George C. Herring Format: Hardcover, 416pp .ISBN: 0811717003 Publisher: Stackpole Books Pub. Date: March 1994

South Vietnam adds to memory of JFK era

Paul Maxwell

All of us who were in the Vietnam era also were part of the Kennedy era

Having marched in his inaugural parade, then later standing as one of the honor company he reviewed in 1962 at West Point, he was the only president I had ever physically seen just a few steps away.

Years later, I was to have another strange relationship to add to my memory of the Kennedy era.

On January 27, 1967, I was in A Company, 229th, and we were operating out of Hammond LZ on the coast and working the usual areas in and around Bong Son. On this particular day, I was flying resupply for one of the battalions and it all started out as just another boring day carrying mermite containers to grunts, who weren't always where they thought they were.

In the early afternoon, I got an urgent call from operations to immediately go over to the runway and join up with a 227th gaggle forming for an emergency assault north of Hammond on the coast. This was one of those rare occasions when both lift battalions were operating in the same area supporting different brigades.

When I got over to the runway with my wingman, we were designated Purple 1 and 2. The Orange flight was made up of other A/229th slicks that had arrived before us, and two more slicks joined me to complete the purple flight. As usual, we knew nothing of what was going on and simply followed the leader. I don't recall stopping en route, so we must have loaded up the infantry company at Hammond.

As we approached the LZ, all the chatter indicated it was a hot LZ. The first sorties in were taking fire and several aircraft were hit. I believe one or more made precautionary landings on the beach just a short distance away.

We heard all of this as we were approaching on final to the LZ. That was one bad thing about being a Purple flight, you had advance notice it was going to be a pucker situation.

As I came in on short final, CWO Larry Hurst in the Orange flight just ahead of me was climbing out and called me. He said there were wounded lying around the LZ, and asked if I could pick them up.

I told him I if I saw them I would pick them up. As we landed, I looked around as best I could and didn't see a soul anywhere.

We unloaded and, as I was pulling out, I asked my crew chief, Miles T. Reid, and gunner John Gregoire, if they saw any wounded. They said yes and I asked them if I were to come around again could they find them? Again, they said yes.

As soon as I cleared the palm trees surrounding the LZ, I did a low-level 360-degree turn back into the LZ. On short final, I saw some wounded lying behind row of hedges.

I sat down with my tail rotor just forward of the hedges. After what seemed like a long time, I realized no one in the LZ was going to get up and bring the wounded to us, so I said: "Get out and get them."

Without hesitation, Reid and Gregoire unbuckled and jumped out. I looked back and the two of them were standing hopelessly on the LZ looking at me. They hadn't seen the wounded behind the hedges as we came in and had no idea where to find them. Later, describing the look on their faces seemed amusing, but I'm sure it was not amusing to them at the time.

After some wild gesturing, I got them headed behind the aircraft to find the wounded. About the same time, I guess the grunts figured out what we were there for and they too started moving to load the wounded on the ship. I don't remember how many we picked up, but at last we were done and I started to pull pitch to get out of there before our luck ran out.

Before I could get light on the skids, the company first sergeant came running over and jumped on the skid next to my window. He said the company commander had been hit and asked if we would hover over and pick him up. I nodded "OK" and proceeded to follow him at a low hover to the other side of the LZ.

They quickly carried the captain to the aircraft. I looked back and was dismayed at what I saw. As they carefully lifted him into the aircraft, one of the troopers had both hands holding the captain's brains in his head. The top of his skull had been blown off. I remember thinking at the time, "What in the hell am I doing sitting here risking my crew for a dead man?"

I departed the LZ and, as fast as I could fly, got the wounded back to the Medevac pad at Hammond. After refueling, we went back to the runway to await further action, but it never came.

As we were waiting, the infantry company first sergeant came trotting over from the Medevac area. He had an arm wound and we had brought him out with the captain. The arm was freshly bandaged and he asked us to take him back to the LZ.

I told him we couldn't, because we were on standby and he would need to go find the 227th flight leader to see if he could get a lift back in. Although this was the truth, in reality I knew I probably couldn't find the LZ again, since we followed the leader in and, after all the excitement, I didn't pay any attention to anything except getting back to Hammond.

A few weeks later, while flying resupply again, I asked the mess sergeant of the battalion we had supported what had happened to the captain. Much to my surprise, he told me the captain was still alive and had been evacuated to Japan. It gave me both a warm feeling to know I'd helped save him, and a guilty feeling that I had written him off for dead and for feeling I had needlessly risked lives.

After a few months, I rotated back to the States and forgot about the incident. Months later, I learned the aircraft I had flown that day had gone down on April 2, 1967, killing John Gregoire and Miles Reid. I later learned John Gregoire was in fact killed; but Miles Reid survived. These two guys were the only heroes that day when they got out of the ship to pick up the wounded.

And Now the Rest of the Story (with apologies to Paul Harvey):

In 1974, I was thumbing through a *Soldiers* magazine when I came across an article titled "Memories of the JFK funeral." Written by MAJ Eugene Bickley the MDW Radio-TV Officer during the funeral, it described his memories of the funeral. As an epilogue, he talked about CPT Michael Groves, the Old Guard Company commander for the funeral and LT Sam Bird the commander of the casket team. On the Sunday after the JFK funeral, CPT Groves collapsed and died of a heart attack.

In 1973, MAJ Bickley, author, learned Sam Bird "went to 'Nam in '66 and was wounded on his birthday, January 27, 1967. He was leading his company - B/2 of the 12th Cavalry - on an assault on the Bong Son plains." Sam was confined to a wheelchair and was to be medically retired.

For some reason, the date and place caused me to be curious. After digging out my old records, I found the award citation and newspaper clipping confirming it was on January 27, 1967, that I had picked up and flown out the commander of B Company, 2/12th. Now I knew his name: Sam Bird.

The real significance of my encounter was not realized until years later. I was reading a *Readers Digest* from May 1998. In it was a

"Most Unforgettable Character" article by B.T. Collins, titled, "The Courage of Sam Bird."

Collins, an artillery forward observer, related the arrival of CPT Sam Bird in B Company, 2/12th. He described over time how CPT Bird's first priority was caring for his troops and, by leading by example; he gained the loyalty and respect of every man in B Company.

CPT Bird had his field duty extended for one month to be able to spend more time with his company. On his last day, also his birthday, the troops had made arrangements to have a birthday cake brought in.

All plans were interrupted when B Company got orders to mount up for an air assault. Sam was hit on landing; slugs shattered his left ankle, right leg, and the left side of his head.

After 17 years of daily pain and paralysis, Sam Bird died on October 18, 1984. During those 17 years Sam was married and never once complained of his plight. He always felt he was far luckier than the ones who didn't come back.

I am happy I had one small role in Sam's life and I thank John Gregoire and Miles Reid for their part in it. I only wish they had known.

A SHAU and PFC Caballero*

*Killed in Action, 24 April 1968

John Fox

In my feeble attempt to give clarity and context to the loss of PFC David Joe Caballero of Corpus Christi, TX I feel it necessary to tell of the A Shau Valley and the events that led to this battle. Operation Delaware by the 1st Cav was the name of the operation. There are many pilots and crewmen I should give credit to, but three were most notable: Ralph Jackson, CO of B/228; Dave Clemmer, wounded pilot; and Andy Dulay, my co-pilot on April 24, 1968.

The A Shau is a beautiful valley that runs north-west and south-east, adjacent to the Laotian border, just south of the DMZ, sparsely populated by Montagnards, a nomadic people. A logging road #548 runs through here. The floor of the valley is 2,000 ft. above sea level and surrounded by 5,000 foot mountains.

In 1963, now retired General Colin Powell arrived as a new Lieutenant serving as an advisor. He declared it had a French Foreign Legion Beau Geste quality without the sand for the six months he patrolled the A Shau. Upon his departure, Special Forces operated a small base camp at the south end. As part of the Ho Chi Minh trail, the North Vietnamese found this to be an ideal sanctuary. In 1965, the Marines took over operation of this area establishing a western base at Khe Sanh plateau, just north of the A Shau. The North Vietnamese continued to build supply caches and a hospital complex. This came to be the staging area for the NVA campaign, Tet '68, initiated in January.

The battle for control of I Corps by the Marines and 1st Cav began. A/228th, a CH-47 Chinook Company, had recently moved to the western edge of Hue Phu Bai under protection of the U.S. Marines. PFC Caballero, MAJ Don Yenglin, and I were new arrivals just days prior to Tet. After many vicious battles, control of most of I Corps was under U.S. control, with the exception of the Marines at Khe Sanh.

We were all battle-weary, but the 1st Cav fought its way past the Rock Pile leapfrogging firebases up the valley to Khe Sanh plateau, rescuing a very happy bunch of Marines. The following months of March and April were spent moving the entire 1st Cav and lead elements of the 101st Airborne Division into I Corps.

The decision had finally come to mount a large force incursion into the NVA supply base, the A Shau Valley. On April 19, 1968 the 1st Cav would air assault into the northern end of the A Shau and the 101st Airborne Division would provide a blocking force at the southern end of the valley. The first day of the assault by the 1st Cav resulted in the loss of 25 aircraft of which five were CH-47s and one CH-54. One CH-47 was mine. This battle was extremely intense.

As I approached the designated bomb crater on the side of Tiger Mountain with a sling load of artillery ammo, the Chinook began to strain due to the high density altitude at approximately 3,000 feet above sea level. To our right side and down the bombed hillside small explosions were occurring. Our gunship escorts reported we were taking fire. Behind the Chinook and the bomb crater were several denuded trees that would be a flight hazard.

While lowering the ammo into the crater, the load hung up on the forward edge. There was not enough power to lift the load to reposition it to the center of the crater. Struggling with the load would lengthen our exposure time to the enemy fire, but the gunships continued to cover us. Looking out over the crater we could see down the mountain side in front of us where LZ Tiger lay, near the end of a dirt logging road that ran beside us and next to the mountain.

Suddenly, the helicopter lurched right, then left, and was followed by a large explosion in the rear. My adrenalin rose as I attempted to maintain control, knowing we were going to crash on top of all this ammo. The nose and cockpit were extended over the crater's edge and it was rocking as if it would slide down the mountain head first. I started shutting down the fuel switches and pulling the fire extinguisher handles.

Apparently I was too slow for the other pilot, Doug Martin, who had already exited the cockpit through the companion way. The intercom was not working, so I didn't know what action was taking place in the rear of the Chinook. After gathering my weapon and maps, I looked into the companion-way, but it was filled with a raging fire. The only way out was through the left cockpit emergency exit door. I pulled the handle, and the door popped off and slid down the mountain. The sloping surface was 15 feet directly below me and it was nothing but pulverized clay from the bomb crater.

Flames were now in the cockpit. I tried to jump but I couldn't move! The voice in my head said: "**STUPID!** Unbuckle your safety harness!" With panic building, I finally jumped out onto the hillside and slid down the mountain into full view of the enemy. Just then, a gunship made a low overhead pass that was very comforting. I knew proceeding down the hill was not an option because our troops were back up the hill behind the burning Chinook. Still wearing my flight helmet and chest protector, and carrying an M-16 rifle, I struggled to climb uphill in the steep, very loose clay. It was one step forward and slide back two.

In front of me appeared two young troops that raced down the loose clay, like mountain goats. They grabbed me underneath the arms, and up the hill the three of us flew, into the safety of a group of trees and a platoon of the 5/7 Cav troopers. All of my crew was accounted for. Kenny Sager, the tail gunner, was being treated for burns of the upper body by Medic Norm McBride. The 5/7 Company XO CPT Mike Sprayberry **, had assisted in removing the crew and, thankfully, had seen me slide down the hill.

After ensuring the rest of the crew was not wounded, our option was to proceed down the mountain side to the logging road, and then to LZ Tiger where the troops could be airlifted out. Although they would be exposed to enemy fire, I sent them down at a fast run. The tail gunner Sager, now had his shirt removed and was lying on the ground being treated with a balm for his burns. He was awake and had been given two morphine shots in his legs. There was no way to medevac him by helicopter from this location. He would have to be moved down to the LZ for evacuation. Kenny assured me he was okay and could walk down.

We got him up on his feet and started moving towards the road, after thanking the troops for their help. As we moved out, we strolled easily down the road in full view of the NVA. We talked casually as Kenny told me it was just a light sun burn. I knew better! Not a shot was fired at us! When the two of us reached LZ Tiger, we were met by the Battalion Surgeon, Dr. Jeff Kahler. Kenny began to get weak so we laid him down on a stretcher. Soon shock began to set in with his body trembling violently. The surgeon looked at me with a shake of his head, indicating his situation was not good. Shortly afterward, a resupply Huey landed and took my crew and the stretcher aboard. There was not enough room for all of us, so I remained behind. This was the last I saw of Kenny Sager.***

I headed to the two-man fighting position where the Pathfinder (Air Traffic Controller) was located. There was barely enough room for us to squat down, yet there was a good view of the surrounding area. He was very busy directing all types of helicopters and there were lots of delays due to small arms fire and incoming mortars. Looking back up the mountain, I could see our Chinook burning on top of the exploding artillery rounds that were cooking off. Several more Hueys had been able to land but there was no time to pick me up. The exploding artillery rounds were causing a delay.

A CH-54 Crane began to make its way down the mountain with a bulldozer on a sling, looking for a place to set down. They continued to move forward until they were over the top of the Pathfinder and me. Still unable to find a place to set down their load, they were contacted by a Command & Control Huey (pilots LTC Speedman and MAJ Ralph Jackson) offering to lead them to another LZ. The Pathfinder with me kept trying to contact the Crane to advise them not to fly out into the valley due to a reported NVA .51 cal. machine gun that was active. The Pathfinder's radio was being overpowered by the C&C ship's radio. A few moments later, the frantic Pathfinder turned to me saying: "We lost that Crane! The Crane was lost in an explosion!" We were very saddened. We watched as more helicopters were shot up. Then another Crane pilot (Ted Jenkins) came in to drop off a sling load and his ship departed safely. Finally, a Huey resupply ship was able to come in and airlift me back to Phu Bai.

It had been a long, sad day for friends, Aviation, and the First Cavalry Division, learning another Chinook from my company, A/228th had crashed with pilots, Donald Winskey and Frank Wendt. I later learned the pilots were able to escape and evade the enemy overnight by traveling through the woods to the sounds of chainsaws. However, they lost their crew: 'Bodies Not Recovered'. Not so lucky were the Crane pilots, Charlie Millard and Art Lord who were listed as MIA, also 'Bodies Not Recovered'. Both were friends of mine. I had served with Charlie in the 11th Air Assault at Ft Benning, GA and with Art at Ft Rucker, AL as instructors and neighbors.

On April 24, 1968, Andy Dulay and I would receive a tactical emergency mission to resupply a 105 artillery firebase SE of LZ Tiger. The unit was in danger of being overrun. An external load of 105 ammo was rigged, and internally we loaded some classified ammo with additional artillery troops. Camp Evans was carrying weather of 100 and ½ with tops at about 8,000 feet (weather with 100 foot ceilings and a half mile visibility). Our flight plan would be to climb out IFR to VFR on top. We were then to proceed out to the A Shau and rendezvous with two UH-1 gunships which would escort us down through a VFR hole in the clouds to the valley below.

Since we were close to the Laos border, our descent would be a rapid spiral of 6,000 ft. to the valley. The descent was so rapid and tight we would drift in and out of settling with power. The final approach was from Tiger Mountain, SE parallel to the valley floor to the hilltop firebase. On short final, we were able to see four or five destroyed UH-1 aircraft around the boundary of the firebase. Within 50 feet of the firebase perimeter, we began to receive small arms fire directly underneath the left side. This gun fire seriously damaged the radio compartment, and the #1 hydraulic system began to lose pressure.

The left waist gunner, Caballero, took a round just below his armored chest protector, which proceeded upward and killed him instantly. The crew said he simply crumpled to the floor. They were not sure what happened to him.

We began our ascent with the #1 hydraulic pressure now at zero. Our altitude would be limited to 6,500 feet; just enough to clear the 5,000 ft. mountains, but we would remain in IFR conditions for the flight back to Camp Evans. Knowing an IFR approach would be required, I began announcing 'Mayday' on both the emergency frequencies. Carl Hess, of B/228th heard the Mayday and relayed our intentions to Evans tower and that we had wounded on board.

After completing an ADF approach, we landed in the Bravo Co. area. Since there was no room on the helipad to land, we set down the sling load. We then moved forward to the edge of the pad touching down our aft wheels and lowered the rear ramp to unload the ammo and troops. We were met by medics. PFC Caballero was taken to the hospital where he was pronounced dead and transferred to the morgue. The aircraft was reviewed by B Co. Commander Ralph Jackson and his maintenance officer to determine its flyable status.

I was again met by medics requesting I come to the morgue for identification and to receive his personal effects. As I observed PFC David Joe Caballero, it struck me he appeared so small lying on that cot, pale and in a peaceful sleep. So young! Just a boy!

Of all the emotionally difficult things I've done, this would stay with me always! The next day I would fly again, the battle would go on. From then on, I don't look at the name or personal effects. Just keep moving.

It would be many years before I would pursue this man's name. My search took me through the VHPA Directory and the national archives, waiting months for the final answer on the report DA Form #1. Thanks to Julie Kink and Gary Thewlis for their assistance.

This was a tough war for tough young men. Doing their duty in a war they didn't understand, nor were they appreciated by the American people. Recently I participated in a radio talk show in Shreveport, LA. The movie 'We Were Soldiers Once' has generated a lot of interest in those of us that were involved. The public timing may be a little late, but there is a new generation and if we can find ways to remember those we lost, such as the final roll call in the movie, recognizing these were real young men whose lives were not fulfilled.

In retrospect, most of us have returned to homes, businesses, marrying and raising children in the freedom they purchased for us. God Bless them all! Thank you for reading this story.

I was saddened, believing that Kenny Sager had died, until 30 years later he would call me. God bless you Kenny! Forty-six years later, Art Lord's daughter, Susan Lord Bizaillion would call me. It must have been Divine Providence!

**Captain James "Mike" Sprayberry would be awarded the Medal of Honor for his actions in the A Shau Valley on 25 April 1968.

***Kenny Sager and John Fox have since been in contact with each other, happy to find the other man alive. Kenny joined John at the 2015 VHPA Reunion

.

The Improvised Secret Weapon

Stephen Cover

Now everybody knows all war stories are obligated to start with "This Ain't No Sh*t"... But, this one really is the truth.

Back in late summer of 1967 (Statute of limitations is well past... I hope) I was a helicopter pilot for D Troop 3/5th Cav. It was a few weeks before I qualified as command pilot in our unit flying the UH1-D Huey.

About 8 or 10 miles south of our base was a watermelon patch. My Aircraft Commander, "Igor", would say we needed to get ourselves a watermelon every time we flew past.

One day, about half of the melons in the field were gone; they were being harvested. That was good enough for Igor. We swooped down on our way back from a mission and landed near the biggest melon in the patch. Our crew chief grabbed the melon and we were off. There's nothing like an armed helicopter for an escape vehicle.

Back at base we eagerly plugged the melon. It was still white inside. We hadn't considered they were picked green so they would ripen up in shipment. Duh!! That brought up the problem of what to do with the evidence. We were sure our CO would enlarge our afterburner vents with a glowing poker if he found out about our larceny.

Well, the solution was obvious. There was a corner of a field just off Highway 5 that always produced some enemy fire. Even though this was in a free fire zone, Command had pretty much decided one

VC shooting at helicopters that were at least a half mile out of range wasn't much of a threat and therefore there was no need to mount an attack on him as long as he stayed where he was. That VC became "The Prime Target."

Design of our secret improvised weapon was discussed for some time - probably three to four minutes. We finally came up with the idea of stuffing the purloined watermelon with grenades to "wipe out" the lone VC at the corner of the field. We cut three holes in the watermelon, putting a frag grenade in the center, and a WP (white phosphorous grenade) on either side of it. When the time came to drop our secret weapon, the crew chief would pull the grenade pins, and throw out the Bomb. The grenade handles would be held in place until the watermelon burst on impact..in theory that is.

That afternoon, we were sent on a recon mission. I think Igor volunteered for it, but I don't remember. On the way back, we drifted over to the target area. Back in those days we flew at 1,500 ft AGL (above ground level) because 30 cal tracers would burn out way before they got to our altitude, making hits on a helicopter with small arms an iffy prospect at best. At 1,500 ft, Igor started our bomb run. The order was given to "Arm the weapon"... The pins were pulled... Naturally, all of the communications on the intercom would have made a B-17 crew proud with both waist gunners on the lookout for ME 109s.

As we approached the target, the Bombardier located the stream of tracers and advised the command pilot of the precise (?) location of the source. Igor made a slight course correction, and as we passed over the offending jungle, I hollered, "Bombs away." The crew chief threw out the watermelon and we started a tight turn so Igor could see the results.

Yep, we hit the jungle. Not too close to the VC, but we did hit the jungle. A cloud of white smoke rose from the trees showing our watermelon had shattered as planned when it hit the ground releasing the grenades. The tracers stopped. I doubt our VC target had ever been shot at before. Unsure of our results, we returned to base.

The next day, Igor took us back to the target area. You guessed it, a line of tracers arced up out of the usual place in the corner of the field. We were our usual 1/2 of a mile away and safe. Oh well, It was an unusual adventure anyway. The war went on.

Routine Autorotation

Dave Baggott

On March 18, 1971, we took off from Tuy Hoa Airbase in one of the 21st Signal Group's Hueys, call sign Manifest 593, on a routine ash-and-trash mission to Dalat. I was Aircraft Commander, CW2 Gary Blanton was Pilot. SP4 Jim Faulk and SP5 Lucas were door gunner and Crew Chief, respectively. We had a full load of "Souls on Board" with our crew of four plus nine pax, including a Lieutenant Colonel.

I was on the controls as we set up to do the DEAR (Daily Engine Analysis Report) Check. A DEAR Check was performed during the first flight of each day. It involved leveling off at 1,000 feet and 60 knots, and recording EGT (exhaust gas temp) and the N1 Tach readings. Gary noted these in the logbook as he read them off. I don't recall the numbers, but I do remember commenting we have a strong engine, as the numbers were a bit better than usual. As we started the climb to our cruising altitude, I pulled in power to reach a rate of climb rate slightly faster than our normal climb, but well within the Huey's capability.

As the coastline approached a few moments later, there was a sudden loud noise and the aircraft yawed; I instinctively lowered the collective and entered autorotation. The sound I heard at the time was like shoving a yardstick into a big fan. Lucas said later that from his seat in the hell hole, right by the engine, it sounded like a shotgun. Almost simultaneously, I heard Gary on the radio: "Mayday, Mayday; Manifest 593, engine failure, two miles south of Phu Hiep." Gary had experienced two engine failures while solo-piloting OH-58s; I'm not sure I would have had the presence of mind to make that Mayday call.

Thanks to luck, good Army training and the grace of God, almost before it had registered on my brain what was going on, I had made a 120° turn into the wind and lined up on a seemingly endless beach. Moments later we cushioned onto the sand.

Lucas and Faulk did a great job of off-loading the pax and moving them away from the aircraft, then dismounted the M-60s to set up a defensive perimeter, although there was no sign of human presence anywhere around. Lucas popped open the cowling to see the extent of damage - a large hole had blown in the compressor section, with pieces of compressor blades and housing scattered on the engine deck.

I was impressed that before the rotor had stopped turning, there were at least two fixed-wing aircraft orbiting over us, and our partner Huey had turned back from the Vung Ro Pass to assist as needed. A Dust-off Huey arrived shortly. We had no injuries, so they merely collected our passengers and took them back to Tuy Hoa.

We were still near enough to base to talk to our operations office on the FM radio. One person in Ops said later it was the first time they had ever heard me get excited. Well, other than the engine failure.

I had to report the tide was coming in, and each wave washing over our skids was causing us to sink a bit! We needed a Chinook to lift us out. The longer it was delayed, the more concerned we became, and we started removing the radios and anything portable. At long last, a

Chinook arrived and we watched 593 being slung back to base while we hitched a ride on the other Huey.

Since we touched down without damage, it was quickly determined to be an incident rather than an accident which could have grounded me pending an inquiry. As it was, we were simply assigned a different Huey and we were soon on our way again to Dalat.

I'm not a swimmer, and in any event escaping from the pilot's seat of a Huey in the water would not be an easy task. I've often thought back on this day, that if the engine in Manifest 593 had held on for another two minutes or so we would have been down in the choppy waters of the South China Sea, and some of us likely wouldn't have survived; I surely wouldn't have. I'm always grateful circumstances gave me a chance beyond March 18, 1971 to have a wonderful family and a fulfilling career.

For the remaining month of my tour in Vietnam, I always flew IFR - as in "I follow roads!"

Dumb Thing to Do

Stan Gause

I guess I did my share of dumb things, but one stands out most in my mind: an incident that occurred in late summer of 1968. I was fire team leader of a Devil fire team based out of An Khe. We were the only gun team between An Son and Pleiku. In addition to supporting a battalion of the 173rd Airborne Brigade operating around An Khe we also had the job of protecting Highway 19 - a job we enjoyed very much since we had the freedom to do pretty much anything we wanted.

We had a free-fire area for roughly 10 klicks (km) north and south of Highway 19 all the way from An Khe Pass in the east through Mang Yang Pass in the west, a distance of probably 30 - 40 miles or more. This was a very desolate area of flat terrain and low rolling hills with maybe 30 - 40% open area, sparse vegetation in some places and dense jungle in others. There were no villages and any people found in the area were assumed to be enemy. Perfect gunship country!!

In addition to convoy escort for the first convoy of the day we usually made a recon of our area of operations at first light and often just before dusk. There were also recons during the day and we worked closely with army FACs (Bird Dogs) to provide fire support on any targets they found. For a gunship pilot this was a great deal of flying and we loved it. We had carte blanche approval to shoot anything that moved.

During our recon missions we normally flew with the lead ship very low (25-50 feet AGL) with weapons systems armed and fingers on the trigger. Often, as we came over small hills or ridgelines we could get a fleeting glimpse of people (NVA/VC) scrambling for cover and we had only a split second to aim and pull the trigger before the target disappeared. Our CEs and gunners were incredible. They had eyes like an eagle and reflexes like a cat. Often, before I could even focus on a target they had already nailed it. They were awfully good! They could spot targets where the pilots saw nothing at all. CEs and gunners like this were worth their weight in gold, and we had the best.

My experience on these daily recon missions convinced me there was no way the new Cobra gunships could provide close ground support like a C model Huey with a good crew. I was convinced (and still am) the 134th had the best gunship crews in Vietnam, probably the best there ever were.

During one period of a few days we caught maybe six to eight people, including one woman, in the open on our recon missions and the CE, gunner or copilot (with the minigun) cut them down before you could even think about whether we should have held our fire. I had some doubts about whether some of these were in fact NVA or VC and felt a little bad about it. The AO was a long-standing free-fire area and our rules of engagement allowed us to shoot anything on sight. No friendlies were supposed to be in the area. However, some of the enemy we encountered appeared to be farmers and I wondered if they were possibly innocent people who had somehow blundered into a free fire area.

On one typical day, we were on a routine patrol of the AO when we topped a small hill and spotted a man running across a clearing. He saw us about the same time and stopped running. I immediately told my crew and wingman to hold their fire; although he certainly was way out in the boonies, the man might be just an innocent farmer.

The man stopped then continued walking rapidly away from us toward a tree line a short distance away. We flew over him and circled back for a closer look. I slowed to maybe 20 knots and dropped down to 15-20 feet. Almost at a hover I slowly approached. He continued walking rapidly away and looking at us over his shoulder. I approached to within 40 - 50 feet and considered the possibility of trying to take him prisoner. At this point he suddenly stopped, reached down behind a bush, pulled out an AK-47 and sprayed a line of bullet holes across our windshield. The six or eight holes were about eye level but luckily they came in at a sharp angle, missing everyone and going out the roof.

We were momentarily stunned and too close to bring our guns to bear. The door gunner probably could have taken a shot but he was so stunned he didn't get one off. I pulled pitch and banked away to come around for a shot at him. The man made a dash for the tree line maybe 20 - 30 feet away. Just as he disappeared into the trees, my wingman hit his position with a burst of minigun fire; then we followed up with a few rockets. The vegetation, however, was pretty dense and I don't know if we got him or not.

It all happened so fast we didn't have time to be scared but after it was over and we had time to think about, it was terrifying - and very stupid!

After this episode I didn't hesitate to shoot first and ask questions later, especially in free-fire areas.

A Few Good Men

Michael J. Brokovich

Over the years I have taken a lot of flak about being an Aerial Rocket Artillery (ARA) pilot. The constant yapping about the ARA guys flying so high they needed oxygen is the most prevalent. What many of these critics don't know is the ARA batteries of the 101st Airborne Division (Airmobile) were avid participants in the famed Command and Control North (CCN) missions out of Quang Tri and Hue Phu Bai. For those detractors who state only the gun companies of the 101st Airborne Division (Airmobile) - the D/101 Hawks and D/158 Redskins - flew the CCN missions, they obviously weren't there. The distinctive crossed cannons in red bordered in yellow on our ammo bay doors were difficult to miss. Additionally, the 2.75" FFAR (Folding Fin Aerial Rocket) was the CCN weapon of choice, and the ARA standard configuration for its Cobras consisted of four 19-rocket pods. The standard gun company configuration was two 19-rocket pods and two minigun pods.

I had the honor of leading the B/4/77 ARA (Toros) section on its first CCN mission out of Quang Tri in April 1969. We were flying UH-1Cs with two 19- rocket pods each as our new AH-1Gs had not yet arrived. I was sent as the section leader as I was a second tour gun pilot. My section consisted of WO1 Al Hansen, my peter pilot; CW2 Barry Shreiber, AC of my wing ship and a recent transfer from the Hawks; 1LT Willie Lawson, Barry's peter pilot; and me. Willie, Al, and I were original Toros, having formed up with the unit at Ft. Bragg, NC and then deployed with it to Vietnam.

We flew north from Camp Eagle and landed at the CCN pad at Quang Tri and walked past the other players' aircraft. There were two VNAF CH-34s (Kingbees) led by Dai Uy Ahn, a number of UH-1H slicks from B/101 (Kingsman), and two Marine UH-1Es. We went into the operations hooch where we were welcomed and told to take a seat for the initial briefing. Until then, none of us had a clue as to what CCN missions were all about. When the CCN folks uncovered a map with no large body of water to the East showing the (South China Sea), and sprinkled liberally with red indicating the enemy anti-aircraft positions and Top Secret labels all over it, I began to feel a little uneasy.

My other three compatriots were poker-faced, but then again, only Barry Shreiber had ever heard a shot fired in anger. Al and Willie later admitted they were scared to death but thought Barry and I looked calm and cool, so they tried to do the same. We all had a good laugh from that. We also were assigned different call signs for the mission. The ARA birds were called Yellow Jackets when they flew out of Quang Tri and Dragonflies when flying out of Hue Phu Bai. The first mission went well, and we started a solid working relationship with the Marine gun pilots; the slick drivers, who were frequently rotated by unit; and, the VNAF, particularly Dai Uy Ahn.

We quickly became part of the team, and our pilots eagerly volunteered for the CCN missions because there were fewer restrictions on rules of engagement and they knew there would always be action. This thirst for action became more intense when the unit was fully equipped with our Snakes. The Toros and the Griffins (C/4/77 ARA) flew many exciting CCN missions; in fact, I flew a bunch myself. Rather than bore you with details, I've opted to describe one mission that I'll never forget. I call it "A Few Good Men."

The Marines flew UH-1E gunships which were a lot like our old UH-1C gunships, except theirs had an odd turret mounted on the nose with two 7.62 mm machine guns mounted side-by-side. They carried a crew of four, had a very short range, and were a whole lot slower than our Cobras. This particular CCN mission was to locate a platoon-sized element in Laos for extraction. The Marines normally flew "low and slow" to locate the troops while the two Cobra ARA section provided overhead cover and fire support, if needed. On this mission, we had four Cobras because of the size of the extraction. The other Toro Aircraft Commanders were my wingman CPT Bob Davis, CPT Bert Lanstra, and CW2 Jim Dailey. When the troops were located, slicks (I don't remember which 101st slick company was providing the UH-1Hs this day.) would be brought in to lift them out. Since the platoon was deep in Laos, the mission would become more difficult if the NVA found them before we could get them out.

As we passed to the west of Marine Firebase Vandegrift (a Marine base near the Rockpile), the Marine UH-1Es dropped in to top off their fuel tanks prior to crossing the border. Our flight of four Cobras flew on planning to rendezvous with the Marines in the vicinity of the extraction site. When we arrived in the general area, the platoon frantically radioed, "Prairie Fire! Prairie Fire!" This meant they were in contact and needed support right then, essentially an SOS call. The Marines were about thirty minutes behind us, so I told Bob Davis to cover me as I went down to positively identify the platoon's position. I dropped down to the treetops and flew as low and slow as I could to pinpoint the platoon. I flew down among the branches for what seemed to be forever and didn't even realize I was being shot at until Bob Davis yelled over the VHF, "Get out of there, Yellow jacket Lead; you're drawing fire!" I nosed over and pulled in more power as I quickly accelerated away from the ridge line in a hail of automatic weapons fire. On the way out, I heard the platoon radio I had just flown over them. Now, we knew exactly where they were.

About this time, the two Marine UH-1Es arrived, and I briefed the flight leader on the platoon's location as well as the enemy situation (I translated this into "heavy automatic weapons fire") on the ridgeline. He acknowledged my transmission, and, to my amazement, flew across the same ridgeline, only he was lower and slower and presented a fatter target. He immediately drew heavy ground fire. We were unable to lay down suppressive fires because we were too close to the location of the platoon on the ground. Our four Cobras fell in behind the stricken UH-1E, two on each side and to his rear. He apparently had been hit several times by automatic weapons fire as he radioed, "Mayday! Mayday! I'm hit and losing power." He started to turn east and head back to South Vietnam. He had been hit in the fuel cell and a cloud of fuel vapor began billowing out the left side of his helicopter.

At this point I yelled to my front seat pilot, Bill Gurski, to start taking pictures with my Kodak Instamatic camera. I figured he might as well be doing something useful as the turret was totally inoperable. Neither of us dreamed we were about to get some fantastic shots of a helicopter going down in flames. Meanwhile, the UH-1E started heading toward a clearing by a bend in a river to get on the ground. Our Air Force O-2 controller, Covey, told him not to land in the particular clearing he was approaching as there was a large unfriendly village nearby and he would be better off landing on the near side. He started to make a descending right turn away from the village area, and the fuel vapor cloud burst into flames. He slipped the helicopter to keep the flames out of the crew compartment and lined up with the river, intending to put it in the water to extinguish the fire. When the helicopter descended to about seventy-five feet, the tail boom fell off. The helicopter inverted and crashed into the river upside down. Pieces of rotor blades and helicopter went everywhere along with large amounts of water and debris that splashed up when the helicopter hit.

When everything cleared, the helicopter was underwater. Kingbee Lead, commanded by Dai Uy Ahn, flew down to the river to look for survivors while our four Cobras put a wall of steel around his CH-34. They picked up two survivors (the Aircraft Commander and the crew chief) about one hundred yards downstream. Kingbee Lead then hovered back up the river to the crash site to check on the other two crew members. His crew chief hung out of the side of the CH-34 with his monkey straps and determined the pilot and gunner were still belted in and obviously dead. This was an outstanding demonstration of bravery on the part of Dai Uy Ahn as he was under heavy fire the entire time.

Since there was no more that could be done for the two KIAs and the ground fire was becoming quite heavy, we all departed the area to get the two survivors out, and for us to refuel and rearm. We told the platoon to hold on as we would be back to get them and flew back to Quang Tri to rearm and refuel. At the rearm point, I checked over my Cobra for hits and found seven holes. (I harassed Bill Gurski at this point as he had been in the front seat of my wingman on a CCN mission less than a month before and had been shot down deep in Laos with Bob Davis. I called him a "magnet ass"; this nickname haunted Bill for a long time.) Several rounds had gone through the rotor blades, but one had missed the 42 degree gear box by less than an inch. An AK-47 round had gone through all the longerons and stringers, which provided structural strength to the tail boom, and effectively grounded the aircraft.

As I was the TC Detachment Commander and unit maintenance officer at the time, I approved a one-time maintenance flight to get the Cobra back to Camp Eagle. The other three Yellow Jackets, led by Bob Davis, went back to Laos with the slicks and covered the extraction of the platoon without further incident. The flight back to Camp Eagle was routine as I carefully watched for strange vibrations and unusual instrument readings.

When I landed at the Bull Pen, the Toro helipad, I discovered I had been luckier than I originally thought and had cheated fate once again.

My maintenance people thoroughly inspected the Cobra and found another round had entered the bottom of the aircraft. It had exploded several rounds of my linked 7.62 mm minigun ammunition in the ammo boxes and had stopped, fully spent, at the last layer. I was lucky the round had not hit me in my right leg.

Ironically, during my preflight inspection that morning, the crew chief for #086, SP4 Jacobs, reported the grenade launcher didn't work. I directed him to remove the grenade drum and fully load the minigun ammunition boxes. Our ARA Cobras normally only carried a half load of grenades and minigun ammo as our primary weapon was the 2.75" FFAR. The extra ammo he loaded made up the layers of linked ammo the AK-47 round had come through before expending its energy short of the floor beneath my leg. If that ammo had not been there, the round would have come straight through unhindered and hit me. I was greatly relieved but had to contend with a very upset crew chief as he felt I had hurt his "baby". The tail boom had to be replaced on #086 as well as the rotor blades and a lot of other sheet metal work, but at least we had the aircraft return to action a short while later.

This was the last CCN mission I flew on with Marine participation. Subsequent missions had the Hawks or Redskins flying the low recon portion of the mission while the ARA Cobras provided cover and firepower. CCN missions were truly exhilarating to all our pilots as we felt we were accomplishing something and were truly appreciated by the CCN people. I'm proud to have been associated with this outstanding team of pilots, soldiers, and Marines. This particular CCN mission was not an unusual one. This was just one of my more exciting ones, and I'm certain there are many untold CCN adventures worthy of being put down on paper. The bottom line of this story is one should not deride ARA pilots without knowing the whole truth of what we did for a living during our time in Vietnam. Contrary to popular belief, we weren't always at altitude in air-conditioned comfort.

Young and Stupid

Phil Marshall

In order to be Old and Wise, One must first be Young and Stupid, (Ancient U.S. Army proverb)

I arrived in Vietnam on the 4th of July, 1969, barely 21 years old. It was an average age for most of the Army helicopter pilots I flew with in the 237th Medical Detachment in northern I Corps near the DMZ. One guy was 19, while the oldest, not counting our Commanding Officer, was the 28 year-old XO, Army slang for the second in command, the Executive Officer. Back home in the real world, my buddies were at the drive-in, drinking beer and looking for a carload of girls to flirt with, just as I had been doing a year or two before.

Even though I had yet to fly my first hour of combat, I had already done many incredible things my high school and college friends could not even dream of. I couldn't have been more proud of myself and my flight school classmates for having come this far. With a fair amount of apprehension, it was now "the moment of truth". Could we really do what we had been trained to do without letting anyone down? We were especially concerned about the troops we were there to support. It was finally time to find out if we had the "gonads" to be combat helicopter pilots.

When I found out I was assigned to be a medevac pilot, I was devastated. In my mind, the only way I would survive the 365 days in Southeast Asia was to be a gunship pilot, blazing my way back to the states, defending myself with miniguns, rockets and grenade launchers. All through flight school, we were taught by gun pilots, slick drivers, scout pilots (although not as many of the scout pilots, as they had a high loss ratio) and oh, yes, one Dust-off pilot. He was an instructor pilot at Downing Army Airfield at Ft. Wolters, Texas in May of 1968. I remember my very first primary flight instructor pointing at him as I listened intently to his every word. "There walks a dead man. He was a Dust-off pilot; a dead man." Meaning he should never have made it back since Dust-off aircraft were unarmed medevac helicopters with red and white targets painted all over them and flew single ship missions. It was a fact that Dust-off crews had three times the casualty rate of other helicopter crews. I never forgot the reverence with which that statement was made, as I began to form a survival plan of action in my mind. I would not fly unarmed helicopters!

Shortly after arriving at Ft. Rucker, Alabama, I learned those of us with the highest flight grades would attend a two week gun school near the end of training, while the rest learned formation flying. I wanted that top 20% and focused all my abilities and energy on making gunship training. I did well enough to make the school along with about 25 of my classmates.

But as the Army would have it, during Friday night formation of the middle weekend of gun school, 24 of us, including 12 in the gun school, received orders to attend Medevac school at Ft. Sam Houston, Texas, immediately after graduation. I told my roommate, "This is it. I won't make it back." Obviously, I was wrong but I didn't know it then. It turned out to be the best thing that happened to me, even though I was wounded before the year was out and sent home before my tour was over. I had no idea of the satisfaction, pride, sense of accomplishment and even elation I would feel in the next six months.

Since I first heard the phrase that is the title of this article, it struck me that those words were exactly what we did as "kids" flying helicopters in Vietnam. As I look back on my own experiences, two things stand out in my mind I consider as "Young and Stupid."

First of all, there was landing on the Navy Hospital ships USS Repose and USS Sanctuary in the South China Sea very near the Demilitarized Zone. While in themselves, those landings were not stupid, the way we got there was! Our single engine UH-1H Hueys did not float in the water very well. In fact, not at all since we usually flew with the doors open, even at night. And what was even "stupider" I suppose was if the doors were closed when we reached the water, we opened them so we could get out easier if we did go down.

Okay, so the Hueys were extremely reliable, and I still love those incredible machines, but for the moment let us discuss navigation equipment on a Huey. And the answer is: "There is none!" Sure, we had a compass and an Automatic Direction Finder, but in the event of an engine failure on the way to the hospital ship, this would have probably been my emergency call. "Mayday, Mayday, Mayday, Dust-off 7-1-1, we're going down over the sea. We're about 5 miles out." Five miles out from where? Maybe it was only 3 miles...no, 7! Shoot, I had no idea! "But, come look for us, will ya?"

But I suppose we would have survived; we had water wings! Mine were draped over the back of my seat, along with my M-16 rifle. It was a well known (and very true) fact that during an emergency exit from an aircraft, if you don't have it strapped to your body, you won't take it with you. If I had gone down over land, I probably wouldn't have taken my weapon with me. If I had gone down over water, I wouldn't have grabbed the "wings" either, because not only had I never tried to inflate them, I had never even tried to put them on. Well, maybe we could have used our survival radio once we were in the water or forced down over the jungle. He he he he....survival radio, what's that? Is that AM or FM? Can I pick up Armed Forces Radio on it? We had no survival radios in those aircraft. So, I guess that makes three "Young and Stupids."

Once out to sea, landing on the ships was an interesting experience in itself, especially when the decks were bouncing up and down like a fishing-bobber with a carp under it. I already knew the difference between port and starboard and it wasn't hard to figure out "beam" and "quartering" approaches. I used to laugh at the occasional Huey slick driver who flew out to let guys from his unit use the shopping facilities on the ships. The radioman on the ship would tell them, "Cleared for a port quarter approach." The silence on the radio was the proverbial pregnant pause and I could imagine the conversation inside the Huey cockpit. "What'd he say?" "Hell, I don't know. Damn Navy talk!" The hospital ship would then radio to the helicopter again, "Just come in from the left and land to the back of the boat." It always got an immediate "Roger!"

It has been said many times by Navy and Marine jet pilots that landing on an aircraft carrier is like landing on a postage stamp. I would never dispute that, but I would argue that putting a helicopter on the tiny pad of the hospital ship is like landing on a corner of that postage stamp. And night time was even worse. The first time I tried to land on the ship at night, I terminated at a 30 foot hover over the deck instead of on the deck and the Aircraft Commander had to take over and hover down to the ship.

That was probably the lowest point of my Vietnam flying experience, and I never forgot it. I promised myself it would never happen again, and it didn't. It wasn't easy and I will now confess my depth perception was almost not good enough to pass my initial flight physical, but I made it. (As an aside, when I returned to the states later and applied for my military driver's license so I could drive the company pick-up truck, I was told I didn't pass the depth perception portion of the eye test and would not be issued the license. I was OK to fly helicopters in the Army, but not to drive a jeep! I asked to take a different test and was able to pass that one!) Knowing my depth perception left little margin for error especially on night approaches, I had to totally concentrate on what I was doing and not relax for a second until we were down on that rockin' and rollin' ship.

The night I was wounded, my new co-pilot Don Study put us right on the deck, but all the while I had visions of my first 30 foot hover when I was a Funny New Guy - an FNG. I knew if Don got in trouble on the approach, I could not be of much help because of the gunshot wound in my left arm, but we were "Young and Stupid" and we made it. I will always thank Warrant Officer Study for his late-night picture-perfect landing on the round end of the boat.

Oh, were we "Young and Stupid" on hoist missions, too; the second "Y & S" thing we did! As medevac helicopter pilots, we flew the only Army Hueys equipped with the electric hoist/winch. The most incredible, dangerous, high pucker-factor, exhilarating thing a man can do with a helicopter is to pull an unsecure hoist mission, day or night. Add to that, it is also the most unforgiving mission flown in a helicopter.

First, one has to understand what a hoist mission is and why we did them. Generally, someone is badly wounded in jungle or mountainous (or both) terrain where a helicopter cannot land on the ground or even close to it. The tactical situation is such the ground troops cannot get the dead or wounded to a secure open area for evacuation. We must now hover over the trees or rocky terrain while we let out up to 150 feet of quarter-inch cable with a jungle penetrator or a Stokes litter attached to it. Translation: "There are bad guys all around, we've got wounded, get in here now before they die or we have more wounded and you have to come back again. We don't have any place for you to land, so just hang your butts out in the open sky for several minutes so any kid with a bow and arrow can shoot you down and gee, those red crosses on your helicopter sure make great aiming points, don't they? When you crash, we'll try to recover your bodies."

We were unarmed and experience taught us that usually, we were better off to quickly fly to the landing zone, get in and get out as fast as possible while avoiding the bad guys and fly straight back to the hospital. If we waited for gunship support, it may be too late for the wounded, so most times we tried to sneak in and sneak out (if that's possible in a clattering helicopter) and complete the rescue before the enemy had enough time to shoot us up....or down.

A hoist mission was just the opposite. We still got there in a hurry, but once there, we hovered over the trees like a target at the County fair 25 cent shooting booth. Five minutes or more seemed like hours while we sat in the air over the ground troops, taxing every bit of professionalism we had. And the reader better believe we had the utmost professionalism. The crewmen I flew with on hoist missions (like me, in their teens and early 20s) were absolutely the best, and I wish I could shake every one of their hands and hug them today. I am so very proud to have served with them. It required every skill we had.

If we had been shot down on virtually any hoist mission, our high hover would not have allowed us to make a safe landing and many would surely die. That was the unforgiving part. It happened many times, and their names are on the Wall in Washington, D.C.

One particular mission I recall was a day hoist. We were an easier target during the day, but unlike at night when we kept all the lights off, we could see what we were doing! When we were on short final approach over the landing zone, I heard small arms fire and my brand new crew chief yelled, "We're taking fire!" I pulled power into the rotor system to get out of there as quickly as I could when the radio operator on the ground called out, "Dust-off, where are you going?" "We're taking fire," I said. "That was us giving you covering fire!" he replied. "OK, I'm turning around" and I did another "Young & Stupid" thing; I made a pedal turn (U-turn) about 200 feet in the air, probably over some bad guys, and hovered back in over the trees.

Normally, one has to push a button to talk over the intercom in a military aircraft, but on a hoist mission, we turned it to "hot mikes" because we all needed our hands for other things. With a hot mike, everything said, every noise, every round fired, every grunt and groan was amplified and transmitted into everyone's headset without touching any buttons. A constant line of chatter was transmitted from the medic and the crew chief to the pilots, who were both on the flight controls in case either was suddenly incapable of continuing to fly the aircraft. One has to realize there was virtually no protection for the pilots from the front and little from the sides or underneath.

"The cable's going out...about halfway down...come right...it's on the ground...looking good....come forward just a little...keep your tail straight....come left...they're on the penetrator..." was typical of the continual commentary from the enlisted crewmembers. As the Aircraft Commander in control of the helicopter, my eyes never left the tree branches touching the nose of my aircraft, but made flight adjustments according to the guys in the back.

The additional weight of patients on the end of the hoist as they were lifted off the ground further complicated the stability of the aircraft. During a hoist mission, we flew with one finger on a button on the cyclic stick that operated an electric solenoid. It would instantly cut the cable should any part of the lift apparatus get snagged in the trees or in any other emergency situation. Otherwise, if we got tangled up, it could cause the aircraft to crash. *I wonder how many grunts would have gotten on the hoist had they known that.*

When I read the quickly handwritten sheet for this particular mission, I knew before we left it was going to be an unsecure hoist, so we grabbed some unsuspecting schmuck, told him to get his weapon and some ammo and run with us to the aircraft. We put him in the back of the cargo compartment with his M-16 and a helmet, hooked him up to the intercom and we were off. I have no idea who he was, but we logged his flight time as, "PP - Patient Protector."

After the first of the two injured soldiers was hoisted on board, the din of the covering fire began to register in my head. With the front of my Huey still kissing the tree leaves and my crew keeping me posted as to what was going on, I took a quick, curious look out my left window to see where the friendly fire was impacting. "Oh, Sugar!" (Not my exact word.) "I can throw a rock in there, it's so close!" was the rest of my thought. I then realized that ole PP back there was just sitting in the hell hole taking it all in, not doing a thing! "Put some fire in that bunker!" I yelled to Private what's-his-name. I guess that woke him up as the next thing I heard was his rifle plugging away at a mound of dirt just outside his door and about 30 feet down.

The rest of the mission went as expected with no more surprises. We took no hits on that mission and as we lifted out of the landing zone, the fact that we cheated death again left me with all the exciting feelings I mentioned at the beginning of this article. There was an adrenaline high, too, and a tremendous sense of accomplishment I have yet to experience since flying my last mission in Vietnam.

The emotions are almost indescribable, but there was one more feeling, relief from being so scared! Being scared in the sense of risking one's life for others, for sure, but also a sense of being scared you won't be up to the standards of your fellow pilots. Scared that maybe, just maybe, you'll fail your mission where someone else just like you would have succeeded. **I suppose that's what kept most of us going in the daily risk of flying helicopters in combat in Vietnam. If we didn't do it, the next guy would and we would have been found to be personally lacking what it took to complete the mission.**

In retrospect, I think that's what happened to one of the pilots in our unit a few months after I left. Warrant Officer One, Al Gaddis, was a tall curly haired kid as I remember him. Always smiling and never hurt anyone, I would guess. On what turned out to be his final mission, they were to pick up wounded on a mountain top, but got caught in heavy fire while making their approach. Whether they took hits at this time or not is speculation, but he tried another tactic. He dropped to the deck a couple of miles out and then screamed up the hill at 120 knots and tree top level, trying to sneak in past the enemy. But this time he definitely took hits from a .50 caliber crossfire, and as he peeled off from the mountain, fuel was streaming from the aircraft.

The gunships escorting him told Al to put it on the ground right away because of the serious leak. "I think I can make it back!" was his last message as the aircraft caught fire, rolled inverted and crashed in flames, killing all on board. My opinion is he was as afraid he couldn't complete the mission as much as he was afraid to die. At least, I believe that's how I would have felt had it been me. We always at least tried to complete the mission and felt we let someone down if we didn't.

On one particularly difficult night medevac in the mountains, all of our windows fogged up as we dropped from 7,000 feet through a hole in the clouds to pick up a soldier with a head wound. It took all of our skill and luck to avoid flying into the valley walls as we stuck our heads out the windows to find our way to the LZ without "balling up" the helicopter. With the patient finally on board, the radio operator with the ground unit "rogered" our departure message with a "Thanks a HELL of a lot, Dust-off!" Those brief and simple heartfelt words meant more to me that night than anything else ever said to me during my entire tour. We risked much in a totally dark valley that night and there was no doubt someone appreciated us.

So, were we really "Young and Stupid"? Yes, most definitely young, but stupid? I don't think so. *We all volunteered to do something that only a year or two before we could not have even dreamed we would be doing. Something only a very few could ever experience; something for which only a very few could even qualify.*

Those of us lucky enough to come home learned from the excursion, and were without question, changed men and no longer wide-eyed boys. I think some of us changed for the better, but some of us didn't.

I tried to use the opportunity to prove to myself I could accomplish the goals I set for myself and do them well. In fact, we all did well. As a group, we helicopter pilots did what we had to do, and then some. We sacrificed our youth and innocence; we achieved above and beyond the call of duty on a daily basis. Not only were we not found to be lacking as youthful aviators, as a whole we far exceeded the expectations. We are now "Older and Wiser", and for that I am very thankful.

Chinook Medevac from Nui Ba Den

Gary Roush

The most prominent terrain feature in III Corps was Nui Ba Den, the Black Virgin Mountain which protruded 3,235 feet above the rest of the area. It was visible for many miles on clear days and was great as a navigation reference. Its prominence was important for allied communications as well as a relay communication station and observation point for the Viet Cong (VC) and North Vietnamese Army (NVA). The summit was first occupied by American forces in 1964 and was a frequent target of the Viet Cong who occupied most of the rest of the mountain. Nui Ba Den had numerous caves and supposedly contained the enemy headquarters for all of South Vietnam, COSVN. This key communications center was used by more than ten U.S. units including radio intercepts for intelligence purposes. In May 1968, the top was completely overrun by the VC/NVA and all of the U.S communication equipment was destroyed, so the 25th Infantry Division deployed A Company, 3rd Battalion, 25th Infantry to the top of the mountain on the morning of 17 August for its defense. This timing turned out to be very lucky.

The approximately 180 signal corps, engineer and infantry troops stationed on the top of the mountain relied entirely on helicopters for all support, including water. Most of this support fell to the 242nd Assault Support Helicopter Company, Muleskinners out of Cu Chi. As a result, we flew to the mountain nearly every day delivering supplies and replacements from Tay Ninh.

In August 1968, I was a newly appointed Aircraft Commander (AC) with the Muleskinners and loved flying to the mountain, so I volunteered for those missions. We were restricted to flying no more than 120 hours in a 30 day period and I was always at the max so I did not fly to the mountain every day. Mountain flying was challenging and exciting. With the combination of high density altitude, hovering out-of-ground effect in very tight quarters, coupled with high and gusty winds, it was definitely challenging. One day I was hovering over a spot on the mountain while my air speed indicator showed 50 knots. It was a blast. Unfortunately, we got shot at occasionally too.

Unbeknownst to the Muleskinners, the Battle for Tay Ninh began on 17 August 1968. This battle lasted until 27 September 1968 and would prove to be a very busy time for us. On 18 August, my crew and I took off at first light for Tay Ninh to accomplish our missions on Nui Ba Den. Unfortunately, the only other crew member I remember who was on that flight was flight engineer SP5 John D. Labelle. The Muleskinners had outstanding crews. The guys in the back were extraordinary and were highly respected by the pilots. Without them, we could never have done our job. You will see the value of those guys in a moment.

The monsoon season was in full swing, so weather was a constant challenge during August and September. We tried to complete all of our sorties before mid-afternoon; when the rain would start. On 18 August, the visibility was good but there was a cloud layer at about 2,000 feet. With the good visibility, we could see Nui Ba Den shortly after take-off from Cu Chi and with the low ceiling it was obvious missions to the mountain would have to await clearer weather. The mountain top was covered in cloud.

When we got within FM radio range, we called the mountain to tell them there would be a delay in their daily resupply. We then discovered they had been overrun during the night and were desperate to get 23 wounded medevac'd to Tay Ninh.

At 02:34 hours, the VC/NVA made an attempt to disrupt the communications into and out of Tay Ninh by attacking the top of Nui Ba Den with an estimated company size unit. They attacked with small arms, automatic weapons and rockets against the bunker line defended only 14 hours earlier by A/3/22 Inf 25th Div. This was a coordinated attack matching the attack time on several locations between Tay Ninh and Nui Ba Den including Fire Support Base Buell II. The VC were successful in breaching the bunker line in the helipad area and managed to blow up one generator. (We helped replace that generator later, but that's another story.) After over three hours of close quarter fighting, the Americans finally drove the VC off the summit at about 06:15 hours.

The VC left behind 15 dead and several weapons including 100 satchel charges and 20 RPG rocket rounds. The Americans suffered eight killed in action (KIA) and 23 wounded. The attackers failed in their mission to cut off American communications but now the Americans had another problem – how to get their wounded evacuated.

According to our radio call to the unit we were supporting, Dust-off Hueys had attempted to land at the mountain top helipad without success. They were desperate to get some help and the company commander was practically begging us to try. So into the clouds we went feeling our way to the mountain top. Man was that a bad idea or what!? The man on the radio would say, "We can hear you but cannot see you, keep on coming." We did this twice. All I can say is we were very lucky not to have hit the mountain. Just as we were about to give up as the Hueys had done, someone in the crew came up with the idea of flying down to the base of the clouds and hovering up the side of the mountain. Our Chinook was empty, so we had lots of power to hover at this altitude. So that is what we did. Because of my many sorties to the mountain, I knew the terrain very well and could picture the helipad in my mind along with its surrounding obstacles. Now all I had to do was get to the helipad. No one in flight school taught me how to hover up the side of a mountain in the clouds!

But wait! The VC/NVA had just broken contact about an hour earlier so where were they now? My reasoning was no self-respecting VC would ever dream of a big lumbering, very noisy helicopter hovering right over their heads shortly after a major attack. So my logic was it would be such a surprise they would not do anything about it. I also rationalized that if our troops could not see us, neither could Charlie. Just in case though, I instructed my left door gunner to shoot anything that moved. I also instructed the left gunner to help by calling out obstacles. I was at the controls flying from the left seat. The pilot read off the instrument readings for vertical speed and altitude to give me some idea about where we were in relationship to the top and everybody looked for obstacles. Oh, by the way, I had been shot at recently from this side of the mountain and took six rounds.

Now, all I had to do was find the helipad and not the bank of antennas. After hovering for what seemed like an hour, we finally came to the perimeter; barbed wire, bunkers and finally the landing pad appeared. Needless to say, I was glad to have all four wheels safely on the ground. After a few seconds, I started looking around. The scene was like it had come out of a horror movie. In the swirling mist of the clouds, I could just make out the outline of bodies, and they were lying everywhere. The rotor wash from the Chinook was slowly clearing the area right around the landing pad, revealing the nightmare our troops must have experienced minutes before. Directly under my feet through the chin bubble was a gook (enemy soldier maybe?) with half of his head missing. Next to him was another grotesque figure of a Viet Cong and then the American dead and wounded lying neatly in a row on the edge of the resupply pad, giving us just enough room to land. The nearby uninjured troops who were on guard never took their eyes from the now-breached perimeter. This was not characteristic, since we were normally the center of attention, with everyone watching us perform our hovering feats.

Fortunately, we could take all 23 of the wounded at once, because I certainly did not want to go through this again, but what about the departure? My memory recalled the antennas straight ahead, still covered by the clouds, and on both sides the bunkers with high RPG fences, also in the clouds. So a vertical or 180-degree turn departure were the only two reasonable alternatives, other than hovering back down the side like we had done coming up and I certainly did not want to do that again.

I had one instructor during primary flight school at Fort Wolters, Texas teach me how to do backward takeoffs, and my instrument instructor, CPT Adam Runk, at Fort Rucker taught me 0/0 takeoffs under the hood. Doing one was crazy, but putting both together was suicide. A vertical takeoff was certainly possible, but how high did the clouds go and how would we avoid the mountains on the way down? The only logical procedure was a hovering 180-degree turn and then a 0/0 standard takeoff on the back course of a normal approach until we were sure to be clear of the mountain, then a standard instrument descent out of the clouds just like a VOR approach. Sounds simple, but how do you hover under Instrument Flight Rules (IFR) in a tight LZ?

To get high enough to get all four wheels off the ground, the cockpit would be in the clouds and I would not be able to see the ground. No one thought to teach me how to hover IFR! But wait, I have made this turn hundreds of times in good weather, so with a little care and concentration on the instruments and the help of the other four pairs of eyes to stay over the landing pad, it should work. There was no way I was going to stay on top of that mountain until the weather cleared.

The plan worked. Throughout the 180-degree hovering turn, at least one of the four other crew members had sight of the ground and gave me, in turn, the necessary directions to stay over the landing pad. Since the Chinook is so large and most loads in Vietnam were carried externally, out of sight of the pilots (the cargo hook was about 30 feet behind the cockpit), we were used to getting reliable hovering directions from the crew. I was not able to see the ground from shortly after lifting the front wheels off the ground until we broke out of the clouds well away from the mountain. This marked my first and last 0/0 takeoff and landing in actual weather. There were other low-visibility landings due to monsoon rains, but no other below acceptable visibility takeoffs. After dropping off the wounded at the Tay Ninh Field Hospital, we went back for the KIAs but decided it was not worth the risk. Another Chinook picked them up after the weather cleared.

Because of limited space on top of the mountain, it was decided not to burn the Viet Cong bodies there, as was common practice. Instead, they were put in a cargo net to be hauled as an external load to a suitable burning site by a Chinook flown by my hooch mate, Mike Ryan. Shortly after takeoff with the sling load of enemy bodies, the sling became disengaged from the cargo hook, dumping the contents over the adjoining small mountain. Since the Viet Cong owned that mountain they were given an unexpected chance to recover their dead.

The interesting thing about my experience is I did not report it because I thought I might get into trouble for unnecessarily risking the lives of my crew. In hind-sight we probably should have gotten medals for what we did, but the satisfaction of helping out our wounded soldiers was enough of an award. I have often wondered what happened to those 23 wounded. Perhaps this article will help me find out.

Twenty Minutes of Terror

Stan Gause

My unit, the 134th AHC based out of Phu Hiep, had a fire team on temporary duty at An Khe Golf Course (main heliport) in the summer of '68 to provide convoy escort, and support Highway 19 defenses from An Khe Pass in the east to Mang Yang Pass in the west.

I was fire team leader with two Charlie model gunships. We were scrambled one night around 01:00 to provide fire support to a ground unit protecting one of the bridges roughly 20 minutes west of An Khe. The weather was poor with low clouds, intermittent rain, patches of fog and maybe a 1,000 foot ceiling. But what the hell, when our guys are getting shot at and ask for help, you don't pay much attention to the weather. You just get your butt out there as fast as possible, no matter what.

We made it to the bridge and identified the friendly positions. We could see muzzle flashes and tracers from both the friendlies and VC. We worked over the VC positions with rockets and hosed it down with miniguns until the firing stopped. Our folks on the ground said the fire was on target and had stopped the attack. We remained on station another half hour or so to see if anything else would happen and then started back to the Golf Course around 02:30.

In the meantime, the weather had gotten worse with a ceiling of 200-300 feet, drizzling rain and increasing ground fog. In just moments, we flew into a patch of fog, lost ground contact and sight of each other.

The old pucker factor was rising fast. Fearing I was too close to the ground, I stayed on course straight east, sucked up the collective, and started climbing at 1,000 feet per minute. I told my wingman to turn 30 degrees to the south and also start climbing. I hadn't flown much IFR and was praying I wouldn't get vertigo.

We kept climbing through the soup hoping to break out of the clouds and by some miracle be able to see An Khe. I finally broke out at a little over 7,000 feet and found my wingman, but there was a solid floor of clouds beneath us. I realized there was no way we were going to make a VFR landing and then terror set in. I could see us splattered all over the mountain beside the Golf Course (the one with the 1st Cav. patch, I forget the name). I tried not to panic but fear was rising. My first thought was to try to make it to another airfield. I called Qui Nhon tower, the closest airfield 35-40 minutes away, and learned it was still VFR there. We had been flying, however, for almost two hours, and I knew we didn't have enough fuel to make it to Qui Nhon.

After another minute or so my 20 minute warning light flashed on. The Peter Pilot looked over at me and didn't say anything. I could see the fear in his eyes and I'm sure he saw it in mine. I got on the horn and talked to the tower at An Khe to prepare for my last straw, a tactical ADF approach. I wasn't aware An Khe had radar but the tower operator informed me of it and said they could give me a GCA approach (after all, gunships don't fly in the clouds!). There was one hitch; the radar was turned off and had to warm up for five to ten minutes and the radar operator was in bed.

At that point, the 20 minute light had been on for two minutes. I told the tower operator it was an extreme emergency and if he wanted to save the lives of eight people to PLEASE turn the radar on and send someone god-awful quick to find the radar operator. He sent someone for the radar operator but didn't know how to turn the radar on. We waited for what seemed like an eternity, becoming more terrified by the minute. What if they couldn't find the radar operator?

We were circling over An Khe at 7,000 feet when finally the radar operator came on and said he needed at least five more minutes for the radar to warm up. The 20 minute light had been on for just over ten minutes, and I decided we had to start down. My wingman had roughly ten minutes more fuel than I had, so I began descending first; homing in on an FM radio in the control tower. Sweating like crazy, I stayed in a race track pattern on the east side of the radio signal since I knew there were no mountains on that side. Descending initially at 1,000 feet per minute, I slowed to 300-400 feet per minute after passing 3,000 feet (field elevation was a little less than 2,000 feet I believe).

Just after passing 2,500 feet, the radar operator came on and said he had my position just east of the airfield. He set me up on approach and we broke out of the fog at less than 50 feet, right over the runway. I hovered over to the POL pad and set down. The engine ran out of gas just as the crew chief was putting the nozzle in the tank. I sat there in my seat listening as my wingman came in on a GCA. I was shaking so bad that I just sat there for another 15 minutes or so.

I had planned to go see the tower operator and radar operator the next day to thank them in person and buy them a beer, but we were called back to Phu Hiep the next morning and I never saw them. To this day I feel bad about not being able to thank them in person.

S.E.A.L Missions

Eric Bray

I flew out of Can Tho with the 162nd Aviation Company (Assault), the Vultures, from December 1969 to December 1970. There were three flight platoons in the company; two were slick platoons – the Vultures, which flew H-model Hueys; one was a gunship platoon – the Copperheads, which flew C-model Hueys. I was assigned to the second platoon. My call sign was Vulture 22.

Over the year they were there, a few of the Aircraft Commanders who also had Command and Control orders seemed to develop a reputation for being very good at flying a particular type of special mission. Often, when the operations officer needed someone to fly one of these special missions, the expert in that field was assigned to fly that day. In the latter part of my tour, I became one of the pilots who flew many joint services missions with the Navy SEALs and sometimes combined command with Navy helicopter pilots. In fact, I later learned the SEAL teams were requesting my services.

The Navy pilots flew L-model Hueys with a smaller cargo capacity than my H-model and used a less powerful engine. They were also modified to fly off of ships; this included a mast brake to stop the rotor from spinning in the wind after the helicopter landed on a moving ship. The Navy pilots were often fascinated by the size of our cargo bay. The Navy worked out of a base located south of Ca Mau on a collection of steel barges lashed together floating in the mouth of a small river in the middle of the U Minh Forest code named "Sea Float."

One of the barges was a floating fuel tank containing the JP5 the Navy used instead of the Army's JP4, and served as the landing site for helicopters. It was just large enough to have two Hueys land and sit side by side. There the SEAL teams would live along with all of the other Navy personnel supporting the base. One of the nice things my crews liked about flying the SEAL Missions was they got to eat Navy food, which even I must admit was much better than the food we were eating in the mess hall back at our company.

River Boats tied up on the side of "Sea Float"

Photo by Jim Ewart

SEAL missions always started with the operations officer calling you to the operations hut the night before the mission and giving you a set of coordinates. When you went back to your hooch and plotted the coordinates you were given, the site was always in the middle of nowhere out in the U Minh Forest. After the second mission I flew with the SEAL teams, it became quite obvious to me those coordinates were very near where the center of the action would be the next morning. It was just someone's way of letting you know where you were going and letting you obtain a map with greater detail of the action area.

The SEAL teams used photographic maps taken by some surveillance aircraft and would offer you a copy before the mission. I didn't like them and always went to supply to get a nice, detailed topographic map of the action area. During my tour in country, I flew many SEAL missions, many of which were routine. The SEALs would go into the area, perform their mission and after several hours call for an extraction. There were two SEAL missions, however, that stand out vividly to this day, some thirty-one years later.

The first of these occurred in the early summer of 1970.

The pre-mission briefing started out as usual with the SEAL team and the helicopter crews going over each other's call signs to be used for communication using the FM radio. Next, the main objective of the mission was discussed. It was explained that their intelligence sources had obtained very reliable information indicating a meeting in a specific building near a creek bed in the northeastern sector of the U Minh by a visiting North Vietnamese. Their mission was to disrupt the meeting and capture the Colonel for interrogation back at a secure location such as Sea Float. The location of the building, as shown by the SEALs' photographic map, was right on the bend of the stream where most of the structure was not too exposed from the surrounding tree line. There wasn't a good landing zone within 1,000 meters of the building but we all felt this was a good point because it would allow the SEALs to egress to the area without too much attention.

At about 08:00 hours we started the two C-model gunships, my H-model Huey, and the Navy's L-model Huey which would serve as the chase ship for this mission. As we approached the LZ with the entire SEAL team ready to exit the cargo bay, the SEAL team leader then asked me how quietly I could approach the LZ. I thought to myself, "Now he asks about the *&%$# noise Hueys make on landings!" I told him I would take care of it. I then cut the throttle back, dropped the collective and auto-rotated into the LZ from about 1,200 feet. Just as I started my flare at 75 feet, I increased the throttle back to 6600 RPM, pulled up the collective, and kicked in left pedal bringing the ship to a three-foot hover. The SEAL team vanished into the tree line and called me, whispering on the radio, to say they were on egress and would call me if they needed me.

The entire flight remained on station at 1,500 feet and about 6,000 meters east of the target building for about an hour "cutting donuts" in the sky. I had the chase ship remain on station while the gunships and I took a five-minute flight to Ca Mau with our radios tuned to the action frequency to hot refuel with JP4, so our fuel tanks would be topped off in case of an emergency. That took about ten minutes and when we all returned, I sent the chase ship back to top off their fuel tanks with JP5 at Sea Float.

When we all resumed cutting donuts, the FM radio came alive with the voice of the SEAL team. They informed us they were ready for pick up and were located about 2,000 meters due west of the building on the other side of the stream and they would pop smoke at their location when they saw us overhead. We all headed toward that location; when we arrived all we saw was a nice lush green growth of beautiful trees. Suddenly, there was a fine wisp of red smoke floating to the top of the trees that grew heavier and heavier as the seconds ticked away ever so slowly.

I called to the SEAL team, "This is Vulture 22. You guys are in a pretty dense area. What's the plan?" They called back, "We are going to make an LZ." The next thing the entire flight saw was tree top after tree top, starting at the red smoke as its epicenter, falling away in an ever increasing circle with the opening to the ground getting larger and larger with each explosion. Finally the SEAL team called, "Is that big enough?"

I sent the gunships down to scout the new LZ area and estimate the relative size of the new LZ. The gunship leader stated the area was clear and it looked like a Huey could hover down to the near-ground area. The pilot flying the mission with me in my ship was a relatively experienced pilot; the 162nd never sent pilots with less than two months in-country time on SEAL missions. Suddenly, his voice came over the intercom and asked, "Are we going to land in there?" I said, "Yes. Are you ready?" and told the gunships I was going in with a "High Overhead Approach and Landing."

This maneuver is done by overflying the landing target at 1,200 feet and doing a spiral descent down to the landing target. Away we went, coming to a hover just above the tree top level over the opening in the forest. Slowly, I brought the Huey down into the hole in the trees with the gunships circling within fifty meters of our position. The tree stumps were all about four feet high so the Huey could go no lower and the SEAL team threw their prisoner, whose arms and hands were tied behind his back, into the cargo bay and then climbed in right after him.

To this day, I have never forgotten the expression on the face of that NVA Colonel when I glanced back to see how things were in the cargo bay. It is the reason I have never forgotten this mission. It was a look of astonishment [What is this machine?], surprise [How did I get here?], and fear [What is going to happen next?] all rolled into one, just before one of the SEALS placed a blindfold over his eyes.

Now came the hardest part of this mission. I had to bring this loaded Huey out of this hole in the trees and then attempt to get airborne from a hover at tree top level. I told the crew chief and door gunner to watch for blade strikes and I began to increase the collective and push in left pedal while watching to make sure the torque meter didn't exceed our company's limit of 40 pounds of torque. The ship began to rise out of the hole in the trees and about 3/4 of the way up we all heard a loud bang - one of the tree branches on the ground had blown up and struck one of the rotor blades. The ship continued upwards until the skids got to tree top level. I slowly pushed the cyclic forward gaining airspeed at an increasing rate until the Huey began to gain altitude and we were safely on our way back to Sea Float.

When we landed at Sea Float, the SEALs got off with their prisoner and took him into an area somewhere in the back of the barges. We stopped the engine and examined the main rotor blades. There was a small dent in the leading edge of one of the blades but there was no break in the surface. I still would have to write it up and fill out an incident report when I got back to Can Tho.

I went looking for the SEALs and found one of them sitting in a room. I wanted to know how they knew about the NVA Colonel. He just smiled and never offered an answer. Later that day, the L-model Huey took the blindfolded NVA Colonel and a couple of SEAL team members to some unknown location. Weeks later when I would ask what ever happened to him or what information did he reveal, I was told he was now just a POW and any information he had was obsolete.

The second SEAL mission I will never forget occurred when the operations officer called me at the Officer's Club right after dinner and ordered me back to the company headquarters. The mission started right then with me being given a set of coordinates located somewhere in the lower U Minh forest, very close to the Gulf of Thailand and also being told my crank time was 03:00 hours at Can Tho.

The onsite briefing was unusual in that it started at 05:00 hours on Sea Float. I was informed the mission had already begun the night before. The SEALs had arrived in the target area by gunboat. They were expecting the Copperhead fire team of 2 UH-1Cs and the Vulture UH-1H command and control ship to assist the SEAL team with any support they may need at first light. There was also a chase ship assigned to the mission that was this time another Vulture UH-1H aircraft. The SEAL team's mission was to infiltrate the area of a known enemy base camp to search the area and destroy any enemy facilities they found.

When the fire team, chase ship, and C & C were over the assigned coordinates at first light, a call was made to the SEAL team on the ground over their assigned FM frequency. They informed us they were able to get into the base camp area and destroyed a great deal of equipment. The SEAL team also informed us they had commandeered a number of sampans and would be paddling them out of the area on a nearby stream that emptied into a river that eventually connected with the bay off the Gulf of Thailand. The SEAL team was asked to pop smoke so their position could be determined by the gunships and the gunships could start their air support. The gunships found the SEAL team's position and began to scout the area. The SEAL team informed the gunships they would be paddling out, but didn't know the disposition of the enemy troops. They were sure a few of the enemy soldiers had escaped the initial assault and were in the area.

Now came the eventful part of this mission. The ground forces team was a mixed group of combatants, consisting of American SEALs and South Vietnamese Marines or Commandos, These members had infiltrated the enemy base camp and now started to paddle the sampans down the stream that emptied into the river. The gunships began to fly in a race track fashion around the small group of sampans firing their machine guns, 40 mm grenades, and rockets into the tree lines on both sides of the stream. This continued for quite some time as the paddlers went from the stream to the river where the tree lines on both sides of the river became denser. For some reason, the last sampan in the group of sampans paddling out of the enemy territory was manned by a single South Vietnamese soldier who was working very, very hard to keep up with the rest of the group. From the air, it looked like he was going to die from overwork before he would make it to the small bay the river emptied into, several miles away.

The Copperheads kept up their fire for the entire length of the sampan's journey out of the enemy's territory. It was a textbook case of the gunships providing suppressive cover perfectly with exacting precision.

I had been told in the pre-mission briefing the gunboat would make contact with us and they would rendezvous with the SEAL team and pick them up and take them out of the area. I climbed to 2,500 feet in an attempt to could catch sight of the gunboat coming toward the SEAL team from the Gulf of Thailand. Just to the northwest of where the river emptied into the bay, I could see the gunboat traveling toward the SEAL team in a southeasterly direction. I told the gunships and chase ship to monitor the SEAL team on their FM frequency and switched my FM radio over to one of those awfully low FM frequencies the navy uses for their communications.

Contacting the navy gunboat, I informed them to continue on their southeasterly direction and I would vector the SEAL team toward them. Switching my FM radio back to the SEAL team's frequency, I advised them to continue on in a northwesterly direction once they reached the bay to meet the gunboat. The lone man in that last sampan, however, was starting to fall behind the rest of the group; but the Copperheads were still making sure he was supported by lengthening their race track formation around the entire flotilla. He was still working very hard trying to keep up.

Switching back and forth between the SEAL team's and the Navy gunboat's FM frequencies, I vectored the two parties until they sighted each other. I took one last pass over the flotilla and there was the last sampan with just one soldier paddling, trying his best to close the little gap that had opened up between him and the rest of his comrades. They all went on to rendezvous at the edge of the bay and the Gulf of Thailand with the Copperheads flying cover until they were well on their way back into the Gulf of Thailand. It looked like everything was going to be all right, so we all headed back to Ca Mau to refuel and head on back to the Vulture's roost and the Copperhead's snake pit back in Can Tho.

This is the only mission I ever participated in Vietnam where the navy inserted the ground forces and army aviation served as the both command and control and supplied the air support for both the ground forces and the navy assets in the water.

The LRRP Mission

Andrę Garesche

It was November and cold for Vietnam. The monsoon season with low ceilings and drizzle had arrived. There was little flying and it seemed as if everything had ground to a halt. The summer had been busy. I had flown 25 missions between July 20th and August 12th. Several of us had been awarded the Air Medal for that stretch of duty. We received our awards sometime in late September or early October on the basketball court of the company compound. The whole company came out in formation. It was the first time I had ever seen the 134th in a company formation. The gun crews were in more ragged and soot covered flight suits compared to the two slick platoons. Five or six of us were called up front and given our medals. But now it was winter.

"Charlie" didn't mortar us anymore, although we were still waiting for one every night. Mark Igoe and I along with our crews took over for the previous primary team at 06:00. We were the primary standby gunship team for the base. It was a 24 hour shift, fully dressed, boots and all. We had to standby at the scramble shack next to the helicopters. All four A/Cs and co-pilots, did a thorough pre-flight of our ships and then went through the checklist flipping only the switches that wouldn't draw power off the battery, but getting everything ready for an immediate start-up. Last thing was to set the "chicken plate" on the seat. It was an armored chest protector we wore. I stuck two packs of Winstons in the plate's front pocket - just in case. And then was it was back to the scramble hooch to sit and wait.

There were two rooms: the back room with bunks which was kept dark 24 hours a day, and the ready room up front. Some guys slept. Some played cards up front. The rules of the scramble hooch were simple. Obviously no booze, keep the noise down for those who wanted to sleep and no gambling lest someone waste time gathering up their winnings when the buzzer went off. I always played cards.

We had been scrambled dozens of times. It was always the same jolt. It was a frenzied ballet, but it was still a ballet. Wing A/C cranked while his co-pilot buckled in. Lead's co-pilot cranked while the A/C got coordinates and frequencies. Door gunners untied the blades. Crew chiefs oversaw everything to make sure we were squared away and clear. It took maybe 30 seconds. The igniters clicking; the turbines whining to power; the smell of burnt JP-4; the adrenaline pumping; the feeling of being scared to death was exhilarating…and we loved every minute of it.

The ballet wasn't without its occasional flaws. On one of my first scrambles, the buzzer went off and we, well, scrambled. It was a night scramble. I ran outside and my crew chief, who had been sleeping in the ship, was holding my chicken plate like a matador so I could just run into it, sticking my head through the hole and just slapping the Velcro together. The weight of the plate caught me off guard and I went diving head first into the sand. Got up in a second and proceeded as if nothing had happened. No one ever said a word. I don't imagine it was the first time it occurred.

But at any rate, that was life at the scramble hooch. We were just sitting there playing the same game, spades, bored as could be, knowing any second the buzzer could go off. We were playing our robotic game of cards. We weren't asleep. I could still sort my hand and follow suit, but really, who cared. Then the buzzer went off!

The whole hooch exploded with action: boots thumping on the floor in the back room, cards thrown down. Normally, there was one blast on the buzzer. This time there were two. As I was running to the ship I heard the third blast. This was not good! The mission was unusual, actually radical. Tactics and procedure went out the window from the get-go.

"Tuy Hoa Tower, Devil 47. Scramble pad for ASAP departure! Vagabond 36!"

"Ah! Roger…47…winds are from the east at niner, ceiling at…ah…500…, no make that 700 feet."

We were already crossing the active runway.

"Godamnit Tower! I didn't ask for a godamn weather report. I asked for clearance. We're already across your active! Out!"

Mark gave me a quick mid-air briefing. A LRRP team from Charlie Company, 1st of the 75th Rangers, was hiding under a tree with a platoon size patrol of NVA coming right toward their position. They had their backs to a small ridge line and a small river to the front and no place to go. They were whispering in the radio; when that got too risky, answered only with clicks of the mic. Two for yes. One for no. This was shaping up to be some bad shit!

Mark was senior in flight time and in country even though I had graduated a month before him. I was the unit IP, but he was flying lead and I was flying wing. We made a great team and I actually liked flying wing because it required more radical flying to always be in position to cover him. We thought as one. The situation was just ten minutes north of us.

"45...7...I'm going up and in IFR."

"Right behind you 7!"

"Bull Shit! What do you want, for us all to go up in a f***kin' mid-air? Hang in the valley and circle at my entry point. I'll call back when I see what's shakin'! If I go total IFR I will call Tuy Hoa and fly an instrument approach back. Hang tight!"

"Roger...but I don't like it!"

"Click Click"

I circled for what seemed like an eternity. Actually it was probably only two loops.

"5...7!"

"Go!"

"Alright. Here's the deal. Go north three clicks from my entry point and go straight west. Climb to 1,500. You'll go IFR. Level at fifteen for a minute and a half, two tops, it won't be long, and then come down fast. Keep normal air speed and you won't kiss the mountain. As soon as you go visual, bank hard left. They should be right in front of you. You'll be right on top of them. They're NVA. Come hot with everything. You're going in alone buddy. I'm going south a ways so I don't spook them. Copy?"

"Roger!"

"They won't expect you because of the clouds. They know we don't fly in this shit. The trail is on the east side of the river. You'll see it. The friendlies are east of the trail 50 yards under a big tree. They'll pop smoke as soon as you go hot. Any color counts. Do it on one pass. No cover for you! One chance! Their cover will be blown once they pop smoke! As soon as I see you, I'm coming back to cover you and clean up. Copy?"

"Roger!"

"Alright. Go for it!"

"Roger!"

I went north for what I thought was three klicks, but was probably only two. The crew chief and door gunner locked and loaded their 60s. Dixie, my co-pilot, lowered the mini-gun sight. He was seasoned, and cool; good at what he did, and probably scared shitless as I was.

"Dixie! When I go IFR count time!"

"Roger!"

We headed west towards the ridgeline and into the clouds. I had been under the hood in flight school but had never flown real IFR in my life. This whole day was going to be a first. Suddenly white all around! I stared at the altimeter and air speed. Fifteen hundred! Oh hell, sixteen can't hurt!

"30 seconds!"

"Roger!"

"One minute!"

"Roger! Arm it! Get ready to go hot on my call!"

"Roger! That's it! That's it. Minute and a half going on two!"

I nosed over, probably too much. I just wanted out. F**ing clouds!

River, ground. Yes! Bank hard left. Shit! There they were! Charlie knew our tactics as well as we did. Helicopters don't fly in clouds, let alone drop out of them and right on top of them…with a gunship no less. I turned too much and had to correct. Lined up and let loose with four rockets. I could barely see them when I fired the first four rockets, but they were NVA. Dixie fired a burst of mini. Four rockets. Burst. Four. Burst. Four. Burst.

Someone was screaming, "Ass…Ass…Ass…Kick Ass!!! It wasn't my crew. It was one of the Rangers. Mark was coming straight at me.

"5…7…Comin' straight at you. I'll pass to the Whiskey."

"Roger."

He went speeding by. I did a cyclic climb, pedal turn and fell in on his ass as we went down the river. It felt good to be a team again. Dixie had some mini left. I was out of rockets. It didn't matter. There was nothing left to shoot at. We did a hard 180 and flew back over the target. Some grass was still smoldering. And there were bodies. Just about all of them face down.

"Devil 47…Demon 26."

"Go ahead 26." It was the slicks coming in for the extraction. "26" was a captain and good. I was glad it was him.

"Roger 26. Standby one. 5….7…You clean?"

"Roger. I'm out. Maybe one burst of mini left."

"Roger."

"Devil 47…Widow 6." Devils; Demons; Widows. What next! Our call signs I guess were meant to speak of death.

"Go ahead Widow 6"

"Man you be some kinda bad. Tell 45 he has a red star comin' his way." He was referring to a 9 mm pistol with a red star imbedded in the pistol grip. Only officers in the NVA carried them.

"Roger….You copy 5?"

"Roger"

"Okay 5. Let's get you out of here." Dixie started putting up his mini gun sight.

"I can stay."

"Nah. It'll be crowded enough when I get the slicks in here."

"Roger. I'll fly south a klick, climb to 2 and head east for 5 before starting a slow descent."

"Roger."

"Try and keep the slicks out of my way since I'll be IFR."

"Roger that. See you at the pad."

"Roger."

"Demon 26…Devil 47."

"Go ahead 47."

"I've got wing comin' out IFR. Keep to the November and Echo and watch out for him. There's no telling where he'll be dropping out."

"Roger. November and Echo. We'll get a little lower and watch for him. We'll give you a call when he's out."

"Roger. Give him 5 mikes."

"Roger."

And off we went into the soup again.

"Give me a five count Dixie."

"Roger."

We went for about three minutes and I couldn't stand it anymore. I didn't like instrument flying. The longer we were in the soup, the greater the chance of getting disoriented.

"What do you think Dixie? We gotta be past the ridge by now?"

"Man, I'd think so."

"What do you think guys?" I said to the whole crew.

"F**k man. You're the godamn pilot! I'm just along for the ride!"

Casey, my crew chief didn't normally talk like that to me but I didn't care. I was too busy on the instruments and, besides, I was just as scared as he was!

"Let's go kids!"

The hell with the slow descent theory. I dropped fast. If I was going to smack a mountain I was going to do it right. No tumbling flips, I was going to kiss it. Literally!

Once I had my descent established, I braced my arms on my legs and closed my eyes. My crew didn't know it. My visor was down.

"We're out! We're out! Oh, son of a bitch, we're out!"

"Oh Sweet Baby!"

"How you doin' Dixie?"

"Just fine now."

"Well then you've got it." I said giving him the controls.

"I've got it." He said, sitting up and taking the controls over. I dug for a cigarette and lit it.

"Say, Mister 'G'. About what I said back there, well that was, well you know."

"Don't worry Casey. You'll have plenty of time to prepare for your court martial." Someone chuckled with an open mic. Maybe Wilson the door gunner. Then the anvil landed on my head. We could still hear the radio from back in the valley. We were used to hearing several conversations on the radio going on at the same time. I held up my hand for everyone to shut up. The Rangers had made it down to the target site. They were doing a body count while they were gathering intelligence. They called in 6 confirmed KIA.

Man that was double what the whole company had gotten in the last six months. There was more radio talk and I heard a single shot while the mike was keyed.

"Hey 47….Widow 6…..make that 13."

"Roger."

"Devil 47."

"Go."

"Devil….you guys are some kinda bad. We're going to need more slicks in here." I took the controls from Dixie and started to circle. "We got 19 now. Can you get more slicks ASAP? You know how the "man" is about the "body count."

"Roger…Demon 26….Devil 47…..Can you get more slicks?"

"Makin' the call right now. You want two or three?"

"Shit man…I don't know….make it three."

"Roger."

"47…Widow 6..we're at…25…Shit there's more…29..30…shit 31 man….that's it….I can see that was where the first rounds hit….No blood trails….no tracks…you got em' all…Get me those slicks so we can get out of here…..I think Charlie's gonna be pissed."

"Roger that….45….you still on freq?"

"Roger," I said almost in a whisper.

"You copy?"

"Roger."

It had been a 31 man patrol. There were 31 KIAs…confirmed!! I gave the controls back to Dixie. Jesus Christ! That's 28 more than the whole company had gotten the year before. I was stunned…beyond stunned! Nobody said a word. We just flew.

"Tuy Hoa Tower…Devil 45….request a Vagabond one eight."

"Roger Devil 45…you're cleared for a Vagabond. Is Devil 47 with you?"

"Negative…he's working with the slicks."

"Roger. Could you tell him Operations would like to see him when he gets back."

"I got it!" I said taking the controls.

"You got it."

"Tuy Hoa! Maybe you can tell him! He usually comes home this way. How long you been in country?"

Another voice came on deeper and more authoritative. It was the major.

"You may as well come along too, 45."

"I usually do after a hot mission, SIR!" When I said Sir he knew that I knew it was him. He never answered the call.

I went to POL and cut back to idle while we refueled, then hovered over to the scramble pad. I set down and shut down. The arms truck pulled up and Casey and Wilson started re-arming. Dixie tied down the blades. I had taken my helmet off and wiped off some sweat. I looked at my watch. The whole thing from start to finish hadn't been more that 40 minutes.

I went around and gave each a double pat on the shoulder for a job well done but there was no joy and nothing was said. Everyone looked sad and tired. I went back and just sat in the cargo door of the ship and watched, waiting for Mark to get back. I lit another cigarette. We weren't supposed to smoke next to the ship but I didn't care.

31 KIA confirmed! Jesus Christ! What had I done! 21 years old. You hand a kid a Huey gunship and send me out there like I'm going onto a football field. I saw a few blurs diving for cover and the rest were hidden by smoke from the rockets and explosions on the ground. 31! My God! What have I done!

I slapped on the old beat up, salt stained cap I wore. CW2 bars with wings above it. It had actually been blown off my head and went up through the main rotor blades once leaving a distinctive gash. I was ordered several times to get a new hat but I never did. It was like an old friend…and if ever I needed an old friend it was now!

After three more cigarettes, Mark came hovering back from POL. He set down and shut down. A Huey came hovering by with the Ranger team. The Rangers were sitting in the cargo door with their feet dangling. They gave a "power salute" fist clenched and arm in the arm. They were followed by three Hueys with what appeared to be firewood from a distance, but I knew better. They followed the Rangers to their bivouac area.

Mark's crew started re-arming. All the gun teams shifted status. The secondary gun team went to primary, stand down to secondary. Mark and I went to stand down which was standard procedure after a hot mission. He threw his gear in the back of the jeep and we headed for Operations. Not a word was spoken.

The brass had turned out. A light colonel; the major; and our platoon leader, a captain was there. The major started out trying to show off for the colonel.

"Garesche, as unit IP you know better than to go IFR." I didn't answer. He didn't like me because he knew I wore beads and a peace symbol on a chain under my flight suit. He had seen me without my shirt. And he hated my hat. I had taken it off but left my sunglasses on.

"Well?"

"Sir! I was flying wing. I was just doing as lead instructed." I thought to myself, "Nice try asshole!" I wasn't setting Mark up and Mark knew that. It was a matter of limiting the crap. Chew one of us out, but not both.

"You two cowboys have just about run your course here…. Garesche, in that case we will just …de-brief…lead! You're dismissed!"

I didn't respond. Just turned and left. I sat in the jeep waiting. The clouds actually started to break a little and a few streaks of sun came through. I felt a little of the tension ease, but I sensed intuitively, that what had happened out there in that river valley was something that was going to stick with me.

Twenty minutes and four cigarettes later he appeared. I could tell by the way his hat was cocked on his head and his jaunt Mark had gotten an ass chewing….and he didn't give a shit! His Irish temper was up but he wasn't going to give them the satisfaction of knowing it.

"Now what?" I asked.

"Oh, I got a five minute chew for taking off before we were cleared. Then I got five more for splitting up the gun team, and then more for going IFR."

"Assholes! What a bunch of d**kheads!"

"Shit man, don't mean nothin'….the Capt. was cool….he didn't say shit."

At that, my thoughts turned back to the 31 KIAs. Don't tell me it don't mean nothing. I had a lifetime of that ahead of me to deal with.

"Club?"

"Club."

We drove to the O' Club.

"Hey! Bourba wata…Scot wata…Where you been? Long time, no see." Yeah. That would have been two nights ago. The barmaid returned with two Scotch and waters for Mark and two Bourbon and waters for me. We always ordered two at a time. It saved her travel time.

The word must have already gotten out because people were staring at us, including guys from other units that we didn't even know. We just drank. I kept my sunglasses on. If the eyes were the window to the soul I didn't want anyone looking at my soul at that moment. Maybe not ever!

We ordered rib eyes and fries. Some war! Kill 31 men and boys and get drunk, have a steak and listen to rock & roll. I could tell this was going to affect me over time as it began to sink in.

We got tired of the scrutiny and left to go back to our rooms. We were both senior enough to have our own private rooms. The plan was to shower, shave, put on clean flight suits and return the jeep. Then head to the flight line. I was finished first. I grabbed a half full bottle of Jim Beam and two cokes and went across the hall to Mark's room. He was just finishing up. We went to the scramble hooch. The pilots were playing spades in the ready room, the crews sleeping in back on the bunks.

"Anything shakin'?" Mark asked.

"Naw, nothing man. Everything's quiet."

"They're poppin' flares," Mark said referring to those mortar flares they shoot that drift down on little parachutes.

"Just some little shit happenin' on the perimeter. You know…the usual." He just shrugged and threw down a card. Nothing was said to me or about the day. In hindsight, I realize it was the beginning of my isolation. Mark and I went outside and sat on the L-shaped revetment protecting the ship I had flown that day. I didn't normally drink whiskey straight, but I took a draw and followed it with a swig of coke. We weren't supposed to smoke on the flight line, let alone drink. We didn't care. I spoke first.

"Since I've been here I've only fired into jungle, man. You know, ground pops a smoke. You shoot north or south, east or west, a couple of hundred yards or whatever. Hell, you don't even know if anything is down there! Shit man! 31!"

"Hey, you better let it lie."

"Yeah, but think of the others: the mothers and fathers, brothers and sisters, aunts and uncles, cousins. Everything changed for them in 30 seconds…hundreds of people!"

"You better put a lid on that shit man or you're gonna end up with a section eight making baskets in a VA hospital somewhere. It happened. So, there it is, man." He took a long draw on his scotch. "Besides, the Rangers probably took out some of them….Dixie got some…your door gunners…! Hell, if you want to clear your conscience, just tell yourself they killed them all and you didn't kill any!"

"Hell….I was the A/C. I flew it. I fired the first shots. Those guys didn't stand a chance."

"So...I guided you in...What do you think they sent you over here for, to play cards all day?"

Maybe I was looking for sympathy...or a shoulder to cry on. I wasn't getting any help from Mark. He had his own ghosts - and not just relating to Vietnam. He didn't even have to be in Vietnam. He had an older brother, also a helicopter pilot, who had been killed in Vietnam. He was exempt but came anyway. I lay down on my back watching the flares drift down on their little parachutes. They cast an eerie light that reflected off the side of my bourbon bottle.

"How long you got to go man?" I asked.

"What time you got?"

I looked at my watch in the flickering light of the flare.

"01:00."

"47 and a wake up."

"Hey man, that's your call sign."

"Well, I'll be damned. You're right. How about that."

I laid there looking up at the flares drifting down. I felt the cigarette slip from my fingers. Later the bourbon bottle must have fallen from my other hand.

Wet n' Wild

J. Bruce Huffman

Slashing Talon 6 and his First Sergeant had grabbed their gear and were running toward the TOC (Tactical Operations Center) at Phouc Vinh when the call came for WO Bard Davenport and me to "saddle up" and make our way to get briefed. I sent Bard ahead to get the ship running, along with my crew Waller and Harper, while I ran to the TOC.

I entered the TOC, step for step with WO Hebert Valencia, Cavalier 26, leader of the two-bird Cobra Fire Team. There we joined the LRP commander already engaged in a hasty brief with our Operations officer. The mission was simple: Slashing Talon 32, a six man LRP team, had encountered an enemy point man; in the effort to capture the NVA, he had taken a round or two. The LRPs were moving south toward the river and were in a running gun battle with the pursuing enemy. Our task was to find an LZ, evacuate the wounded NVA, and extract the LRP patrol.

My crew couldn't have been better picked by anyone for the work we had to do that day. WO Davenport was a big guy from Maine and talked in that monotonal, thoughtful manner of the folks from those parts. Bard would do all the flying from the right seat, and I'd be the Aircraft Commander (AC) handling the radios.

SP5 John B. Waller kept the cleanest lift ship in Charlie Troop. "Little John" was not great in stature, but the great care he took with his work inspired our confidence in the quality of the maintenance.

SP4 Allan G. Harper would be manning the M-60 on the right side. Allan was another guy, like Waller, from California where everyone got labeled, like it or not, as a "surfer" but you could be sure you were never going to poke the tail rotor into a tree on his side unless you heard about it first; loudly and often.

We were quickly airborne to the west and began a climbing left turn south-bound headed for a river terrain feature known as the "testicles", for the river's eerie resemblance to a well-developed male scrotum. The Cobras had raced ahead to support the LRP team and to sort out the tactical situation. Less than 20 minutes later, we were on station and square in the middle of a monumental FUBAR*.

The LRP "snatch" ambush had gone badly wrong. The soldier they bagged was walking point for a much larger NVA force strung out along the trail in column. The LRP team had carried their wounded prisoner as fast as they could down the trail, while fighting a rear guard action to keep the gathering NVA at bay.

The LRP team found themselves pinned against the rapidly flowing river at their backs with no LZ, and the bad guys were deploying in an attempt to flank them. They quickly realized there was no way they could get the prisoner down the river bank, into the current, and onto the helicopter while laying down covering fire. Slashing Talon 6 made a snap call and asked us to go down and get as close to the river bank as we could.

Not exactly sure of what was going to happen next; Bard brought us to a low hover over the river, keeping enough distance from the bank to prevent tangling our main rotor in the overhanging vegetation. Both Cobras had set up an orbit to our right and were laying down some seventeen-pounders less than 100 meters north of the LRP perimeter.

The LRP CO had un-strapped and, along with his First Sergeant and SP5 Waller, had jumped into the current to reinforce and assist with the extraction. Waller hadn't exactly asked me for my permission; he just left. They took a short swim and joined the LRP team's perimeter and quickly got on the radio to coordinate the extraction.

The plan was to come back in when the LRP CO, First Sergeant, SP5 Harper along with one of the LRPs, had moved the wounded NVA into the water suspended on a poncho. They would then swim out to the helicopter, put him on board and climb up themselves. The remaining LRPs would fold in their perimeter, swim out to the Huey and we'd "get the hell out of Dodge" while the Cobras provided suppressive fire. Great plan?

We came back in and took up our low hover as the swimmers struggled with the wounded NVA in the river's swift current. When they got to the helicopter, they quickly realized they couldn't lift the wounded prisoner in the poncho since the water was over their heads. Bard held us as steady as a rock while Waller went out on the right skid, hanging from the M-60 pylon knee-deep in river water, as Bard carefully lowered the pitch while we took "Mr. 'H' model" for a swim. Waller was up on intercom calling out tail rotor clearance above the river until the water level was inside the cargo compartment. The swimmers, with some help from Waller, were able to float the prisoner inside still on the poncho, and we could pick up the hover a bit as we waited for the rest of the LRP team to board. The remaining five team members came on board while Bard eased us out of the river. The Cobra Fire Team rained high explosives and flechette rockets along our right side as Bard struggled to get us flying. Cavalier 26 cheerfully called to let us know "we were sporting a rooster tail" of dripping water that lasted for at least five minutes after we cleared the riverbed headed for Long Binh and the pad at Charlie Med.

Our wounded prisoner looked terrible as we flew toward Long Binh and medical care. I called ahead to ensure they were ready for our arrival and knew the condition of our patient. The medics off-loaded our prisoner and the LRPs decided to disembark as well to decompress a bit while we went to refuel for our short flight back to Phouc Vinh.

On returning to the pad, we were concerned and saddened to learn the prisoner was still in the casualty holding area and had yet to be treated. Our entire LRP crew was gathered in one corner of the landing area quietly talking to one another, when Bard stepped out to find out how long we'd be and to roust some attention for him.

What none of us realized was a medical assessment team had earlier triaged the badly-wounded prisoner and determined he wasn't going to make it. While we stood watching, he gasped once and died, provoking an emotional and tense response from Bard and SP5 Harper. This was directed toward the medical folks who just couldn't grasp or begin to understand the depth of our emotional connection to the dead enemy soldier.

We got everybody loaded up and made the short flight back to Phouc Vinh in silence, certain we had done our best and gratified we'd pulled it off and were still all in one piece. Slashing Talon 32 was coming home.

FUBAR. F%& up beyond all reason.

Epilogue

The letter I mailed to Bard following my DEROS contained a packet of Orange Kool Aid, intended to spoof those left behind who had to still drink the crap until their own Freedom Bird was "gear in the well", was returned on 13 May 1969. It was accompanied by a letter from LTC Thomas C. Adams, Commander, U.S. Army Mail Terminal, San Francisco stating *"The enclosed mail, addressed to WO Bard Davenport, W3 159 711, bears your return address. I regret that it was not possible to have delivered this mail to him."*

On the 27th of March 1969 aircraft UH-1H, 66-16714 was lost to hostile fire at XT 636587 in Binh Long province Republic of Vietnam. Killed that day were WO 1 Bard Elton Davenport, WO 1 William Don Potter, SP4 Allan G. Harper, and SP5 John Bussy Waller.

I've kept the letter, in its original envelope unopened for all of these years, to remind me of Bard and of the valor and bravery that had become just routine behavior for some of the wonderful guys I had the honor to know and serve with.

Vultures of Vietnam

FIRST IN & LAST OUT

Robert M. "Bob" Shine

The following story is dedicated to some of the bravest men the U.S. military has ever witnessed; the helicopter pilots and crews who flew during the Vietnam War. The machines came in many shapes and sizes, as did the men who flew them, and each service had its favorite, but the one they all had in common was the Huey. I'd like to relate some of the adventures with which I'm familiar as a Huey Slick H-Model pilot in Vietnam.

To get a feel for who these men were, go to a local high school graduation and picture that class of young men, just out of boyhood, at 18 and 19 years old, going off to war to fly million dollar aircraft at 150 MPH with people shooting at them, trying to kill them and these same men flying into that machine gun fire repeatedly to get the mission done. It's a sobering scenario.

They became men because of the job they did and the selfless heroism they performed on a daily basis. Many thousands of helicopter crewmen were wounded and/or killed before their 21st birthday, the legal age to drink and vote during the Vietnam War. One out of every five pilots was killed or wounded.

There wasn't much these brave young men wouldn't do when it was required of them. The missions were many and varied, with too many hours and days without rest and a lot of missed sleep. Gunships acted as protection for rescue and medevac ships. Slicks carried troops, supplies, ammo, wounded and dead. They sprayed Agent Orange, Blue, and White to deny the enemy hiding places in the jungle, and were told the stuff was not harmful. Getting shot at and shot down was not an uncommon occurrence. And, they flew in any and all types of weather, sometimes with disastrous results.

Helicopters and the Vietnam War are synonymous, especially the Huey. Made by Bell Helicopter the machine was first called the HU-1 by the Army. In Army jargon, the letters stood for Helicopter, Utility and for those of you in the service you know how they love their acronyms.

As with the Jeep of WWII, the word derived from the letters GP for "general purpose" so in staying in the tradition of making words out of letter sounds, the Bell Turbine Helicopter became known as the Huey after the cartoon character "Baby Huey" and the shape of the aircraft only helped to confirm the name. The letters of the machine were later reversed to the present UH-1, another command decision.

The 162nd Assault Helicopter Company used H-Model Hueys for its Slick platoons who were called Vultures. The Gun Platoon used C-Models and was named Copperheads. These models were used from 1968 until the unit was deactivated in 1972. Less powerful B and D models were used before that time.

The Huey was, and still is, a most amazing aircraft. It first saw service in 1962, when most of the future pilots were still in grade school. The pilots and crews counted on this thin-skinned - think Coke can - machine to get them out of dangerous situations; the grunts, for whom the helicopters existed, loved the sight of an incoming ship. It could mean food, beer, ammo, clean clothes, or a ride to R&R or a replacement and a ride home! The Huey was pushed well beyond its safety envelope many times out of combat necessity or simple mistakes. It could do 110 degree banking turns, get in and out of some very tight places and it also made one hell of a tree trimmer when the need arose.

One mission I flew was a combat assault with a flight of five slicks into a hot LZ in the U Minh Forest, a very heavily defended enemy stronghold in the Delta. The ARVN (Army of the Republic of Vietnam) were in very heavy contact and wanted out fast. Our flight of five approached the LZ to discover only three helicopters could fit into the hole in the trees at one time. That left the last two aircraft hovering over the tree tops waiting for the first three ships to get their passengers loaded and get out.

No one wants to be the last one out of a hot LZ. The ARVN were highly motivated to vacate that very hot LZ. Not wanting to wait for the two hovering Hueys and not caring about overloading as many as could fit, piled on the three aircraft. One of the best pilots I know, CW2 Coonrod, came limping out of the LZ with 21 troops and the four man crew, for a total of 25 people on board! Eight troops was a normal load. Watching the Huey claw its way into the sky from the rear, I could see the rotor blades slowing down due to the maximum power requirements. Coonrod later said his rotor RPM was bleeding off rapidly, and by luck and much skill he was able to get the thing flying and away. The sight of arms and legs sticking out of the open cargo doors was unforgettable.

CW2 Easthouse and I finally got our turn at the LZ and still being shot at; we picked up the last remaining troops. We each got three! The battle damage these machines could take was amazing. I had my ship blown up by a rocket from one of my gunships, while I was on a defoliation run. Luckily for us it was only the 10 pound high explosive war head. If it had been a 17 pounder it would have blown us apart. I headed to the Medevac pad at Navy Bien Thuy to drop off wounded crew members and then back to our base at Can Tho with more shrapnel holes than we cared to count. It was pouring fuel and Agent Orange defoliant heavily from all the holes.

By the time we got back to Can Tho, a five minute flight, I couldn't see out of the windshield due to the brown colored Agent Orange. I started to shoot an approach to what looked like the runway, only to be told by the tower I was headed for the South Swamp just to the west of the active (runway). I had to stick my head out the side window to see where to land at the end of the runway where the tower directed us. The ship never flew again.

Then again, one well-placed bullet in the engine, transmission, or tail rotor could bring the ship crashing down in flames, which happened many times. The only armor on the Huey was the pilot's seats and the "Chicken Plates" the crew wore on their chests. Some crew chiefs and gunners also sat on one. These would stop small caliber projectiles. One problem, of many, was the enemy didn't always use small calibers. They also used large calibers, rockets, or mortars. They also wired artillery shells in trees to detonate when the rotor wash hit the tree branches. I learned to fly slumped way down in the seat, thank you very much. Most pilots in my company carried pistols in cowboy-type hip holsters. These were twisted around so the gun and holster rested between the legs when seated. This was a false sense of protection at best, but was better than nothing. That part of the anatomy is very important to a 20 year old, or for anyone aged 5 to 85 for that matter!

Hueys have long been doing maneuvers not thought possible by a tilt rotor machine. In an autorotation (as in losing the engine) it could safely touch down and still have enough inertia in the rotor system to pick the ship up to a hover and do a 180 degree pedal turn and land again. It could autorotate and land backwards just after takeoff from a tight LZ if there were no place to put the ship down straight ahead or to the sides and no time or altitude to make a 180. I know of one pilot, someone near and dear to me, who decided to do a little showing off to anyone willing to watch. The scene of the "demonstration" was an airfield in the Delta called Ben Tra. The helicopter took off and accelerated along the runway to the maximum speed of 120 Knots (about 150 MPH) and the pilot slowly pulled back on the cyclic to initiate the climb and not promote mast bumping which can snap the rotors off the helicopter (not good!). It was a beautiful smooth climb out. As the ship neared the apex of its climb, I noticed I could look up and see the runway that had just been behind me in the overhead greenhouse window. A very unusual sight in a helicopter! I figured it was a good time to nose the aircraft over into level flight again, only to discover the cyclic and foot pedals had gone limp and lifeless. The helicopter was now hanging by its nose in mid-air about 150 feet off the ground and as pilots of all aircraft know, gravity always wins. What saved the crew's bacon was the superb flying ability of the pilot (read luck). By pulling in more power on the collective, the torque of the system spun the body of the helicopter to the right and straight back down the runway; right back the way it had just come. During the short dive, the controls came back to life and the helicopter pulled out of the very steep dive, leveled off and climbed away. It was a thing of beauty. And a lesson learned the hard way. Everyone watching and the crew, was very impressed. One of my fellow Vultures (#10) watching from the ground later told me "I thought you were dead." Since the saying of "no old bold pilots" didn't arise out of nowhere, it was a learning experience for many. And a maneuver not repeated by one suddenly much older and wiser Aircraft Commander.

The missions were many and varied but they came down to either Combat Assaults or Ash & Trash missions. The A&Ts were usually dull delivery-type flights, but as with everything in Vietnam even they didn't stay dull for long. I was told a radar site on the Cambodian Border needed parts for its ground radar ASAP. It was located on a canal line near the West coast of the Delta. Taking off and heading there wasn't much of a problem. It was night and starting to rain. It got very dark as we approached the site and the wind was picking up quickly. It went from very dark to pitch black. I circled the compound, but those circles turned into large ovals due to the very strong wind. I set up the approach, shooting for a small hand held flash light on the ground. It felt like trying to approach a lightning bug in a pitch black room. The airspeed indicator showed 40-50 Knots and we were just barely creeping up on the light. As we landed without a landing light, we could see the rain going by, parallel to the ground. We knew from the type of station it was there were antennas all around us but it was too dark to see. The only instruction we received from the ground personnel was where not to head.

We departed and headed back to Can Tho. We were on total instruments due to the poor night time weather conditions so I decided to give Saigon a call for a vector back home. He gave me a heading and we were flying along fat, dumb and happy at 2,000 feet. This is where pure luck plays into the picture. I knew we were in the Seven Sisters Mountain region and that Nui Koto went 5,000 feet straight up out of the rice paddies. I also figured Saigon wouldn't put me into a mountain. I was almost dead wrong!

Just by pure chance, luck, or our time not to go, a flare ship on the other side of the mountain lit one off to provide illumination for a Cobra strike on that side of the mountain. It silhouetted the mountain in front of us. We saw, to our horror, we were headed directly into the side of the mountain at 120 Knots. I immediately pulled in maximum power and banked sharply up and to the right. I can still see the tree tops brushing against my chin bubble as we flashed by. I climbed away from the mountain, which was being pretty well lit up by the guns and flare ship and called Saigon to let him know he had just vectored us into a mountain. His reply, "Well, you didn't give me your altitude!" A couple more new lessons learned on that flight.

Being the new guy in country you were next to the lowest of the lows until you had proven yourself. Also being new meant you flew as a "Peter Pilot" to do what you were told when, where, and how high, by the Aircraft Commander (AC) who was the Captain of his ship. I was still a Peter Pilot and we were up by Moc Hoa on the Cambodian Border flying support and combat assaults with the ARVN in the Plain of Reeds. We were told that morning the VC had captured a mini-gun (capable of firing 2,000-6,000 rounds per minute).

The day started off badly when, in a two-ship formation, we were to pick up found weapons. The lead ship was on approach and swerved to the right on short, short final. I then saw why. He had landed next to a pile of mortar bases and tubes to extract. This left me landing next to a pile of dead ARVN with no body bags on them. They were piled on the ship like so many bloody sticks of cord wood. Their arms and legs twisted in many grotesque positions because rigor mortis had set in. The smell was indescribable. I looked back to see the gunner cringing in his gun well because of the dead ARVN that was staring right at him with wide open eyes. Because of the wind rotation in the helicopter we were soon covered with various bodily fluids from the dead men, and it was still morning. We didn't smell good all day. And it's a smell you never forget.

After returning to the rest of the flight at Moc Hoa, we mounted up to go extract the company of ARVN we had dropped off in the LZ earlier. My AC was letting me fly in the chalk 2 position of a flight of five. We were in a V formation when the whole windshield and both side windows filled up with tracers all around us. It was the captured mini-gun. As the flight started to climb away, I noticed as I was pulling in power trying to stay with the flight; we were going down. I told the AC this and he took the controls. We continued our semi-controlled landing while still taking mini-gun fire. The crew chief stated bullets were ripping up through the floor between us and him. We managed to land in the Plain of Reeds and were soon chest high in swamp water that smelled like a sewer.

We got the radios out along with the guns and another Vulture Slick flew in to pick us up. I sat on the edge of the open cargo door with my legs hanging out, as I emptied my .38 caliber Smith and Wesson revolver back at the enemy position. Small consolation! We were dropped off at the end of the runway at Moc Hoa, cold and smelly, but alive. It was getting darker by the minute and an operation was underway to recover the downed H-Model. Soon it was too dark and our guys lost sight of the ship. The VC didn't. They managed to sneak up to it and blow it up. Then it was real easy for our guys to see it; it made a grand, million dollar bonfire. One that I never got to see because we were still waiting on the ground at Moc Hoa until the operation was completed.

One of our missions was to take two Copperhead gunships along with a Vulture Slick (I was the AC at 20) who would be the Command and Control ship (C&C) and pick up a local "Back-Seater" familiar with the area to be hunted. We headed for an area east of Can Tho on the Mekong River and soon found the bad guys and they were willing to fight. The gunships rolled in and made repeated runs at the trees. One of the gunships got hit and shot down. He managed to land in a small clearing in the trees alongside the river. With no hesitation on our part we went in under fire and returning fire, got the crew, guns, and radios out, fast. Now we were the ones who needed the help. We didn't like leaving good C Model gunships. After all, it only had a few bullet holes in it, so we put in a couple of calls to get some extra help and get the Charlie Model lifted out and returned to base for repairs and to fly another day. Those things weren't cheap.

First I had to get a flight of five Slicks to put troops into the LZ to secure the aircraft. Along with the Slicks came their own Cobra gunships. My helicopter was still on station and fighting mad. A Chinook Heavy lift helicopter had to be called and since these aircraft were and are very expensive, more gunships came along to help keep things calm. So, here I was, a 20 year old CW2 Aircraft Commander in charge of more than 100 men and 14 aircraft. I was using so many different radios with their different frequencies I had to have my pilot (name forgotten with apologies) dedicate himself to turning the radio knobs to the right people at the right time. He did a great job and I'm happy to say the ship was recovered and no one was hurt. Everyone did a fantastic job! I was later told by this same pilot that he had written me up for the Silver Star, but because I didn't write myself up for it, I didn't get it. We weren't really big on "Atta Boy Buttons" in the 162nd. The real Heroes of that day were all the flight crews and ARVN on the ground that made it all possible.

Hero is still a word that has meaning and substance, unlike the words "star" or "superstar" which is overused to the extent that someone who has 15 minutes of fame on TV becomes a "Star". The word Hero does apply to those men who manned their helicopters and fought in spite of the unpopularity of the Vietnam War and its politics. They did their duty with honor and courage. These men didn't get to be called men because of their age. Some of them started flying for the Army at 18 years of age and were flying combat at 19. They were considered old men in the group if they were 23 years old or older. Most were proud to have been there and done their duty and most would do it again in a heartbeat if they had to. It was the most intense time of our lives. Of course, in our 50s and 60s and in some cases 70s, it is probably best left up to the younger generation to earn their wings and "fly above the best." Heroes in the making; America can be proud.

The Rest of the Story

Graham Stevens

"By direction of the President of the United States...the **Distinguished Flying Cross** is awarded for exceptionally valorous actions while participating in aerial flight evidenced by voluntary actions above and beyond the call of duty...his actions were in keeping with the highest traditions of the military service and reflect great credit upon himself, his unit, and the United States Army."

These words are not the ones I would have conjured up to describe the events surrounding any action in which you are getting shot at; however, as another of my colleagues had observed about our year in Vietnam, "Great guys and a fun place."

That was also my first impression of the 334th Aviation Company (Aerial Weapons) when I first arrived in Bien Hoa, Vietnam in early September 1969. After my graduation from flight school in June, I had attended the aircraft qualification for the AH-1G Cobra in Savannah, Georgia. Man had just walked on the moon, and I was a really cool, new Cobra pilot, molded in the image of Chennault's Flying Tigers, and on his way to battle the "wily, elusive, yellow hordes of communism."

Yes, now I was invincible. I had a new flight jacket, shiny new wings, and my badge of courage, a Cobra patch. To quote Dan Grossman of the 48th Blue Stars, "little did I know that for better or for worse, for all the fun times, for all my personal ups and downs, I never expected to have had some of the best times of my life intermixed with many of the worst nightmares of that life."

There is a real bond among air warriors. But since man first strapped a gun on an aircraft, we aerial gunslingers have been different. Oh yes, we're all pilots, but "gun pilots" take that dashing, daring, death dealing, devil may care, white silk scarf image a step further.

The 334th was divided into three gunship platoons, the Playboys, the Raiders, and the Dragons; a maintenance platoon, the Gun Runners; and the headquarters platoon, the Sabers. The 334th and its predecessors had built a solid reputation for themselves dating back to July 25th 1962, when advanced elements of the Utility Tactical Transport Helicopter Company (UTT) arrived at Tan Son Nhut Air Base. The 334th was the first fully armed helicopter unit in Vietnam.

Flying with the 334th AHC in III Corps during the period from September 1969-September of 1970 was, to say the least, interesting. The terrain varied from flat marshy rice fields in the southern portion close to the Mekong River, to rolling hills and rubber plantations, left over from the French occupation years, in the north. The unit supported everyone: Americans, Australians, New Zealand Kiwis, Vietnamese, Thai, and Special Forces units. They all requested our support. After three months, a pilot would work with almost every unit in the Corps. The one thing that never changed though was the tenacity of the enemy. It never ceased to amaze me how much firepower they could muster in the middle of nowhere. We owned the day, they owned the night.

I remember my rite of passage in the drinking of the "Green Dragon Cocktail" at the Bien Hoa Officers Club, and later being advanced from a "Peter Pilot" front-seater to Aircraft Commander. I don't, however, remember much after I finished vomiting up my rite of passage. In the interim, there were days and days of flying and learning how to stay alive. There were lessons on how not to get fixated on your target during a rocket run, and fly into the ground, especially at night; lessons on how to apply immediate action emergency procedures, to avoid spinning into the ground after losing your tail rotor; lessons on which hospital to take a wounded co-pilot or pilot to if he got shot during a mission. Above-the-shoulders wounds went to the 21st Evac Hospital, and below-the-shoulders wounds went to the 93rd Evac Hospital.

One could go on forever about experienced incidents and operations in general; but, perhaps this story will speak to the many similar actions that reflect a synopsis of the Vietnam experience for some of the Dragons, Raiders, and Playboys of the 334th Aviation Company (Aerial Weapons). Sometimes we did incredible things and overcame unbelievable obstacles and still came home to laugh about them over a beer in the club. Sometimes we weren't so lucky.

Probably the most important missions the 334th conducted at the time were scrambles. Scramble teams consisted of Cobras fully prepared and ready to cover anyone in III Corps, anytime, day or night. Within five minutes after receiving the call for assistance, the Cobras were in the air and on their way. Scramble missions were never routine, because the same conditions never occurred twice.

It was a day just like any other day, except this day we would standby and scramble if needed from a little airstrip close to Tay Ninh, only minutes outside of Cambodia. After an early get-up and an "aviator's breakfast" of a cigarette and a coke, we took off for Tay Ninh.

We knew if we scrambled, it would be into Cambodia. President Nixon had announced to the world during the last week of April 1970 that armed forces of the United States were to cross the boundary line separating South Vietnam and Cambodia to destroy enemy supply caches and base camps. That decision had a tremendous effect on the entire world. Nowhere was it felt more acutely than by the aviation units like the 334th.

We arrived at Tay Ninh with our fire team of two Cobras, shut down and waited for something to happen. Being the second oldest of the four, at 21, I also happened to be the Flight Leader. My wingman, Larry Pucci, was 19. Our front seat co-pilots, Wayne Hedeman with Larry, and Johnny Almer flying with me, had both been in Vietnam for some months and were already seasoned pilots. As seasoned as we were, however, we were soon bored with just waiting, and began to play. Our attention turned to throwing rocks at a smoke grenade we had tied to a tree by the safety pin. As mid-morning approached, the temperature rose into the mid-90s and, of course, the humidity was already 100 percent. No one had yet hit the darn grenade. As we continued to smoke and joke we removed our shirts to "catch those rays", and stay somewhat cooler.

Finally, someone hit the smoke grenade and out popped the pin, followed by a little puff of smoke. There was much disappointment, however, when no colored smoke appeared. Next, two things happened almost simultaneously. The radio crackled to life with our order to scramble our aircraft to a location in Cambodia, and we were hit with the invisible vapors of the riot gas grenade we unknowingly exploded. Being hot and sweaty and being exposed to riot gas is not an exciting experience on the ground, but when you have to go fly, well…

So with eyes burning from the gas, off we flew in search of an Army of the Republic of Vietnam (ARVN) mechanized Infantry Company. The ARVN company, with its American Army advisors, was in a hot firefight with a reported battalion of North Vietnamese Army (NVA) regulars. Twenty minutes later, we identified the location of the ARVN unit by their signal smokes. These were smoke grenades units would "pop", and we would identify the color. The enemy was sometimes clever in that they would wait until the friendly elements would pop their smoke, and then pop the same color smoke to confuse us. That day we didn't have any problem finding the location of the enemy. Angry red and green tracers were coming at us from everywhere.

I immediately radioed to the unit on the ground we would begin our rocket attack oriented on a West to East azimuth. Then, in we dove, rockets flying and mini-gun spraying bullets at 4,000 rounds per minute. I had a good fix on the bad guys shooting at us; however, as I broke off my rocket attack I saw out the left side another anti-aircraft position. Suckered! About the same time I saw the gun emplacement, the enemy rounds started coming in the cockpit just like in the movies. Plexiglas was splintering, and warning lights were coming on. The #1 and #2 hydraulics OUT lights were glowing, and my wingman reported to me over the radio, that I was on fire! Great, thanks for confirming I'm in deep doo-doo!

The bullets, remarkably, missed the human targets, but had taken a terrible toll on the aircraft. We were going down. Your first thought is to get as far away from the enemy as possible, but Cobras don't fly too well without hydraulic pressure to the flight controls, so all I wanted to do was get the aircraft on the ground. Just about the same time the controls began to freeze up due to loss of hydraulic fluid, we touched down. We threw open our canopies, jumped to the ground, and ran as fast as we could over to a bomb crater. It was here the two of us realized we had no weapons. I had not put on my survival vest prior to takeoff because my tearing eyes made me forget to do anything but get the helicopter started and take off. My front seat, Johnny Almer, had his vest with him, but had dropped his pistol upon leaving the aircraft. So, all we had managed to escape with was one survival vest and one survival radio.

What an ignominious end! I'm thinking we'll both be shot dead in a bomb crater just like the end of the "Bridges at Toko-Ri" when William Holden and Mickey Rooney get shot. Well, not just yet!

It suddenly occurred to us both we were not really that far away from the good guys. After peeking about, we scurried out of the bomb crater and ran the hundred yards to the ARVN position. What a relief, friendly faces. With the aid of the infantry company's radio we reestablished communications with our sister aircraft. They had been orbiting a way off, waiting for the situation to cool off some.

I'm sure the commies were dancing about after their victorious shoot-down of our aircraft. Eager to get back into the game, Larry Pucci in our wing ship wanted the location of the bad guys who shot us down. I told him the machine gun, which we referred to as a "high speed 30 caliber" (7.62mm machine gun on two wheeled cart), was located at the corner of the tree line we were attacking. With that, Larry brought his Cobra about and lined up on the long axis of the tree line and began his attack.

Whoomp! Whoomp! Whoomp! The 17-pound High Explosive rockets threw mud, trees, and enemy up in the air. What an awesome sight. As was customary with our tactics, the front seat copilot would begin to cover the break with 7.62 mm mini-gun, spraying the area with bullets at an ear shattering rate of 4,000 rounds per minute as the aircraft broke around for another pass.

Halfway through the turn though, the mini-gun stopped shooting. I radioed to Larry, "Everything okay?" Through the crackle of the radio I heard him say, "Front seat is hit." I radioed back, "How bad?" His reply sent shudders down my spine. "I don't know." Larry said. "All I can see is a hole in the back of his neck." Because the pilot and copilot sit in tandem in the Cobra, it is difficult for the back-seater to see anything below the shoulder level of the copilot in the front seat. Larry radioed me he was breaking off and heading for the hospital in Tay Ninh. A thirty minute ride with Wayne slowly bleeding to death and there was nothing he could do about it.

This is one of the times we weren't so lucky. Wayne Hedemann died enroute to Tay Ninh. He was old - twenty-two years old and a graduate of the University of Hawaii. We used to kid him about what a Major in Agriculture and a Minor in Soils was all about? The aircraft he was flying in took one hit. The armor piercing round entered on the left side of the aircraft went through his jugular vein and out the back of the neck through the spine. More than likely, Wayne Hedemann never knew what hit him. The aircraft flew back to our home base where the small hole in the side was patched and the blood was washed out. We would need the aircraft the next day with a new crew and a new mission.

Wayne's luck ran out as so many others did during those years. The youth, the life, the blood, just ran out. Those of us who are left, however, know "their actions were in keeping with the highest traditions of the military service and reflect great credit upon themselves, their units, and the United States of America."

"Welcome to Vietnam"

Jim Thorne

After Class 67-10 (Yellow Hats) finished flight training at Mother Rucker, I stuck around for another six weeks and went through gunnery IP and got checked out as an IP in the Charlie model (UH-1-C) gunship hoping this would give me a leg up in getting assigned to a gun unit when I got in country. My orders were to the 173rd Airborne Brigade. I had not yet been told about the "pipeline" and would leave CONUS (Continental United States) on the Big Bird as a young, naive First Lieutenant thinking that's where my ultimate assignment would take me.

After two weeks leave, I checked into Travis Air Force Base on September 10, 1967 for my flight across the "Pond" to my new home in the Republic of Vietnam. After crossing the International Date Line somewhere over the Pacific we landed at Bien Hoa sometime during the day of September 12th and were immediately shipped off to the 90th Replacement Detachment in Long Binh. There we were shown to our quarters in beautiful Camp Alpha where we would spend the next few days waiting for orders.

After what seemed like an eternity waiting to find out when I was going to be sent forward to the 173rd, I was told by a young buck sergeant that *"my orders didn't mean squat, the needs of the service and all that, you know?"* It wasn't long after that my journey down the pipeline began. First stop was the 1st Aviation Brigade, then to 12th Group and then to an intermediate stop at the 145th Combat Aviation

Battalion where officer assignments were made (Warrant Officers were assigned directly to Company level).

After being unceremoniously dropped off at Battalion Headquarters at Bien Hoa I reported to a MAJ Bell, the Battalion S-1, for further assignment. In proper military fashion, I knocked on the Major's office door, marched up to the proscribed distance from his desk, and saluted smartly. The Battalion Sergeant Major had preceded me into Major Bell's office and presented him with my orders and personnel records. The good Major was kind enough to let me stand at attention while he reviewed my records for an appropriate amount of time and let me rest after the long ride from Long Binh. He then slowly rotated in his swivel chair to study the Battalion manning chart on the wall directly behind his desk and after a few seconds of study announced that the next opening in the Battalion for a Lieutenant was in the 2nd lift platoon of the 68th Assault Helicopter Company, Top Tigers, and I was to become a "peter pilot slick driver."

I stood there unable to speak while waiting for the full effect of his devastating pronouncement to sink in. SLICK DRIVER!!! I immediately began to explain the error the Major had just made. I was a qualified instructor pilot in the UH-1-C gunship and all the weapon systems. The only assignment for someone with my training and qualifications would be a gunship assignment. After what seemed like an eternity of pleading my case to the S-1, he "Locked my heals", called in the Sergeant Major, handed him my service records and told him to call the 68th and have them send a jeep to transport me to my new home.

As I stood there in shock having just had the rug pulled out from underneath me, I heard MAJ Bell say "Lieutenant is there anything else I can do for you before I throw you out of my office?" I stuttered for a moment before I could pull myself together and tell the Major that I needed some orders; to which he replied "the Sergeant Major is taking care of that. What else?" It took me another minute to understand what he was telling me and then I clarified my request. "No sir, not my transfer orders; I meant my promotion orders." "What promotion orders?" the Major questioned accusingly, looking at the silver bar on my fatigue collar. I then explained I was a First Lieutenant when I left the States on September 10th but my PED (Promotion Eligibility Date) to Captain was September 11th. I had been a Captain since we crossed the International Date Line a few days ago. I could see the anger building on the Major's face as he turned around in his chair to once again study the Battalion manning chart.

The seconds seemed like hours before the Major turned back around, but when he did there was no mistaking the anger on his face. His hard fiery stare went through me like the Sword on the 1st Aviation Brigade shoulder patch. Finally, he composed himself and called the Sergeant Major into the office, and with a noticeable unsteadiness in his voice, said "Sergeant Major, have someone cut CAPTAIN Thorne some promotion orders and call the 118th Assault Helicopter Company and have them send a jeep for their new 3rd platoon commander. The 3rd platoon, Bandits, was the gun platoon of the 118th AHC. *It was the ONLY vacant slot for a Captain in the Battalion!* I had the privilege of commanding the Bandits from September, 1967 until June, 1968.

Footnote:

Many years after the war, I ran into MAJ Bell at a VHPA (Vietnam Helicopter Pilots Association) convention in Washington D.C. As I recounted the story to him I could tell it was something that he did not recollect. But after a moment, I could see a small glint of recognition in his eyes and slight grin came on his lips that told me that he had just pulled this event from the recesses of his memory. It was one of those things you just never forgot.

"BREAK RIGHT!"

Immediately after being dropped off at the 118th AHC flight line I was introduced to our Commanding Officer, MAJ Bill Bradner, and the man whom I was to replace as the 3rd Platoon Commander, CPT Jeff Thomason. My new moniker would become Bandit 36. Jeff gave me a tour of the Hideout, the name given to the gun platoon revetments, and then took me to the Bandit hooch where he briefed me on the status of our eight UH-1-C gunships, our 17 other pilots and 30+ crew chiefs, gunners, armorers, etc. He concluded his briefing by letting me know he was going to Saigon early the next morning to meet his wife, a Registered Nurse, who was assigned to 5th Evac

Hospital, and they were leaving on an R&R together to Tokyo before heading back to the States. If I was lucky, he said, he might see me before he and his wife caught the Big Bird back to the US. ANY QUESTIONS? Two things immediately came to mind! First, "what the F*%K, OVER?" and the other, "who was the most experienced pilot in the gun platoon?" I got an answer only to the second question…WO Warren "Pappy" Spencer. So-called, because he was the oldest pilot in the Guns at 28-years old; whereupon, I immediately went looking for one Pappy Spencer. It was several hours later when the company returned from a CA (Combat Assault) that I found Pappy Spencer. He was not one who had been blessed with an excess of oratory. The many questions I shot at him in rapid fire were answered with either yes sir; or no sir; or I don't know sir. After an hour of this jousting it was getting late, and since I was getting nowhere fast, I told Pappy we should take a break and get some chow. We could resume our discussion after dinner.

That evening, MAJ Bradner introduced me to most of the other pilots in the Company. After some small talk and a few hot beers I found Pappy and re-engaged him to continue our discussion regarding aircraft status, pilot makeup, and other general information one would consider important to running a platoon. After several hours of prying out this critical information, we hung it up for the night and agreed I would ride with him on the mission the next day and consider that my in-country orientation. After a few days of riding left seat with Pappy, I was deemed qualified as an AC (Aircraft Commander) and finally assumed command of my platoon and my aircraft, Bandit 8, an M-3

Hog. It was then I informed Pappy I had made a command decision. He was being relieved of his position as a flight leader and given the awesome responsibility of becoming my wingman; his primary and sole mission was to keep my ass out of a sling and to ensure my aircraft and I returned to the Hideout at the end of each day in one piece, more or less.

Things went well for several weeks and, for a FNG (f#*king new guy) I managed not to embarrass myself more than once or twice. Then the inevitable happened. We were on a CA out near the Parrots Beak west of Duc Hoa that very quickly turned into a GRF (giant rat f#*k). We had just inserted the grunts and I had left one fire team on station to cap the LZ. I took my fire team to Duc Hoa for refueling and rearming and after a quick turnaround, we returned to the LZ to relieve the fire team on station so they could go and do likewise. About five minutes out, I called them on the radio and told them to break off for fuel. Pappy and I proceeded to the AO (area of operation) and upon arrival flew over the LZ to pick up a cap. As soon as we were dead center over the LZ, mortar rounds started detonating on the ground. I immediately laid the aircraft over in a 45-50 degree turn, punched the transmit button and screamed in the radio for Pappy to "break right." The reply came calmly and clearly, "Why right, dai uy?" It was a question that you did not, should not, and I would not, try to answer. I immediately realized the stupidity of the question; whose rounds were they, where were they coming from? Questions only a FNG with only a few weeks in country would ask. Weeks went by and the events of that day were never mentioned again. It was a testament to Pappy's code of honor; and, my promise to have his ass if he ever repeated the story to anyone.

Less than two weeks later, the Company picked up an "Ash and Trash" mission. The Guns were given the mission of providing a light fire team to one of the Province Chiefs in northern III Corps. We spent the entire day chasing shadows here and there and were not released until almost dark. Since we knew it would be EENT (end evening nautical twilight) before we reached Bien Hoa, and this would be my first flight at night in Vietnam, I told Pappy to take the lead and I would fly off his right wing back to home base. I took up my position at a 45 degree angle and an appropriate distance behind and to the right of his lead aircraft and we proceeded to navigate home. Piece of cake! Per our SOP (Standing Operating Procedures) we had turned on only the rotating beacon on top of the helicopter and the instrument panel lights so as not to give Charlie a brilliantly lit up target to shoot at from below. As the sky fully darkened, as it does in RVN, it was as if we had walked into a closet and someone closed the door. There was no light. No horizon. NO NOTHING, except the Grimes light on top of Pappy's ship which I kept my eyes fixed on knowing that if it ever became lost, I was doomed. And then it happened. IT WAS GONE! There was nothing in the entire universe (only those who have flown at night in Vietnam can appreciate the claustrophobic feeling of being IFR at night in country). Again, with a strangle grip on the "push to talk switch" I screamed "Pappy where in the hell are you. I've lost your light". Then with that same calm, clear voice came the reply. "You're 180 dai uy" (when you are following directly behind another aircraft, the rotating beacon on top of the aircraft is blocked out by the vertical fin on the end of the tail boom), thus another event, the details of which were never to be repeated to anyone.

Warren "Pappy" Spencer continued to keep my chestnuts out of the fire until he rotated back to the States in the summer of 1968. He went on to receive a direct commission and rose to the rank of Major. In 1991, while serving as a platform instructor at Fort Rucker, Alabama, Pappy was diagnosed with lung cancer and shortly thereafter passed from this earth. We had kept in touch over the years and when his wife called and told me of his condition, I immediately went to Dothan, AL where he was living. It was spring break at Texas A&M University where my daughter was a senior. I stopped on the way and picked her up to go with me. Pappy and I spent the next afternoon and most of the night reminiscing and telling war stories to the great delight, and sometimes horror, of my daughter and Pappy's wife. We left the next day and I was home less than a week when his wife called to tell me that Pappy was gone.

Were it not for Pappy, who faithfully fulfilled his charge by saving my ass more times than I care to remember, I most likely would never have returned from Vietnam; would never have met my loving wife, Earlene, and would never have been blessed with two wonderful children, Traci and Stephen. I will forever be in his debt.

"BANDIT ESCORT"

It was sometime in early 1968 just after Tet when we got word MAJ Bill Bradner, the Commanding Officer of the 118th AHC

(Assault Helicopter Company) was about to DEROS (Date Eligible to Return from Overseas) and his replacement, MAJ Evans Guidroz, had arrived. At the same time one of my gun drivers, WO Bobby Bell, got his orders to return to the "Big PX in the Sky." They both were ordered to report to the 90th Replacement Detachment (Camp Alpha) for out processing and the flight home. As was the tradition in the 118th, when one of our pilots was going to catch the "Freedom Bird" home a number of us would get together and drive over to Long Binh to the Officers Club and have a send-off party for our departing comrades; and so it would be for MAJ Bradner and Mr. Bell.

We finished our mission early on the day of our Farewell Celebration and CWO Warren "Pappy" Spencer and I loaded up in my jeep and headed for the O-Club at Long Binh. It's probably best to simply describe the going-away festivities by saying that late into the night and after hours of saying the last farewell to our friends, that it ended only with the NCOIC (Non-Commissioned Officer in Charge) running the O-Club announcing the "Absolute Last Call" a little after midnight. Only after many handshakes that eventually turned into hugs, did Pappy and I finally find our way back to my jeep and started the long trek back to Bien Hoa. After a long interval of absolute silence, I said "we can't just let them leave without doing something they can take home with them." After a few more miles without either of us saying a word, I finally came up with an idea born from too much scotch and too little sleep. "LET'S GIVE THE FREEDOM BIRD A GUNSHIP ESCORT OUT OF BIEN HOA!" Pappy immediately called my sanity into question. However, my compelling logic and cunning oratory prevailed and somewhere between the Long Binh POW Compound and the Bien Hoa Air base the plot was hatched; my position as his commanding officer and superior rank had overcome Pappy's many objections, sound though they were.

Once we arrived back in Bien Hoa I looked up SSG Jimmie Pirtle, my platoon sergeant, who was still up with 1st SGT Dale Kinney, the Company First Sergeant, plotting how to win the war over a couple of beers. I told them of our plan and instructed SSG Pirtle to get two gunships and strip them of everything not necessary for sustained aerial flight. We would need all the power available if we were to be able to hover the aircraft enough to maneuver around the many obstacles between the Bien Hoa runway and taxiway. After a brief discussion during which SSG Pirtle and 1st SGT Kinney summarized their opinion of my plan in more-or-less proper military protocol, they saluted smartly, did an about face and rushed away to comply with my orders. The deed would soon be done.

For the next hour or so, I continued the tactical and administrative planning of our mission. It was decided the crew requirement for the aircraft be kept at a minimum; one pilot per aircraft ONLY, Pappy & Me. The rationale behind this decision was simple; everyone I told about the plan thought it was absolutely insane and I didn't want a mutiny on my hands. This had to be a fait accompli.

Next, I needed to coordinate this exercise with the Air Force AOD (Air Officer of the Day) on duty that night. After getting the Tower Operator on the horn I had him wake up the Officer on duty. After visiting with an unhappy Air Force Major for a few minutes his anger at being awakened at 2:00 AM in the morning became overcome with the hilarious absurdity of my idea. In the end, however, he agreed to my plan, gave me the frequency of the Freedom Bird, instructed the tower operator to allow my aircraft to hover from our side of the airfield to the area between the Bien Hoa active runway and taxiway, and await the Freedom Bird's departure. At this point we decided to take a break and try to get an hour or so of sleep. What earlier had been a happy buzz was now rapidly becoming a mild hangover and we would need all our wits about us if we were to pull off this gig in less than two hours.

After an hour or so of trying but failing to get some sleep, I finally got up and went looking for Pappy so we could get the show on the road. Suddenly he appeared, trailed by WO Kenny Dolan, another Bandit. Pappy had evidently recruited Kenny for our courageous mission without telling him the details of the plan... Now we were three. (At this point I must confess the ravages of time do not allow me to recall whether or not anyone else was involved in this sinister plot. My recollection is I was flying a single pilot ship).

At about 04:00 hours, we mounted our trusty steeds, called the Bien Hoa tower for clearance, picked up to a high hover (and yes, you can hover a UH-1-C at 4:00 AM after it's been stripped of door guns, ammo, c-rations, chicken plates, etc.) and maneuvered over to the runway. We sat at flight idle on the gap between the runway and taxiway watching in envy the Freedom Bird loaded with its precious cargo of soldiers, waiting to take off for the land of the Big PX. Suddenly, I heard the whine of the jet engines as they began to turn and without notice my radio came alive. "Bandit aircraft this is Freedom Bird 1234. Are you monitoring my frequency?" Our moment was upon us. I responded in the affirmative and the Captain of the airliner began giving me admonitions regarding jet wash, vortex hazards on lift off, etc. and ended with a sincere "thank you" since Charlie had a habit of taking pot-shots at aircraft departing Bien Hoa Airbase at night. After all the preflight admonitions he felt appropriate for our mission, he called the tower for permission to taxi to the active runway. He began to move.

Once Big Bird was in place and holding at the departure end of the runway, Pappy and I took our places off each wing of the big Boeing 707 (you really don't appreciate just how big they really are until you're sitting on the ground next to one of those beasts). I got the Captain on the horn one more time to thank him for going along with this circus and to ask that he make an announcement over his intercom that "onboard he had MAJ Bradner, the Commanding Officer of the 118th Assault Helicopter Company and one of its finest gunship pilots WO Bobby Bell and it was our intent to give them a gunship escort off Bien Hoa airfield to ensure no harm came to them as they departed for the Land of the Big PX." MAJ Bradner told me years later the pilot did, in fact, make that announcement and it was received by cheers from all aboard!

Just as the Boeing 707 started to roll, the Captain came on the air again and admonished us to pay particular attention to the vortices created by the big wings as he began to rotate the jet. That was when the turbulence would be the most severe. We added that caution to the many other things we were concerned with which included clouds of dust stirred up by the four jet engines, the myriad of radio antenna scattered about, cinder block huts containing electrical equipment, etc., all of which were scattered in our immediate flight path. Away we went!

As we picked up to a hover and began to accelerate alongside the jet, it at first seemed that we were going to outrun this behemoth down the runway. That feeling didn't last long. As the jet picked up speed and passed us, we began to feel the turbulence from the jet engines and when they eventually lifted off it seemed as though something or someone picked us up and tossed us about uncontrollably. Then all was quiet. Our comrades were airborne and on their way home to the Land of the Big PX. And we were still in Vietnam!

We quietly high hovered back to the Hideout, the Bandit revetments, and shut down the aircraft. The adrenaline rush was over and the emotion of seeing our friends leave soon faded. It was time to get ready for another Combat Assault scheduled to lift off in a matter of hours. The deed had been done!

Three Hundred and Sixty Five Days

Paul T. Kearns

With Letters to Home

What follows is a narrative of my personal experience as a helicopter pilot serving in the U.S. Army in the Republic of South Vietnam during the years 1968-1969, and portions of my army flight training experiences prior to my combat duty service in Vietnam. It is a recollection of what I experienced then, and can recall now, some thirty five years later. History books tell the facts concerning the battles and politics of that war, what led up to it, how it was won or lost, and how it ended. My perspective, described herein, is much more limited and personal. It is my story, and to a limited degree, a story of others who shared the three hundred and sixty five day tour of duty with me.

This version of my memoir has excerpts taken from personal letters I wrote to my family during this period.

MY ARRIVAL

The date was May 30, 1968. It had been a very long flight from McChord Air Force Base near Tacoma, Washington to Cam Ranh Bay Air Force Base in South Vietnam. I was 21 years old, three weeks past my graduation from the United States Army Aviation School at Fort Rucker, Alabama. The moment I stepped off that airplane I was the newest arrival amongst the steady stream of mostly young men going to Vietnam to join the occupational army consisting of some 500,000 Americans. I was scared, and very lonely.

Almost to the day, three years earlier, I had walked down the aisle at La Jolla High School in San Diego, California to receive my diploma. My life had undergone some major changes during those past three years; it would be changed more during the next.

COLLEGE

1965 was near the end of the period which America stood proud after the Second World War. During the preceding 20 years (1945-1965) the American people looked upon their country as being beyond reproach...an America that had not yet lost a war. All of this would change. The nation was just beginning to pass into a new era. President John F. Kennedy had been assassinated only two years earlier, and his brother Bobby, along with Martin Luther King, would soon also die by assassin's guns. The Cold War was at its midpoint. America was confronting communism throughout the world.

What had started in Vietnam as advisory assistance had escalated into a major military commitment. President Lyndon Johnson found himself being drawn ever deeper into a conflict on the other side of the world. Many young Americans were being told to serve their country as their fathers had only a few years before in the Korean and Second World Wars. The military buildup required a draft that was soon inducting thirty thousand young men a month to fulfill the needs of the ever growing manpower requirements of the Vietnam conflict.

As the escalation of the war in Vietnam was taking place I graduated from high school and went off to college.

I went off to college for the wrong reasons. After three semesters I wanted to enlist in the armed forces - this despite much well intended advice to the contrary from many friends, and my family. I had made the first major decision of my life.

Aviation had always been of interest to me. As a youngster I built my share of model airplanes, and loved to read of the exploits of aerial combat during the World Wars. When I began to seriously consider joining the military, I naturally gravitated to the possibility of becoming a pilot. Lacking a college degree, my best chance of becoming one was through the army's Warrant Officer Helicopter Flight Training Program. I started the application process at the local army recruiting station in Spokane, Washington where I was attending Whitworth College.

I left college on a cold winter day in January of 1967. On March 27 of that year I was inducted into the U.S. Army at Oakland, California. I was two weeks short of my twentieth birthday. The Army soon had me on a plane with three other helicopter heroes-to-be, headed to Fort Polk, Louisiana. We had orders to attend Army Helicopter Flight School at the completion of basic training.

BASIC TRAINING

Basic training is an experience one never forgets. I was a middle class white boy who was used to a middle class lifestyle. In military basic training, one is stripped of his identity and given a new one. The process takes about eight to ten weeks. You get a shaved head and surrender all civilian clothing. Your mind is tested for aptitude and your body poked with needles. You are given your military serial number and told to memorize it. We were given army underwear, army pants, shirts, boots, a jacket, a hat and a duffel bag to put it all in. We were then loaded into a large truck and transported, like cattle, to our basic training company area. It was here we were introduced to the drill sergeants. The drill sergeants were not nice people. We were made to stand at attention while they screamed at us. The next three hours were a succession of pushups and running. We had to dump the contents of our duffel bags into a pile so the drill sergeants could rummage through, looking for anything not issued to us. We were assigned a barracks and bed. We were issued sheets and blankets. It was late that night before I found myself in that bed. We were awakened many times and told to fall into formation. The next day started very early. Welcome to basic training, Private Kearns.

There is no privacy in basic training. You eat, sleep, and eliminate in the presence of others. I learned how to act and look like a soldier. I was taught the Military Code of Conduct and learned how powerless I was, and what I could expect should I stray from those rules. I learned how to march, whom, and how to salute, to shoot and clean a rifle, how to crawl as if my life would depend on it, and how to put on a gas mask while in a gas chamber filled with C-2 tear gas. I learned how to kill someone; in fact, I was pushed to the point where I learned I was capable of killing someone. All of this was basic training. At the completion of basic training I was put on an army bus with other helicopter want-to-be pilots and shipped to Ft. Wolters, Texas, the home of The United States Army Primary Helicopter Flight School. I was sure the hard part was over. Now the fun would start.

FLIGHT SCHOOL

The Vietnam War, with its massive helicopter fleet, required a lot of pilots to fly them. Since the army did not have a large enough pool of helicopter pilots to fulfill the requirements demanded by the war in Vietnam, it had to train many new ones. Over 40,000 pilots were trained during the course of the Vietnam Conflict. Most applicants for helicopter pilot training program were much like me: young, capable enough to learn to fly, and adventurous enough to be willing to fly helicopters in Vietnam. All of us shared the desire for change and adventure. Not many of us, I think, really knew what we were getting into. Whatever our motivations, our lives would never be the same.

The majority of army student helicopter pilots went through flight school as warrant officer candidates (WOCs). Upon graduation, WOCs received the rank of Warrant Officer (WO1) along with their Army Aviator Wings. Alongside the WOCs were a smaller number of commissioned officers (RLOs, real live officers) who went through the same flight and academic training for their wings. We would all serve together after graduation.

Fort Wolters was located in Mineral Wells, Texas. It was there that primary flight training was conducted: first by one month of preflight training, followed by four months of primary flight instruction. Upon graduation from Fort Wolters, the graduates were sent to Fort Rucker,

Alabama for another four months of advanced flight and ground instruction. It was at Rucker where we were trained to fly instruments, received a basic checkout in the Bell UH-1 Huey helicopter and underwent advanced tactical training. Upon graduation from Fort Rucker, the new pilots received orders for their first assignment as Army aviators. Immediately upon graduation, most were given orders to report to Vietnam within a matter of a few weeks.

Instead of the Drill Sergeants of basic, we had a new demon to contend with: the TAC Officer. I remember some of their names to this day: men like CW2 Newhauser and CW2 Duer. The TAC was himself a warrant officer who had served a tour in Vietnam as a pilot. They knew what was waiting for us as army helicopter pilots in Vietnam and they intended to see that nobody went over there who was not fit to do so. Constant harassment and pressure were applied to us. If a WOC could not deal with harassment of the sort handed out in flight school, what would he do in a far more stressful and dangerous situation such as Vietnam?

Picture, if you will, a young warrant officer candidate standing at attention with a TAC about one inch from the tip of his nose. The dialog would go something like this:

TAC: "Candy...date. Do you know you have a bomb in your boot?"

WOC: "Sir, Candidate Kearns, No Sir!"

TAC: "Is that a fuse in your boot...Candy...date?"

WOC: Looking at a stray boot lace not tucked away in a military manner, "Sir, Candidate Kearns, no Sir that is my boot lace sir!"

TAC: "Candy...date Kearns, if I light that fuse would your boot blow up? "

WOC: "Sir Candidate Kearns, no Sir! "

TAC: "Candy...date Kearns. Are you a dhu...d?"

WOC: "Sir, Candidate Kearns, no Sir. I'm not a dud, Sir!"

TAC: "Candy...date dhu...d, I don't think you are going to make it through this program!"

WOC: "Sir, Candidate Kearns, No Sir! uh, I mean, Yes Sir! I intend to make it through this program, Sir!"

TAC: "Candy...date, I think you are a scum ...bag."

WOC: with lips quivering, "Sir, Candidate Kearns, Sir, I'm not a scum bag, Sir!"

TAC: "Candy...date, are you going to be a he...row?"

WOC: "Sir, Candidate Kearns, Sir, Yes Sir, uh no Sir, I mean, I don't know if I want to be a hero, Sir."

TAC: "Candy...date, you better pull your head out of your ass and get with the program!"

At this point the TAC would move on to his next victim. The process was ongoing.

The first month at Wolters was spent in classrooms, the parade field, and our barracks. Our living areas had to be kept in a spotless and orderly condition. The latrines were kept spotless, the hallways waxed, and our personal areas displayed to exacting standards. When the TACs inspected our barracks and found anything not up to their standards we were issued demerits. Too many demerits meant fewer privileges, and often extra hardship, such as practicing close order drill, or extra physical training during what could have been free time.

The academic stress was considerable .If you failed a written examination, you would retake it after a thorough review of the subject matter. If you failed it a second time, you were out of the program. Map reading was my wakeup call. I had to retake no other written exams.

Upon successful completion of the first month flight training began.

Three different helicopter trainers were used at Fort Wolters: Bell OH-13, Hughes TH-55, and the Hiller OH-23D. I was assigned to an OH-23D training flight. We were also assigned our flight instructors.

An early flight lesson would go like this: The small noisy helicopter would be hovering in a large field. The instructor would be on the controls flying it while I sat next to him not knowing what was to come next.

Instructor: "OK Kearns, put your feet on the pedals and keep the nose straight. Remember the nose will move in the direction you push, right pedal right turn. Left pedal left turn. That a boy.

Now, notice when I add power the nose turns to the right, unless you add left pedal. If I reduce power, you must add right pedal. That a boy, you are doing well."

"Now, hold on to the collective stick with your left hand and try to keep it positioned so we maintain a steady height of three feet above the ground. Up collective, up we go. Down collective and down we go. Damn it! Keep that nose straight when you make power changes with the collective! Watch the height! Don't hit the ground! Up! Up! Keep that damn nose straight!"

"Keep an eye on the RPM! If you move the collective you need to adjust the throttle."

"OK, now let's try the cyclic stick with your right hand. Remember, the helicopter will go in the direction you push the cyclic. Left cyclic, you go left. Right, you go to the right. Forward, forward. Aft, you guessed it, aft."

"OK, any questions? You got it. Watch it, not so much control input!"

At this point, the helicopter would begin to drift from its position, slowly at first, but progressively faster and more erratically…in every directional axis: nose up, nose down, nose left, nose right, sideways left, sideways right, up and down. The harder I tried, the more uncontrollable and terrifying it became. Just prior to crashing, the instructor grab the controls and in about 1/2 second have the machine completely under control again, as if by the hands of God himself.

"OK Kearns, let's try it again. You have the controls…"

Even the long-awaited flight training was tougher than I had expected. My relationship with my instructor was not helping me much. His style of verbal abuse, while teaching, was not helping me to learn how to fly. It was nearing time to solo and I was not going to be ready. If you failed to solo within the apportioned period of time you could find yourself terminated from the program, or in some cases sent back to the following class - not a move of distinction.

I gave serious thought to giving it all up and resigning. I approached my commanding officer and expressed my frustration. We had a long talk behind closed doors where he was able to convince me to stick it out. He told me to consider asking for a different flight instructor. He also told me if I left flight training due to my own volition, I could expect to be wading in a Vietnamese rice paddy very soon.

My new instructor, Mr. Saunders, knew how to teach without intimidating. I began to relax more and develop the early skills needed to solo.

Learning a difficult task such as flying a helicopter is accomplished in a series of steps. Motor skills are developed and layered upon each other. Along with the motor skill development comes increasing self-confidence.

I had soloed, but I was progressing slowly with my flight training. I needed to take the next step, that step came for me on a solo flight.

Throughout the training zone, in and around Fort Wolters, were confined landing areas. Some of these areas were on flat land surrounded by trees and brush. Others were located on hill tops and as such called pinnacles. All were marked by old automobile tires painted white, yellow, or red. These color distinctions were used to classify with regard to difficulty of use. Normally, students on solo flights were restricted to white tire areas.

I was flying about on a solo flight in my OH-23, trying to pick suitable white tire areas to practice with. As long as I could make a shallow approach, I felt little intimidation. While practicing with my instructor I had been having trouble with my rate of closure since I feared that approaching too slow would result in falling out of the sky. There was something here I was missing and my confidence level was suffering for it.

While cruising above a narrow Texas road I spotted a large hill. I banked to fly over it and spotted a red tire on its top. A few more orbits and I began to feel an uptake in my adrenaline level. My palms were growing sweaty. A few more orbits and I decided I was going to land on that pinnacle. I made my high recon and set myself up for an approach. All looked well as I approached the red tire while I kept my airspeed up. Over the trees on my approach, still keeping my airspeed up…I continued. I was now committed to land since I had descended below the tree tops I would have had to clear in order to abort the landing. No instructor sat next to me telling me what to do or take the controls from me. I was going land or crash. It was that simple.

As I approached the ground, I realized I was going too fast, the trees were looming up at me to my front. I needed to stop my forward speed now or I was going to indeed hit them with my rotor blades. I pulled back on the cyclic stick and dug the tail stinger into the ground, thus plowing a furrow across the landing area. I came to a stop before hitting those trees. I had survived a horrible approach...barely.

After my heart rate returned to normal, I reduced the engine RPM, frictioned down the controls, and climbed out of the cockpit to survey the landing area. Sure enough, there was a stripe of yellow paint across the rocks I had drug the stinger over, ending where my machine sat idling. I had come in way too fast. I would not make that mistake again.

The helicopter revved back up to operating RPM, the friction was taken off, and the machine and I once again roared back into the air. Again an approach was initiated, only this time my airspeed was correct. My landing was perfect.

On my way back to our training base I felt a little more like a helicopter pilot.

I graduated from Fort Wolters in November of 1967 and reported to Fort Rucker in January of 1968.

Letter to home dated January 14, 1968

"Just a short note to give you my address, and let you know that everything is going better than I expected. They treat us with a lot

more respect here than they did at Wolters. We start classes and flying tomorrow. That's two weeks sooner than I expected. My only worry right now is flying with instruments."

Letter to home dated January 29, 1968

"Well, I have fourteen hours of instrument flying in. I've been having my share of difficulties, but I am coming along. The first big test will be in two weeks when I get a check ride. I will phone you and let you know how I make out on it.

I received my officer dress blues and some assorted items in the mail last week. I sure hope I will wear them some day."

Letter to home dated February 14, 1968

"Things are moving along fairly well. We have taken two tests and I scored 87% on both of them. As for flying, all I can say is that the check ride is due sometime this week. We had so many bad weather days last week that we flew Saturday, but it was worth it since I received a grade of "A". It's the first "A" I have ever received, even at Wolters. If I can fly like that on the check ride I'll have no problem. If all goes well, I will be flying Huey's in five weeks. That sure will be a long awaited moment.."

I failed my first basic instrument check ride.

After five additional hours of basic instrument training, I took another check ride and passed.

In flight school, the army had a tough job to do: that was to try to teach very young men how to behave as officers, as well as teach them to fly. Neither of these tasks was easy. Once again, preexisting values are stripped away and replaced with new ones. Some people have considerable difficulty making the changes and learning these new skills. Time was of an essence. If a student fell too far behind the set pace he was released from training.

Letter to home dated February 22, 1968

"I have struggled through two weeks of advanced instruments. So far I find it easier than basic instruments, but time will tell. It is sure a lot more interesting."

Letter to home dated March 17, 1968

"One more week of instruments, that is if I pass my check ride! It not only will be great to fly the "Huey" but it will also be wonderful to see where I am flying."

Letter to home dated March 17, 1968

"The "Hueys" are great. I can't fly them worth a damn, but I am slowly learning. At least I think I am?"

"If all goes well, I will be a warrant officer and army aviator in seven weeks."

Letter to home dated April 3, 1968

"I passed my first phase check ride in the Huey today. Now this next month we go into tactics. That should be fun. It is in tactics that we start training in areas like mass formations, low level cross countries, tree top flying, external loads and the like. The last two weeks are spent out in the field living in tents and flying simulated missions. We also have to spend a night stumbling around the woods in escape and evasion training. I will phone you as soon as I get my orders."

Tactical was very interesting and almost fun. After all this time, energy, and money neither us, nor the army wanted anything but for us to graduate and fill our slots in the U.S. Army's helicopter pilot rosters. We were senior classmen. We looked upon others in earlier stages of training with distain, they at us with envy.

We had been taught in flight school an army aviator is never really lost, but only temporarily disorientated.

Challenges still presented themselves. One dark night, while performing a training flight with another WOC we found ourselves lost. It was very dark flying over the Alabama flatlands that night. Our navigation aids were only a clock and compass. Our destination was a field where someone waited for us with a small smudge pot for identification. We missed the field. After flying about in the dark, looking for our checkpoints, we had become completely disorientated. So disorientated in fact, we could not find the main airfield from which our flight had originated. At last, we spotted lights on the ground in the distance. Flying over them we realized we were over one of Rucker's airfields. No telling which one though. Having had more than enough of night navigation for this evening, we landed at the airfield, still not sure where we were. We parked in the first available parking slot we came across and wandered about until we discovered that we had in fact landed at our home base. Finding our briefing room was difficult being that our bearings were still completely crossed up. As we sat in the debriefing later that evening nothing was said to us other than to make it known we had failed to check into our reporting points. Every instructor in the room knew pretty much what had happened to us and made us feel very uncomfortable by their smirks and knowing glances.

Letter to home dated April 23, 1968

"Two weeks from today marks graduation. I just hope I can hold on for fourteen more days."

Letter to home dated May 4, 1968

"We have three more days until graduation; it is sure getting close! I guess it is all over except for the shouting. We have finished training and we are now just out processing. I finished this program with an even 215 flight hours and about 540 classroom hours for the thirteen months I was in training."

I made it to graduation. I graduated from U.S. Army Helicopter Flight School Class 68-503 on May 7, 1968. I had silver aviator wings on my chest and was appointed to the rank of warrant officer, WO-1. I had not believed many times during the preceding thirteen months this day would arrive. I was very proud. I had every right to be.

I, along with most of my classmates, received orders to report to South Vietnam. My report date for transport to Vietnam was May 28, 1968.

Tac Officer CW-2 Thomas Duer would later return to Vietnam for a second tour. He would die there when his Boeing Vertol CH 47 helicopter disintegrated in flight.

ON LEAVE AT HOME

Before departing for Vietnam I went back home on leave. My parents lived in Millbrae, California at the time. It was an awkward time for us. The anti-war movement was starting to become daily news. Americans were dying by the hundreds every month and helicopter losses were being reported with alarming regularity. In the early months of 1968, the North Vietnamese launched a massive offensive throughout South Vietnam. What became known as the "Tet Offensive" brought to realization all was not going as well in South Vietnam as some in Washington D.C. believed. If my parents had doubts about the validity of the war, and their only son going off to fight in it, they didn't tell me so.

For my part, I had been sequestered in training for over a year and was not in touch with the mood of the country. It was during this period at home I first encountered the anti-Vietnam mentality of some people. I remember, shortly prior to my departure for Vietnam, a girlfriend and I attending a play on the campus of her school. She was attending college in Santa Clara at the time. We dressed up, her in a green dress, me in my army dress green uniform, wings and warrant officer bars new and shining. Unknown to me, the theme would be anti-war in nature. I was the only person in attendance wearing a uniform. To say I was the wrong person in the wrong place would be simply a gross understatement. Maybe my girlfriend felt I would benefit in some way by being exposed to this prior to going off to Vietnam. Maybe she was just as misguided as so many others. The day to leave for Vietnam came all too fast. I had stored my car in my parents' garage. I hugged my somber father and crying mother, and left them for Vietnam.

At the airport, the ticket agent asked where I was headed. I proudly explained that I was on my way to Vietnam. His response: "That's too bad..."

It was May 28, 1968. I was 21 years old. I would step off the plane into Vietnam three days later.

THE FIRST AIR CAVALRY

Soon after my arrival in Vietnam, I received orders to report to what was to be my family for the next year. That family was the First

Air Cavalry Division...the Cav for short. The Cav had a reputation for living under tent roofs, eating meals out of cans, and having only cold water for showers. I was warned about life in the Cav during my training and had been persuaded it was not really the unit one would choose if given a choice. I was not given a choice.

Letter to home dated June 3, 1968

"This will just be a short note to let you know that everything is going as well as can be expected.

We stayed at Fort Lewis for two days and left for 'Nam' Thursday morning. Eighteen hours later I was in Cam Ranh Bay. We processed into the country there and received our unit assignments. I got a change of orders. I am now a member of the 1st Cavalry Division. They are the top unit in the country and I am glad to be with them.

One drawback is the Cav is 'air mobile', meaning they move around like the horse cavalry used to, only they use choppers. That means no permanent buildings.

We are being sent farther up north tomorrow for a four day school on the Cav's tactics, and jungle warfare in general. After that is finished we will be assigned and sent to the unit in the Cav that we will belong to. I will be able to give you my address then.

It is hot and humid here. The countryside is pretty.

I will write a little better letter when I get organized and get my address."

One, if not the best known, American military unit to participate in Vietnam was the First Air Cavalry Division. The division implemented a new form of tactical operations for warfare: helicopter borne air mobility. The Cav's fighting men moved to and from battle in helicopters, and were supported in their efforts by helicopters. If they fell in battle, helicopters flew them to medical support areas. It was a comfort to know should they be wounded, chances were good immediate transport via helicopter to well-equipped medical facilities could save their lives.

The standard tour of duty in Vietnam for an American soldier was three hundred and sixty five days. You could request to stay longer; some did, most didn't. The majority of new arrivals in Vietnam started the three hundred and sixty five day countdown to departure the first night there.

At the time of my arrival, the Cav's headquarters were located in An Khe, South Vietnam. I flew to An Khe in an air force transport. That night I tried to sleep in a tent that smelled of mildew. My thoughts that long and lonely night were of home, family, and friends; many of whom were attending college...maybe even burning their draft cards as I lay sweating in my cot.

My stay in An Khe was short and unpleasant; I was soon on my way in another air force transport to "I" Corps, the northern most partition of South Vietnam.

CAMP EVANS

I had been assigned to Bravo Company 227th Assault Helicopter Battalion. Bravo Company was what was known as a lift company. Its mission was to transport people and supplies about in what were known in Vietnam as "slicks". A slick was a Bell UH-1 helicopter manned by two pilots. Sitting in the rear, behind the pilots and facing out toward the sides sat two door gunners who manned M-60 light machine guns. The area between the pilots and door gunners was the cargo compartment. It was in the cargo compartment our passengers sat and cargo was carried. It had no rocket launchers nor other armament mounted on its sides. It was from its relatively uncluttered appearance the name slick was derived. It is the images of slicks with infantry standing on their landing skids that are so often associated with the war in Vietnam.

Bravo Company was staged at a large fire base named Camp Evans. The term fire base referred to an encampment, often surrounded by barbed wire and fortifications manned by infantry. The larger fire bases could contain an air strip for fixed wing aircraft. Artillery units protected the fire base from within and served to provide artillery support for troops working in the surrounding area. The larger fire bases would also include so-called rear echelon or support units for the troops operating in the field. Evans was the base of operations for numerous helicopter units. These units were staged about what was called the flight line. It was there the flight and support crews lived. After a day or night of flying, the helicopters were parked in sandbag protected revetments on the flight line. Here the maintenance crews serviced the helicopters.

Camp Evans was a busy place. People and supplies were constantly being transported into and out of its center via air force transports and, of course, army helicopters. Air traffic was very heavy, and at times the weather was less than ideal. I remember seeing a midair collision between an air force C-123 transport and army Chinook helicopter within sight of Evans. After the collision the Chinook immediately began spinning. It continued to do so as it fell to earth and exploded. The transport continued to fly briefly before plunging to the ground. I do not know how many died; rumor had it the passengers on the transport were on their way home. It was becoming evident to me that death in Vietnam was always associated with how much time remained in country for the unfortunate individual. The tragedy of death was more magnified with each passing day of one's 365 day tour.

Camp Evans was located on a coastal plain. Laos was beyond the mountains to the west. The DMZ, which separated North Vietnam from South Vietnam, was a short flight to the north. Highway 1, what the French called the "Street Without Joy", ran north/south just a few miles to the east between Evans and the South China Sea.

It is a testimony to my ignorance when I went to fight Ho Chi Minh's army in Vietnam I had little, if any, knowledge of what had happened to the French there. They had fought Ho Chi Minh's army only a decade prior to America's involvement in Vietnam. Without the benefit of world class aviation support, such as America used in Vietnam, the French were defeated in what was then called French Indo China. Many tens of thousands of Frenchmen died in that war and are buried in Vietnam. They died in places such as Dien Bien Phu, and on the Street Without Joy. I have since read the French buried their fallen soldiers in an upright position, facing France. We Americans chose to collect our fallen and return them home for burial. The body bags containing Americans killed in Vietnam, upon returning home, fanned the fires of America's growing anti-war mood.

Arriving at Camp Evans, I felt as if I had been transported into an American Civil War camp. Everywhere I looked I saw tents, the roads were muddy and the people looked rather somber. This similarity ended; however, with the presence of army helicopters flying this way and that, projecting the whop, whop, whop sound so often associated with America in Vietnam. Dust, or mud, and unpleasant smells abounded. The air was hot and humid and infested with flies.

I hopped a ride in a jeep that delivered me to the company area of B Co. 227 Assault Helicopter Battalion. As was the case elsewhere at Evans, not a building was to be seen, only tents, bunkers and sandbags. I reported to operations where I was greeted with less than exuberance.

I was soon sitting by myself on a cot, in a hot tent, my equipment piled nearby. This was my new home.

I had truly arrived in Vietnam. I could go home in 362 more days.

Letter to home dated June 12, 1968

"I have finally made it to my unit. Barring the unforeseen, I should be with this outfit for the next year. To make a long story short, I think I have been screwed. The unit I am now in lost almost all its aircraft in an explosion about three weeks ago. They are just starting to get some new ones to replace the loss; in the meantime, I just sit around and do nothing.

The living conditions aren't the best over here. There is no hot water, the latrines smell, and my tent where I live has a dirt floor. The heat and humidity are bad, the sky seems to be always cloudy, but it's still hot. Not to mention the insects, you have to use an insect net at night, and even so they get you."

Letter to home dated June 30, 1968

"We have gotten most of the aircraft back, but I am still sitting around. To make a long story short we are short of first pilots so until we train some the older new guys, our newest co-pilots can't get much flight time in. I don't expect to be flying on a daily basis for another month. So in the meantime all of the non-flying officers and

warrants are building new officer's quarters and what have you. I'm getting a good tan out of it anyway."

FNG

Life for all of us in Bravo Company was not very comfortable. The tents being used were called GP Mediums (general purpose) and stood about fifteen by forty feet in size. These tents that served as personal quarters for the warrants housed about ten men each, thus giving each person sixty square feet to call home. Furnishing consisted of a cot, sleeping bag and foot locker. We coveted extra items such as a chair, a table, and perhaps a fan. New arrivals such as me had no extras.

The mess hall was also a GP Medium with folding tables and chairs for dining. There was a field kitchen nearby. Most of the food being served came out of cans. One step above C rations, meals in boxes carried by an individual and eaten cold, at will, but still rather plain. Fresh foods were very rare. Drinking water was treated with iodine to rid it of parasites and bacteria.

Bathing was accomplished with cold water draining from elevated steel drums. The toilets were primitive. To use them you sat on plywood panels with holes placed over shortened oil drums. As the drums filled with waste, the drums were dragged a short distance away where diesel fuel was poured into them and then the diesel-soaked filth ignited. The smoke from this was thick and black, the smell unpleasant. Flies and maggots were rampant.

The living conditions I encountered upon my arrival at Bravo Company were the worst I would see for my whole tour in Vietnam. The primitive living conditions were due in part to a traumatic event that occurred a few weeks earlier.

It was not uncommon for Camp Evans to be the target of incoming mortar and rocket fire from enemy troops in the area. One of these incoming rockets had struck Camp Evans' ammunition dump. The ensuing explosions lasted for hours...wreaking havoc. Concussions from the blasts flattened anything above ground level. Aircraft parked in their revetments were damaged or destroyed. I reported in to a company in the act of rebuilding itself from ruin. Upon my arrival, Bravo had one air-worthy helicopter and 40 pilots.

So, there I sat with nothing to do but help with the rebuilding of the company area. I worked in the hot sun filling sandbags for much of my first month. There was little escape from the tedious boredom and not much comfort from the veterans who saw new arrivals as "f..king new guys"... FNGs for short. Most of these veterans had seen some rough times over the preceding months. Many of them were close to going home. An FNG was treated with little respect since he had not yet proved himself one way or another. As time went on, this situation would slowly reverse, as short timers left and FNGs took their places in the company hierarchy.

With this sort of environment it was natural for people with similar time in country to form friendships. As I labored with the sandbag detail a few other FNGs arrived. It was comforting to see new arrivals for it helped to diminish the sense of loneliness. One of these new arrivals was a flight school classmate of mine: Mike Almgren. Mike was from Chicago, Illinois. Mike and I worked together filling sandbags in the hot sun. At one point, Mike suffered heat stroke and had to be medevaced. We have laughed many times since when he recalls the ice pack being applied to his crotch at the field hospital in an attempt to lower his body temperature.

Upon one occasion, the 4th of July, the old guys decided to have a party. The FNGs were not invited, but one of the short timers felt sorry enough for us to toss a bottle of gin into our tent. Having no ice and only warm tomato juice did not stop us from drinking until we puked. Our hangovers did not exempt us from sandbag detail the next day. I to this day do not care for the taste of gin.

My morale and military bearing began to deteriorate. Suffice it to say my situation in Vietnam was a growing disappointment. I had planned on doing some serious flying. My self-esteem as an officer and pilot was very low. Had I worked so hard in training only for this?

Our commanding officer, MAJ Ginter, was a veteran due to rotate home soon. He had the difficult job of rebuilding Bravo Company. His job was not made any easier by young warrant officers who were beginning to develop attitude problems. A war was going on, he knew that, but I was losing sight of it by beginning to focus too much on my personal disappointments, and not enough on the real situation. I was young and I regret to say, ignorant.

The maintenance of the morale and discipline of their troops is perhaps one of the more challenging responsibilities commanders deal with. Keeping people busy helps to accomplish this. Since MAJ Ginger had bored and disenchanted pilots, such as myself, to contend with he tried to put us to useful purposes. One such useful distraction was guard duty. While Camp Evans was protected by infantry outposts and barbed wire on its perimeter there still was the need to watch over our helicopters on the flight line during the late dark hours. Enemy troops had been known to sneak past a perimeter and place explosive charges around such things as parked aircraft. MAJ Ginter called upon his FNG warrants to perform this guard duty. We of course hated the duty since it required staying up and remaining alert most of the night. On one night a fellow warrant, Mike, and I were posted as guards and instructed to protect a helicopter parked on the flight line. It was late, we were tired; and we both longed for sleep. Mike and I agreed to alternate sleep breaks. It was my turn to watch, but I managed to doze off. MAJ Ginter happened to choose this time to check up on us and of course found two warrants guarding an aircraft, one sleeping atop the revetment, the other on the helicopter's passenger seat, fast asleep. Ginter walked up to our unguarded helicopter, picked up the radio lying near Mike and dropped it on Mike's crotch. The ensuing yell from Mike served to bring me to full attention. MAJ Ginter proceeded to chew our asses with enough vigor to frighten the dead. The Major did not pursue the event further; his point had been well made.

I really was a FNG. I had not really come to appreciate fully the dangers we faced. It is not a pleasant thought for me to think what could have been my fate if while I was sleeping a North Vietnamese soldier had decided to dispatch me with his knife before placing an explosive device in the helicopter I was guarding. This difficult and disappointing period came to pass as more aircraft started arriving to replace the ones damaged by the explosions of the ammunition dump. Bravo Company took back to the skies.

Letter to home dated July 23, 1968

"I am starting to fly now. Not much, but at least it's a start. On my last mission our formation was fired at and the lead aircraft was hit. It's a strange feeling, but not as bad as I expected (getting shot at).

I received a letter from a friend in flight school who came over here the same time I did, but he was assigned down south in the Delta. He has 135 hours already compared to my 16. He also has a private room, hot shower, officers club and cement floors. Somehow, I get the idea that I was screwed when I was sent to the Cav."

IN THE AIR AGAIN

Slowly, as the early months passed, some of the senior pilots completed their year and went home. At last I was given a chance to fly. My early flights were humbling; it was almost as if I had forgotten how to fly, but my rudimentary flying skills returned soon enough.

Letter to home dated July 30, 1968

"I am flying about every other day now. I am averaging about six hours each time I fly. I enjoy it, but I need a lot more practice before I will be any good."

Letter to home dated August 10, 1968

"Today is the first day I haven't flown in five days. It feels great to finally be doing something. I can see improvement in my flying every time I go up; of course I still have a ways to go yet. When I get good enough and have more experience they will make me an Aircraft Commander. That means I will move from the right seat over to the left one. It will put a lot more responsibility on me since I will be responsible for the aircraft and crew."

Letter to home dated Aug 24, 1968

"I will have about seventy five hours for this month, that's not bad considering I had about fifty hours the first two months in country.

They are expecting a ground attack so if we aren't flying the next day we get stuck guarding an aircraft all night, all kinds of fun."

After having spent such a long time performing menial tasks in the company area, I was of course very excited about being used as a pilot. Perhaps, because of that, I took on the challenge of learning the new skills of flying in Vietnam very seriously. My enthusiasm became apparent to those looking for replacements of those old timers who were leaving. I began to fly more and more with an assortment of Aircraft Commanders.

Letter to home dated September 4, 1968

"Rain, rain, rain. It started last night and it is still going strong. I had to fly in it today. You know what a pain it is to drive a car in rainy weather. Well, you can imagine what it's like flying in it. We have to fly about fifty feet above the ground since when the clouds are below one thousand feet you are an easy target if you get any higher. You're safe at fifteen hundred feet, but the clouds ruin that. So we stay low and dodge trees. When I got back to my tent this evening I found it flooded. My bed was soaked...the end to a perfect day."

It was during this period two events took place that had a very profound effect on my attitude about being in Vietnam.

It was a rather dreary day and I was sitting in my tent. I was assigned to an aircraft that was not doing much flying. The Aircraft Commander was the company instructor pilot and the missions rather undemanding; a good situation for breaking in new pilots. Word came through operations we were needed to fly off somewhere. I was happy to get another chance in the air as we started the helicopter and departed Camp Evans heading west toward the mountains. I was busy enough flying the helicopter, but I at last asked the Aircraft Commander what our mission was. With a somber face he said that we had been called to recover the bodies of a helicopter crew that had crashed into the jungle two days earlier. My throat and stomach clamped down.

The approach and landing into the landing zone (LZ) was a bit beyond my skill level so I sat in my seat in silence and watched. Having landed, we waited for a few minutes with blades turning before I heard the sounds of what sounded like sacks of potatoes being dropped on the helicopter cabin floor-a very unpleasant odor soon permeated throughout the aircraft. I was beginning to feel ill. I turned about to look in back and saw the four bodies. The sight of their broken limbs and disfigured faces horrified me. My stomach was now sitting in my throat. One of the dead men wore the rank of WO-1.

We flew the four KIAs (killed in action) back to the graves registration helipad at Camp Evans. Returning to our company area I sat in my tent in silence for a long while. This was my first view of violent death.

My other eye opener was a bit less traumatic but very important none the less. The experience took place on a day I found myself copiloting with a less experienced Aircraft Commander than I had flown with prior. Our ship was one of a flight of six. It had been a busy day of flying in and out of many different mountain LZs (landing zones) inserting troops and cargo. The flying was somewhat demanding in that we were working at high density altitudes into small helipads. As the day wore on, the winds began to pick up making the flying all the more precarious. While I had come a ways toward acceptable proficiency as a helicopter pilot, I was still little help to the poor guy sitting next to me. He had to make the difficult approaches while I watched. I was not aware of it at the time but he was also being tested to his limits.

It was hot and windy. The aircraft had a full load of ammunition boxes... maybe a bit too full. The Aircraft Commander initiated a steep approach to a ridge top LZ. To me all looked normal at first but as we neared touchdown our rate of closure seemed a bit fast. At the point where we should have been transitioning into a hover we instead continued to descend rapidly. We hit the ground rather hard and bounced off the ridge and began to fall off the backside. Our low rotor rpm warning horn was wailing, telling us that rotor rpm was below the normal operating range. It was beginning to look like we would hit the ground again and crash. My mind pictured that dead WO-1 lying on the helicopter cabin floor. The Aircraft Commander was not taking any action to correct our rapidly deteriorating situation. Looking back on the experience I believe he had stopped flying the helicopter and was just holding on to the controls...he was probably frozen in fear. At this point, I remembered lessons from flight school training suggesting pushing down the collective stick when in a low rpm situation during approach. This action would allow for the reduced drag of the rotors to increase rpm. I pushed the collective down a bit, and as it should, the rpm increased, the rpm audio stopped its beeping, and best of all, the Aircraft Commander started to fly the helicopter again…away from the ground. We had to return to Evans since one of the landing gear skids was badly bent from the hard landing on the ridge top. Once again I sat in my tent at day's end pondering the incident. All of those hours spent in flight school learning things such as gross weight limits and tricks of the trade such as lowering collective in a low rotor situation had real merit. These were the things that could mean the difference between life and death for a helicopter pilot. Maybe I should have paid a bit more attention to my instructors. I would certainly do so henceforth.

In my debriefing about the incident I was rightfully criticized for not being more help to the Aircraft Commander by calling out the torque reading and rotor rpm as we approached the ridge top prior to the hard landing. With the exception of pushing the collective down, which was critical, I was more of a passenger than a copilot during those critical seconds when he was running out of pitch, power, and ideas. There was so much for me to learn.

Letter to home dated September 12, 1968

"The 'gooks' sent eight 122 millimeter rockets over our way a few nights ago. There were a few causalities, but none in my unit. It sure broke the routine around here."

AIRCRAFT COMMANDER

I was checked out as an Aircraft Commander when I was able to demonstrate the knowledge and skills required. At the time, I may have had four hundred and twenty five hours of pilot time. I could fly reasonably well and knew enough about the theater of operations to get by. I did not; however, have very much experience. This situation did not deter my enthusiasm, or the Army's willingness to launch me into harm's way.

Letter to home dated September 27, 1968

"Flying is coming along great. They have moved me from the right seat to the left (copilot to pilot). That means I will be the Aircraft Commander. That is a lot more responsibility. I made it with 200 hours of flight time in country; it takes the average pilot about 400 hours. So you can see things are going well, I just hope they stay that way."

I look back on this now thirty five years later and can see the precarious situation I was in as plain as day. I did not see it as clearly in 1968. It was very exciting to strap yourself into a helicopter early in the morning and take off for a day of combat flying in Vietnam. This was exciting stuff, but also very dangerous. It was all too easy to be overcome by the excitement and glory of it all while forgetting or minimizing the hazards. No guts, no glory, you say...perhaps.

I was doing this when only three years earlier I was graduating from high school.

Young Warrant Officer Kearns, fledgling helicopter hero, Aircraft Commander, was going to do his damned best to help win this war--- let come what may, be it over-gross-weight loads, enemy gunfire or weather ducks didn't fly in.

Vietnam was heading into the monsoon season about this time, a season of thick clouds, strong winds and heavy rain. Life at Evans was made even more miserable with the downpours that regularly besieged it. Nothing seemed to stay dry. Most of the tents leaked, requiring us to erect poncho liners over our cots to keep the water out. One does not sleep well in a wet sleeping bag. At one point, our operations bunker was flooded to its ceiling.

Much of our flying was in the mountains to Evans' west. It was here the Cav's ground forces found themselves trying to engage the North Vietnamese regulars traveling south on the Ho Chi Minh Trail. This area was covered with heavy jungle. When the clouds and rain came, it could be very difficult, if not impossible, to safely fly through. Our slicks had instruments for instrument condition flying, and we had some basic instrument training, but this was not an appropriate environment to be doing so.

On a day when the ducks were not flying we were trying to supply an infantry (grunt) company nestled deep in the mountains. The area was obscured in most places with low clouds. I was pushing the weather limits too hard trying to get the needed food and ammunition to the grunts. Predictably, I inadvertently flew into the clouds. I found myself with no ground reference outside the helicopter's plexiglass windows. The army had taught me to fly with reference only to the aircraft's instruments, but in the proper environment with an instructor at my side and the nearest mountain two hundred miles away. Now, Mother Earth was nowhere to be seen. We were surrounded by mountains and in very serious trouble.

Unexpected flight into instrument conditions has probably killed more pilots than any other act of neglect or carelessness. Under such conditions, the chance of losing control of the aircraft, or simply flying into the terrain high. An experienced pilot should see this situation approaching and take corrective action, such as turning around before many a less experienced pilot might, thus avoiding the potential disastrous consequences awaiting there. My crew and I found ourselves with one option for escape. That option was to attempt to climb high enough to clear the mountain tops and head back to the east and Camp Evan's life-saving GCA (ground controlled radar approach).

We kept the helicopter under control as we climbed up through the clouds, praying the whole time we would not plow the helicopter into a mountain. Frantically, we called radar when we were high enough to make radio contact. No voice sounded sweeter than the radar controller's when he told us he had radar contact and started giving us vectors back to Evans.

On another occasion we were once again supplying grunts high in the mountains. I had just landed on a rather marginal landing pad that was little more than felled trees with the limbs bucked off. As the skids came in contact with the trees I reduced power thinking we had safely completed a landing. Upon power reduction the helicopter suddenly settled lower, punching a hole in its belly with a tree stump. I was able to return to base with the hole, but the damaged aircraft was out of service for some time being repaired.

Both of these incidents were indications of an Aircraft Commander who was not really up to the skill and experience levels required for safe completion of these types of missions. I was called out on the carpet for them, but I still continued to fly almost every day, there was, after all, a war going on. I was gaining experience, but at considerable risk.

Letter to home dated October 14, 1968

"We have had some interesting missions lately. Just yesterday we were out in the mountains hauling supply when we were asked to evacuate a POW and a wounded GI out of a company's location in the mountains. It was raining and patches of fog were floating from one ridge to another. The area was too small to land so we dropped a rope down as we hovered overhead. The people on the ground tied the POW on first and we lifted him out and carried him (hanging 150 feet below us) to another landing zone in the mountains. My crew chief said the poor guy was so scared that he passed out while he was down there. I guess I don't blame him. Our next trip was for the wounded man. I let my copilot fly this time and we carried him out the same way. The weather was starting to move in, but things were going smoothly until we were letting the patient down onto the pad, it was then that my copilot took his eyes off the ground and looked into the clouds in front of us. He got vertigo, but did the right thing by telling me. I took the aircraft; if he hadn't told me we could have lost

the whole works and probably gone into the trees ourselves. I must

admit that I was happy to see the day end."

Letter to home dated October 9, 1968

"Just a note to let you know that my mail might be screwed up for

a few weeks since we are on call to move south for a while. If we do

move it will be unorganized for a while and I will have trouble writing

letters or receiving any for that matter."

In October of 1968, the First Cav was moved down south between Saigon and Cambodia. This area contained the routes and staging areas used by the North Vietnamese in the prior year's Tet Offensive. The Cav was being placed into position to deter any repeat of the last year's major attacks on Saigon. Bravo Company found itself in a new environment; our new base was an airstrip on a rubber plantation called Quan Loi. Flight operations continued at a frantic pace to support the new placement of the Cav's forces.

It was our job as helicopter crews to provide transport for the infantry and their supplies to and from the operational areas they patrolled. It was no easy task for the grunts to carry everything they might need to engage, or defend themselves from the enemy troops in the area. The absolute necessities were carried on their backs. It was not practical for them to carry all they might need for extended operations in the field. Slicks provided a means to lighten the load. These supply missions were called "log" missions for logistical support. A typical supply load, or loads, would consist of many ammunition boxes, heavy weapons such as mortars, claymore mines, water, food (both hot and cold), mail, and individuals needing a ride in or out. We also served as medevac helicopter when the need arose to get someone out and to medical care in the rear area.

When the grunts' patrol was completed, they would normally be flown out and back to their support base where they could clean up and rest. This process was reversed when it was time for them to return to the field. These trips into and out of the field were called combat assaults or extractions. Most of these "CAs", as we called them, were routine, some were not. I'll tell more of that later.

Letter to home dated November 6, 1968

"We moved into an airfield someone else had been using so things are built up real well. There are no mountains to speak of around here, but there are a lot of rubber plantations. I like this area more than up north."

QUAN LOI

Life at Quan Loi was an improvement over Camp Evans. A few new amenities such as a wooden dining hall and GP Mediums with wooden floors improved the quality of life. The company area was situated within a grove of rubber trees. This meant shade during the heat of the day. The rainy season had ended, but this forced us to endure a lot of dust. Anytime a helicopter departed or landed a cloud of red dust swept through the company area leaving everything in its wake covered with the stuff. The showers were still only cold water and the latrines the same style steel drums as we had at Evans.

Within walking distance a PX store provided shopping where we could buy extras such as fans and folding chairs. The PX was a real treat. The warrants' living areas began to take on a more hospitable appearance. I had a small writing desk where I could compose letters to family and friends at home while sitting in my new folding chair. My new fan was placed at the foot of my bed so I could bask in a refreshing breeze during the muggy days and nights. I even had a small closet area to hang my uniforms. The living areas were separated by plywood partitions giving a sense of privacy-something in short supply when sharing a tent with nine other people.

At the other end of the airfield was an old villa that had been transformed into an officer's club. It was now possible to spend an evening away from the company area drinking and telling stories with other aviators. It was an interesting place at most times since it attracted all kinds of people with stories of their own, some true, and I imagine, some not.

Quan Loi was infested with rats. Almgren had one walk across his chest one night while he was sleeping. It disturbed him so he began sleeping with a machete in his cot.

The task of cleaning the company area was accomplished by local Vietnamese who would work during the day and return to the local village at night. It was suspected by a few of us some of these locals had a dual purpose in their work: One, to make Yankee dollars, the other, to note where the latest incoming mortar rounds had impacted the previous night. These observations allowed corrections to be made for the next night's barrage.

In the event of incoming rounds, not an uncommon event, we would dash out of our tents and run for the nearest bunker. These bunkers were trenches covered by sheets of metal called PSP (pierced steel planking) covered with sandbags. The bunkers gave me a feeling of claustrophobia so I developed the habit of staying in my cot when the all-too-often incoming rounds came whistling in. This was an act of bravado in an attempt to salvage a night's sleep...something in great demand by me. I felt since I was surrounded by sandbags I was safe from anything short of a direct hit, and understandably avoided the risk of dashing about in the dark, running into rubber trees and seriously injuring myself. This was a situation where I was damned if I did, and damned if I didn't. One night, the rounds did come very close. I bailed out of my bed and started to run. As I ran a round passed over my head. The eerie sound was like a screaming banshee that brought chills up my spine. I was sure the beast would jump on my back any second. I dove to the ground and extended my arms upward to fight off the terror from the sky. I was begging for mercy. I was terrified. The round overshot me and hit the nearby helicopter refueling facility. The jet fuel burned fiercely through most of the night.

Getting a good night sleep was further jeopardized by an eight inch artillery battery also located at Quan Loi. If they had a fire mission that required them to fire over our company area, the sound was deafening, and the concussion would cause the tent sides to flap. The projectiles passing overhead sounded like a winged freight train passing through the tree tops.

BULLET IN MY LAP

Occasionally we would fly South Vietnamese Army (ARVN) on combat assaults. Most of the ARVN conscript troops were not known for their fierce or heroic nature in battle. That should have been a clue to the Pentagon's planners that something was wrong when the people you were fighting for didn't want to do much of the fighting themselves.

On one such extraction things didn't go well. We took seven rounds and had one of our ARVN passengers hit by small arms fire.

Letter to home dated November 6, 1968

"My aircraft took seven hits from enemy automatic weapons yesterday on a combat extraction. We were number three in a flight of six, lifting a company of ARVNs out of a hot area. We had just cleared the trees and were starting to climb when we flew over a small unit of North Vietnamese who were waiting for us in the trees. They cut loose on the whole flight, but they concentrated on us so we were the only aircraft to get hit. One round went into the nose of the ship, came up through the radio compartment, shot out my airspeed indicator and came to rest between my feet. (too close for comfort),

two rounds hit the rotor blades, one came up through the floor and hit one of the ARVNs in the back of the knee and stuck in the ceiling. The other three were scattered along the tail boom. I have the round that almost hit me. I plan on keeping it to remind me how lucky I was."

We made it without further mishap. Afterward I was criticized for breaking formation. We would have been wiser not doing so.

In early November I had been in country for five months. My environment had changed from one of boredom to a state of unreal intensity. For the most part, I had been fortunate to be lucky enough to survive any major mishap despite a tendency to explore the limits of my skills. My luck would change.

THE ACCIDENT

November 7, 1968 started early for me. I was assigned to fly a log mission. My copilot for the day was a Texan named Mike LeMaster. LeMaster was a WO-1 who had been in Vietnam less time than I. He was a likable guy, but had little flight time. I should not have been flying with Mike on that day for the simple reason we were both inexperienced pilots. I should have been flying with a senior copilot and Mike LeMaster with an experienced Aircraft Commander, but that was not our fate on this day.

It was still very early and morning fog patches floated in the area around the grunt's position. As was normal, we had established radio contact with their radio operator. When our arrival was imminent, the landing zone was confirmed with colored smoke from a smoke grenade discharged on the ground. The smoke not only served as an aid in determining location, but also served as a wind indicator. There was not much wind on this morning, just some hungry grunts waiting for a helicopter to deliver their breakfast. I allowed Mike to make the first approach into the landing zone, but when it became evident he was approaching too fast for a safe landing I took over the controls and made the landing. LeMaster was having a difficult time controlling the helicopter.

I remembered my first few days back in the cockpit only a few months earlier and how difficult it had been to regain the confidence level I possessed on graduation day from flight school.

After the cargo was removed from the helicopter, I gave LeMaster control again and told him to make the takeoff. His departure seemed a bit fast to me; nevertheless, I did nothing to slow him down. There was a large tree to our immediate left. LeMaster started a sudden turn toward the tree apparently thinking he had enough clearance to swing around it and head back the way we had come. During these few seconds I sat motionless in my seat not believing he would actually hit the tree when there was no reason to strike it. Our blades struck the tree with a loud thump. The sudden stoppage of the rotors against the tree severed the engine drive shaft and destroyed the rotor blades. Without power to the rotors, and decaying rotor RPM, the aircraft fell to the ground and rolled over on its right side. I found myself suspended in my seat harness looking out the window at a 90 degree angle to the ground. The engine was still running since the broken drive shaft no longer connected it to the transmission and rotor blades. I looked around and saw no one else in the aircraft; I appeared to be by myself. I unbuckled from my seat and climbed to the ground within the cargo compartment. Thoughts began to race through my mind: was the aircraft going to explode, where were the other three crew members, was one of them pinned under the helicopter? At this point I realized it was a good idea to try to shut down the engine. I climbed back between the pilot's seats and frantically tried to shut it down, but in my shock I couldn't put the necessary sequence together to silence it. I climbed out of the wreck. I was still worried about the door gunners and was yelling at the grunts that were standing nearby and watching all this, to help me try to find my missing crew. Someone put his hand on my shoulder and yelled in my ear the crew was safe and standing nearby. Once again my attention was directed to the still running engine. I climbed on top of the wreck and attempted to disconnect a fuel line in order to shut it down. Thank God I was not able to do such a foolish thing. While I vainly struggled with the fuel line another helicopter landed nearby and one of its pilots came over, climbed into the cockpit of my aircraft and shut down the engine. As I climbed off the wrecked helicopter I felt overwhelmed with disbelief and regret. A young aviator who had only a few minutes before felt so proud and confident was now reduced to a total fool.

A few hours later I was standing at attention in front of my commanding officer's desk with LeMaster at my side. There was no justifiable reason for hitting that tree. It was pure and simple pilot error on our parts. That afternoon a Chinook helicopter slung my wrecked machine back to Quan Loi and deposited it at the end of the runway…near the officer's club. I spent some time standing and looking at my mistake trying to find absolution for my misfortune. Finding none, I removed a small plate off the pilot's collective stick, as a souvenir, and returned to Bravo Company and secluded myself in my living area for the rest of the day. Things would get worse.

THE BRIDGE

It had been a very long day. My helicopter was a wreck lying at the end of the airfield, my self esteem was destroyed, my efforts of the prior five months in Vietnam seemed all for nothing. What better way to end it than to go to the officer's club and try to drown my misery? Mike Almgren joined Mike LeMaster and me for an evening of serious drinking. The hours passed and the alcohol had its desired effect. Before we knew it, the time had come to close up and return to the company area, go to bed, and put this unfortunate day to rest.

There were no street lights or lighted paths at Quan Loi. The club was about a mile from Bravo's area and the road between the two somewhat unfamiliar. A group of us, LeMaster and I in the lead, carelessly walked along in the darkness. We could not see one step in front of us. Suddenly, something tripped LeMaster and me at knee level. I felt myself falling forward toward the ground; but when I expected to hit the ground I instead kept falling into the darkness. I landed on my head and shoulder with a painful jolt and lost consciousness. When I awoke a short time later I found myself lying in mud. My head and right shoulder throbbed with pain. As it happened

LeMaster and I had walked directly off the road, at a corner, and tripped on a short bridge wall, falling over it, we dropped about six feet into a drainage ditch. Everyone was laughing except me.

The next hour was spent in the medic's tent where after an examination it was determined I had suffered a mild concussion and a broken right collar bone. I was lucky I hadn't broken my neck.

The next day found me lying in my cot with a very sore shoulder and terrible headache. I could expect to be grounded for at least a month. I was doomed to have nothing to do but convalesce and ponder my failure as a pilot. Every morning my brothers in arms would rise and go off to fly while I sat in my living area with nothing to do but hate my life and choke on dust.

During a soldier's tour in Vietnam a short leave was allowed. This was called R&R, rest & recuperation. There were restrictions on where you could travel to. As I recall the choices were limited to selected locations near or in Southeast Asia. Married men could go to Hawaii to meet their wives, but the single men went to places like Hong Kong, Kuala Lumpur and Sidney. The army transported you to the location you selected amongst the available choices. After four days you were transported back to Vietnam.

Letter to home dated shortly after November 7, 1968

"Just a short note to ask you to please send me a money order for $500. I just put in for a leave and I will need the money. Please try to hurry since I will be departing shortly after the twentieth of the month."

My only hope of retaining my sanity was to take my R&R and get the hell out of Vietnam.

R&R

There is one strong desire on a young man's mind who has been deprived of female companionship for over five months, and been living under conditions of hardship and danger. Moving beyond that, R&R gave ample opportunity to spend what money was left shopping, dining and enjoying the sights of a big city. The hotel was a trip to Heaven. This was the first hot shower, regular bed, and flush toilet I had seen since I had left the USA five months earlier. The food tasted as if it came from the Gods.

Letter to home dated December 8, 1968

"Well, it's back to Vietnam tomorrow. Needless to say I had a good time in Hong Kong and I think I bought some goodies for some good prices.

You should receive my tailor made clothes in the mail fairly soon. The three piece super worsted suit cost me sixty five dollars, the cashmere wool sport coat was thirty eight dollars, and the worsted slacks were fifteen dollars each.

I also bought a 35mm Minolta SRT101 with a F1.4 lens, an electronic flash, and a Rokkor 1:4 F=135mm telephoto lens. These three items plus the cases for the camera and telephoto lens cost me one hundred and eighty dollars.

I also bought a Seiko watch for twenty eight dollars.

I am enclosing a photo of me a friend took while we were on a tour. I am going on another tour this afternoon which will take us past the Red Border.

I received the money you wired me about eighteen hours after I called you. Thank you very much. I believe I will have enough left over to be able to send some back to you when I return to my unit.

So all in all I had a good time and I believe I will be ready to go back to the nitty gritty and finish my six months and days that I have left in Vietnam."

My R&R served its intended purpose; my inner tension was relieved somewhat. I would return to Bravo Company ready to try to pick up the pieces of my career and carry on.

I was forgiven my accident by the Army and put back onto active flight status when I was physically able. I put my accident behind me and found myself flying again on a regular basis. It was December of

1968 and I had about one hundred and eighty days remaining in Vietnam. The next six months would be the most intense of my tour. It was my turn to help take the helm from those before me.

My adversity had served to mature me; I was no longer a carelessly confident young pilot.

DAY IN THE LIFE

By mid December of 1968, the Cav was well entrenched in its new area of operations. Bravo Company was settled into Quan Loi. I was back in the cockpit as an Aircraft Commander. Bob Hope was touring Vietnam. I recall the Christmas season to be very depressing. Most of us received packages from home, but there was little Christmas spirit. It was flying as usual.

Of course, there was a routine to be followed. The routine started in the evening. Before almost everyone had gone to bed, the staff in operations would receive orders for the next day's flight requirements. Operations would then assign aircraft and crews to the specific missions. For the most part, there were three types: log (supply, etc.), air assault (movement of troops), and command and control (flying commanding officers in and around the operational area). There were other types of assignments such as psychological warfare, night reconnaissance, but the basic three mentioned above were the most common. Normally, you would go to bed knowing what aircraft you would be flying and with whom.

The day started with an operation's orderly making the rounds waking us up. You would dress in your fire resistant nomex flight suite, lace up your boots, strap on your sidearm, grab your flight helmet and nomex, and head to the mess hall. Hot coffee and breakfast was wolfed down there. On the way out to the helicopters we stopped by operations and received last minute instructions and information concerning the day's mission. This included things like the radio frequencies we needed, who we were supporting, and where we were going. The crews would then meet at their aircraft for preflight. During the preflight the helicopters cowlings were opened allowing inspection of fluid levels and all critical mechanical parts subject to failure. When the inspection was completed and all appeared well, the aircraft log book was signed by the Aircraft Commander attesting to his willingness to take the machine into the air.

Besides the two pilots the crew consisted of two enlisted men. One was the crew chief who was a helicopter mechanic. Each helicopter in the company had a crew chief assigned to it. The crew chief would perform the required maintenance on his machine in addition to flying with it all day as a door gunner. The other enlisted man was a door gunner who would assist the crew chief during the day. It was not uncommon for door gunners to be second tour grunts who wanted to fly as crew members on the helicopters they themselves had been passengers on during their prior tour in Vietnam. During the preflight, all four crew members would see that all was in order and ready to go for the day ahead. The door guns (M-60 machine guns) were mounted on their stands and crew members put on their armor chest protectors, helmets and gloves. The pilots strapped themselves in their armor seats and at the appointed time hollered "CLEAR" and started the Lycoming T-53 engine.

After the engine was started, the rotor blades began to turn. The generator was turned on, then the radios. Contact was established with operations and any other aircraft that may be flying the same mission. When all was ready, and everybody had checked in, we would lift out of our parking revetments, amidst a cloud of dust, and hover out to the runway and align ourselves in the prearranged order, one behind the other. The flight leader was in front and his call sign was yellow one. The ship behind him was yellow two and so forth. At the time when the Yellow Flight was all in position a radio call was made to the control tower. The tower operator would clear us for departure. Anyone not flying who was still in the company area would be besieged with the howling and thumping of all the running helicopters as well as a good dusting from the rotor wash.

Of the three most common mission types the combat assault was often the most demanding and dangerous. A combat assault flight could consist of multiple helicopters, the number of which depended on the mission. Massive troop movements would combine many flights to total thirty or more helicopters, but normally a flight would consist of four to six aircraft. Each aircraft would have an assigned position in the flight. Yellow one would be the flight leader and Yellow six in a flight of six would be called, "tail end Charlie." Each position would be responsible for some duty such as contacting artillery for flight clearance into target areas, or maintaining communications with operations at some level. All the aircraft would have an assigned position in whatever formation the flight flew. Formations could change depending on the size and shape of the landing zone.

For any combat assault we would arrive at an appointed pickup zone where the grunt unit would be waiting in full combat gear. As the slicks landed, the grunts would board (about six per aircraft) and when all was ready the flight would launch in mass, heading for the landing zone.

The landing zone was often being worked over by artillery while the flight flew toward it. The flight would normally be joined by helicopter gunships that would cover from the rear during the first approach. About one minute prior to arrival at the landing zone, artillery would send a white phosphorus round into the LZ indicating the last shell had been fired. On short final into the landing zone, the door gunners would begin cover fire with their M-60s while the gunships would rake the perimeter from behind with rocket fire. When the slick's skids touched ground, the grunts would jump out and seek cover. Ideally, as Yellow one started to depart the LZ, tail end charlie would be ready to follow. Some of the LZs were large enough to accommodate the entire flight; others required that only a portion of the flight could land at one time. The sequence of events I just described would be complicated greatly if there was hostile fire directed at the troops or slicks. Everyone was very vulnerable despite all the firepower. It was during this phase of an insertion that helicopters could easily be shot down by determined enemy troops who survived the onslaught long enough to shoot back. As the slicks raced back to the pickup zone for the next load of grunts, the thirty or so who remained on the landing zone were vulnerable should they come under attack. Their protection would be the gunships remaining overhead and the artillery which was always on the ready to resume firing into the area should it be required. In the meanwhile, the formation would race back with the next load of grunts, drop them off and return for another load until the entire unit was in place at the landing zone. If all was well at this point, the flight would fly back to base for fuel and either go off on another assault or standby as required.

Once in position, the grunts would begin to carry on with their patrol. They would often stay in the field for days at a time and would require support from slicks flying log missions. Flying log missions was much different than combat assaults. Generally you flew as a single ship and were responsible for all communications and navigation. Your mission was to fly people, food, ammunition, and water back and forth between the grunts in the field and their support base.

Command and control missions were for the most part boring days. I dreaded them. Most of the work required was simply to orbit overhead while an assault or extraction was taking place with a commanding officer and his assistants working radios in back coordinating the missions.

Lunch was often taken out of a can while sitting in or near the helicopter. During slack periods, one might even catch a few winks as best as one could in the shade of the aircraft.

At day's end, it was back to the Bravo Company area where a hot dinner, a cold shower, and maybe some beer or soda waited. Drinking to excess was not uncommon. Drug use was not evident though I have little doubt some people snuck off and tried to escape from the stress that way. Normally, the evening was spent visiting, writing letters to home, or reading. Sometimes, the evenings grew a bit loud with music from someone's stereo. Every evening I would fill in another slot on my "short timers" calendar. There were three hundred and sixty five slots to be filled. There was always much talk of home and what we were going to do upon our return to the real world, The States. My parents saved some of my letters and I ended up with them some years later. It is interesting to note how much time I spent writing about the car I was going to buy when I returned from Vietnam. It was a very common interest to me and most of my friends to spend much time trying to decide what type of automobile we would purchase when we got back home. Most of us gravitated toward names like GTO, Firebird, and 442 (that is what I ended up buying). Before turning in for the night we would walk to operations and check the next day's mission board and see what was in the works for us. Another day had passed and the next was waiting.

Stress management was awfully important. There were times when the stress got to us all. Christmas Eve was such a time. I became very upset with my tent mates when they celebrated the Yule Tide Season in our tent while caring little of the fact that I was on the board for an early flight the next morning. To use the vernacular and say "I lost it with them" would be an understatement. My anger progressed to rage. People came into our tent to see what the fuss was all about. I screamed at them as well. Everyone fled and left me alone while I regained control of myself.

I managed to ruin the Christmas party, and spirit, with my angry Scrooge rendition.

Letter to home dated January 5, 1969

"Well, I just counted up the days and I found that I have one hundred and forty five days remaining in Southeast Asia. Time still seems to be going fast.

Thank you for all the Christmas presents."

SOME EXPERIENCES OF OTHERS IN BRAVO COMPANY

A low flying helicopter was a tempting target for small arms fire. Normally, if one stayed above three thousand feet small arms fire was not effective. There were times, however, when this strategy did not work for us. Larger caliber guns on the ground, or the necessity to fly at times lower than three thousand feet would expose us to effective ground fire. Should a tracer round penetrate our helicopter's fuel cell, located beneath the cargo compartment deck, there was a good chance of fire. There was really no way to put the fire out; we did not wear parachutes. The only recourse was to attempt to get the helicopter on the ground before the fire consumed everyone. One of Bravo's pilots was transferred to another unit. While there, he had a fuel cell fire. Before he could get the aircraft on the ground most of the people on board had jumped to their deaths or were burned to death.

Another Bravo aviator seemed to draw more than his fair share of trouble. One night he was involved in a supply mission to some grunts who were engaged and needed more ammunition. His helicopter was in the process of landing in complete darkness, when it was hit by a hail of small arms fire and all hell broke loose. One round entered the other pilot's helmet and blew it off his head. More rounds pounded into the machine causing an engine failure. They crashed. All of the crew spent that night in the jungle learning firsthand what it was like to be a grunt under attack from enemy ground troops. Some months later our same friend was struck by an AK-47 round in his lower leg. He was bleeding to death, but fast action by the crew chief and door gunner saved him by their pulling the pilot out of his seat and applying a tourniquet on his leg.

Almgren and I visited our friend in the hospital in Saigon. Lying next to him was a young soldier, heavily sedated, with no arms or legs. Our friend was under considerable medication, but considering all, doing well. He had serious damage to his leg and was going to be flown to Japan for reconstructive surgery. The doctors had, at one point, told him that he may lose his lower leg. The response: "If it means I get out of this place then take my leg!" The leg stayed on. I could not get out of the hospital fast enough.

PSYOPS

Psychological Operations, PSYOPS for short, was an attempt to persuade NVA and VC (Viet Cong) troops to give themselves up. On a PSYOPS mission we would mount loudspeakers and a tape player on the helicopter and broadcast messages explaining how disenchanted troops could surrender themselves. We also dropped leaflets containing the same message. I did not care for PSYOPS missions. I found them boring and dangerous. I certainly did not care for flying around below three thousand feet making a target of myself while trying to sell the enemy an idea they did not want to hear.

The day had been as boring as I expected it would be as we flew about, speakers blasting and leaflets flying. Below, an American grunt company was dug in. They called us on the radio and explained they had a problem. Apparently, the night before, they had come under attack and had lost one man. During the fire-fight a VC was also killed. The VC's body lay a few hundred yards from their perimeter. As the day wore on the grunts noticed more Vietnamese in the vicinity of the corpse. The grunts attempted to chase away or kill the individuals they saw, but with no success. They were growing nervous and agitated with the combination of the activity in the air and on the ground. I received an order on the radio to engage the individuals in question with our door guns. The loud speakers were shut off and the

M-60s started to blaze away. Once the Vietnamese realized what was happening they started to run while machine gun rounds struck the dirt all around them. They ran until they were exhausted. We descended until it was possible to see the Vietnamese were unarmed, and women. They had stopped trying to escape and just turned to face us. We did not fire anymore.

DEATH OF A FRIEND

Most of the army helicopter pilots in Vietnam were warrant officers. Warrants had very little military training in command of troops. As a result many of us took our flying a bit more seriously than many RLOs (real live officers) who had other duties. Since I held the rank of warrant officer, I was not considered qualified by the army to lead or command other than as an Aircraft Commander.

As the months passed I became more senior amongst Bravo's pilots. My flying skills improved to the point I was ready for more responsibility. Since the company needed pilots to serve extra duties it was normally the responsibility of a warrant officer to serve as the company instructor pilot (IP). I was asked to become the company IP.

Letter to home dated February 5, 1969

"Well, once again I am grounded, only this time it is for a different reason. It appears that since I have flown over one hundred and forty hours during the past thirty days I am required to take three days off. I think it is a good idea. I needed the rest.

Good news. I am going to become an instructor pilot for our company. I will be giving ninety day check rides to all the pilots and in-country check rides to the new people. Needless to say I am proud of myself since not everybody makes I.P. while in Vietnam; however, just about everyone becomes one back in the States."

My job as an IP required me to become more familiar with the UH-1. I would be giving company check rides to all pilots and would be required to ensure they knew the limitations, systems, and procedures of the aircraft we all flew. It was also necessary to develop skills in emergency procedures such as engine and hydraulic failures. It was a good thing for me as a pilot to hone these skills in any case. I felt good about being an IP.

One of my new duties was to give check rides for Aircraft Commander (AC). The check ride for this endorsement would normally be a full day in length during which the applicant would demonstrate that he was ready for those responsibilities.

I was also given the extra duty of Safety Officer. Perhaps the CO (commanding officer) felt that as a result of my accident I had developed into one of the more safety conscious pilots, making me a good choice for the job. The position required little other than to remind everyone of safety by conducting meetings on the subject and to observe daily operations...looking for safety transgressions. I took this extra duty seriously also.

Mike LeMaster had done a lot of flying since our accident. He had become a candidate for AC by virtue of his time in country and hours flown. He had a few questionable habits as a pilot and had been given the unkind nickname of "Bore Sight." It was a topic of discussion whether or not Mike was ready to be trusted with the responsibilities of commanding a helicopter in Vietnam. Mike felt very adamant that he was ready and should be given a chance to prove himself. It was my job as the company instructor to make that decision.

The check ride did not progress very well. Mike's flying skills had come a long way since our accident, but on this day he had done a few things wrong that concerned me. In all fairness, he was under a lot of pressure. Not only was he the target of peer criticism but he was flying with me---the guy riding next to him when he had flown into a tree a few months earlier. All this aside, I was preparing myself to give Mike a thumbs down on this day. Maybe in a few more weeks he would be ready, but not yet.

I think Mike knew what I felt as we flew along at three thousand feet, but he said nothing. I was flying the helicopter when suddenly our engine failed. I lowered the collective stick and entered autorotation and told Mike to get on the radios and call Mayday! There was a very large rice patty within glide distance and we autorotated safely to it. As I maneuvered the helicopter, Mike worked the radios feverishly. We touched down and came to a stop. My recent practice with power failures had paid off. Meanwhile the rotor blades had barely come to a stop when an air force jet fighter began to orbit us at low altitude. He was soon joined by numerous other aircraft. If there were a Viet Cong who wanted to take a shot at us he must have thought better of it. I was amazed at how many aircraft had responded to Mike's radio calls for help. He had performed admirably to say the least.

I gave Mike LeMaster thumbs up on his AC check ride.

Not long after the engine failure I conducted a safety meeting. The topic for the night was the proper fit of our flight helmets. I invited an army flight surgeon to discuss the subject. We were all asked to put on our flight helmets and allow the doctor to inspect all of our fits. One man, a First Lieutenant, was singled out by the doctor as having a perfect fitting helmet. All the rest of us failed. The remainder of the meeting was devoted to adjusting helmet straps and pads. I felt the meeting was constructive.

My efforts as an Aircraft Commander, instructor pilot, and safety officer were draining me. It was during this time period that I did a great part of my one thousand hours of the flying I would eventually do while in Vietnam. I needed a rest. I was sent to Vung Tau for a few days. Vung Tau was a coastal town used for in country R&Rs. For me it was a boring place, but it was restful and that was what I needed...rest. I remember drinking beer, eating pizza...little else. I began looking forward to returning to duty.

Letter to home dated April 3, 1969

"Fifty six days today. I am starting to get the short timers shakes. I am still flying almost every day and I will probably continue doing so until I leave.

I received my orders. I am going to Hunter Army Airfield in Savannah, Georgia."

Letter to home dated April 28, 1969

"They say the offensive is over but I tend to disagree. The Cav has been hit pretty hard during the past week. I won't be going into details. You can find those in the papers. I am trying to fly as little as possible, but that still puts me up every other day. So it looks like my last month here is going to be an interesting one.

Good news. My C.O. has given me a three day R&R in country. I will be spending it on the coast at Vung Tau. It should be a good break from the old routine. It will start on the third of May. I will see you in thirty one days!"

The accident occurred on May 4, 1969.

Upon my return to Bravo Company I learned we had lost two aircraft in a mid-air collision while I had been away. All eight crewmembers had perished...among them Mike LeMaster and the First Lieutenant with the perfect fitting helmet. The helmet was found still on his head despite him having been decapitated.

The loss of my friends had a depressing effect on me. Vietnam stopped being an adventure; it became a morbid ordeal I had to endure. This was not the first time I encountered death during my time in Vietnam, but it was the first time it visited my family. I knew most of the eight crewmembers well; their passing was felt deeply by all of us who remained in Bravo.

I had twenty five days remaining in Vietnam.

MOST CAME HOME---SOME DID NOT

I had passed into the last phase of my Vietnam experience...I was getting very close to going home. A very "short timer."

The date was May 11, 1969. I was on one of my last flights. It had been an uneventful day and my crew and I were thinking of going home and notching another day off the calendars.

I don't know what kind of day WO-1 Jim Gilbert and Sergeant Paul Rodriquez had been having as they flew their OH-6 scout helicopter. I bet both men had a short timer's calendar and dreamed of a new car upon their return home. I would never have the honor of meeting them.

Late in the afternoon both of our aircraft were contacted by operations. A grunt unit was under heavy attack and running short of ammunition. We were needed to fly in more. The LZ would be hot and too small to land in. It would be necessary to fly the cargo in externally, which meant our slick would be a sitting duck as it hovered with an external load. Gilbert and Rodriquez would go in first and attempt to draw attention away from us as we delivered the load onto the drop point.

Upon initial radio contact with the grunt unit we were advised from which direction to approach from to avoid known enemy positions. The OH-6 scout would be in the lead, helping provide cover fire for us. We made the approach while the scout flew ahead. After dropping off the load, we did a one hundred and eighty degree pedal turn, pulled in maximum power and departed the way we had come in without taking any hits. Gilbert and Rodriquez were not so lucky; their machine was shot down and exploded in flames. Both men died.

In about eighteen days I would be going home. Those grunts we helped had enough ammunition to ward off the attack. WO-1 James Gilbert and Sergeant Paul Rodriquez are enshrined on the Wall in Washington. I do not ever visit the Wall without paying respects to them.

MAY 29, 1969

On May 29, 1969 CW-2 Paul Kearns found himself sitting amongst a group of homeward bound short timers at Saigon's airport waiting to board the Freedom Bird for the trip home. I was a different young man than had arrived three hundred and sixty five days earlier, much older in some ways, still very young in others. My age was twenty two.

While we waited to board, another plane arrived and disembarked a group of FNGs, most of whom had three hundred and sixty five days remaining in Vietnam. A loud cheer erupted from us short timers. Not long after, another loud cheer erupted as our Freedom Bird lifted off the runway and headed east, the dust and smoke of Vietnam sinking behind us.

EPILOGUE

My life was profoundly affected by my experience in Vietnam, and by the country that awaited me upon my return. Most Vietnam veterans found no parade when they returned. Our country was being torn apart by the war in Vietnam. The veterans of it found little praise. Instead, we found contempt and pity. Politically, Vietnam was the first war America lost. At such a young age, it was difficult to separate myself from the political war awaiting me after returning from the real war. People who had not served, and did not understand, ridiculed my pride for what I had survived and accomplished. It would be some years before I was able to put many of those ghosts from that part of my life in their proper place, and regain a sense of balance and understanding. And yes... pride.

America would struggle in Vietnam for six more years after my return home. The last news image of the war I remember is of a helicopter evacuating South Vietnamese from the roof of the American Embassy in Saigon to American ships waiting off shore. I was no longer in the Army. I had recently married and was working as a civilian helicopter pilot when America extracted itself from Vietnam.

May the more than 58,000 Americans and uncounted hundreds of thousands of Vietnamese who died in that war rest in peace, and may the rest of us who came home not forget them.

T.I.N.S.*

This Is No Shit

Bruce E. Carlson

Lowering the nose of his little Red Bird and pulling in an arm load of power, Kev made for the next hill top. This rapidly accelerated the little Red Bird up to thirty or forty knots making them a more difficult target. Then, rolling to the right, his side of the helicopter, he pulled in maximum power and began a zoom climb to the top of the hill. Bam! Bam! Bam! Five, ten, maybe fifteen rounds of fifty-one caliber anti-aircraft fire went off no more than a dozen feet from them. Horrified, Kev and Johnny felt the hot muzzle blast banging on their legs. The two of them didn't exchange a word. No words were necessary. They knew it. The future had become fact and no F-4s were close by to save them.

Abruptly and rudely, the bad guys had transformed them into three dead men flying in a little helicopter! It was only a matter of seconds before the heavy anti-aircraft rounds tore the three of them into hundreds of bloody little pieces. "Break - Break. All Cav aircraft immediately break down the valley to the south! Hit the deck! Heavy caliber anti-aircraft. White Birds do not engage! Number two; follow the White Birds out of the valley at best possible speed. I repeat. White Birds do not engage. Everyone on the Yellow Scarf net, Get the hell out of here! I'll join you guys later." The way Kev saw things, his wing man or the two White birds would get themselves blown out of the sky if they tried to help him. Terrified, Kev wasn't trying to be a hero. However, he accepted that the grim situation was his problem. He had stumbled into the anti-aircraft trap like a rank and raw rookie. Anger replaced fear. This was the second time in a couple of weeks he had stumbled into a trap. Kev was supposed to be the hunter and not the hunted. "Well," he thought to himself. "It will only be my problem for another second or two. Join them later. Now, that's a laugh." Just as suddenly as it had started, it stopped. Unexpectedly, the fifty-one had stopped firing! Finding they were still very much alive and well, the three young men in the little helicopter were surprised and shocked. A heartbeat later, the reason for their reprieve began to become clear to them. It appeared that if they stayed below the crest of the hill, they were safe. At least, they were safe for the moment. The bad guys couldn't depress the muzzle of the heavy, anti-aircraft, machine gun low enough to shoot at them. If nothing else, the Mexican standoff, of sorts, gave them a moment's breather. However, they were well aware their good fortune wasn't going to last all day. If nothing else happened to ruin their day, they would run out of fuel soon enough.

Drawing upon his deep pool of leadership skills, Kev came up with a big fat blank. He didn't have a ready answer for the potentially fatal, problem they were facing. Later that night, Kev wrote in his journal about how he initially felt when the fifty-one opened fire on him. Never let anyone say that when he was totally terrified, that Kevin Paul Johnson was too proud to ask for help. Most likely, I had involuntarily deposited a smelly dark brown coating inside my skivvies. However, I decided not to address the odorific problem of brown and smelly underwear. Putting first things first, I didn't figure I would be the first man to die in combat with a big brown load in his britches. Keying the intercom, I mentally crossed my fingers that someone on this helicopter was a whole big-bunch smarter than I was or that I had been. "Anyone have a brilliant idea or two that you would like to share with me? If you happen to have one, now is a really good time to do so. Because, I am afraid that the minute that we make a break for it and head down the valley, that gun is going to have a clear shot at us. I promise, when they're done with us, it ain't going to be a very pretty picture. By the way, let's keep this little piece of information just among the three of us guys. Between you, me, and the lamp post, I think that we're in some very deep shit. Whatever happens, though, I don't want the other guys coming back to try and get us out of this mess."

People have an incredible variety of responses to danger and fear. Some like Charley Bird, as Kev had discovered months ago, freeze up. Others, and Kev had occasionally done so himself, got twitchy and highly excitable. Some, and Kev truly envied those people, become cool as a cucumber fresh out of the ice box. The largest numbers of folk, grimly grit their teeth, bear down, and do the best they can. These people are usually hesitant to acknowledge their fear. Generally, Kev acknowledges his fear. At times, he seemed to embrace it as something evil with which he must compete. While he was competing with his fear for ultimate control, he usually got a little mouthy and sarcastic. Finally, when he had come up with a plan of action, he then boldly challenged his fear and the source of his fear. This was when ole Kev was at his best and at his worst. The problem was he could become brave to the point of being foolhardy. Two quick circuits around the crest of the hill and Kev won the battle for ultimate control. With that critical battle won, his fangs came slashing out of both sides of his mouth. Uncontrolled, they smashed their way straight through the worn metal floor of the cockpit. He was mad as hell. However, what was worse in his eyes, he was professionally embarrassed by stumbling into another trap. "By God!" He said to himself. "If, I'm going to die, I'm going to die on my terms, and on my terms alone!" Pride and ego are a two-edged sword. It got Kev into trouble. He decided it was time to cut with the back edge of the sword. Kev's fight with the anti-aircraft gun suddenly became very personal.

The heavy gun had surprised him and scared him almost to death. Its profound threat to unarmored helicopters had deprived him of his Cobra gun cover. He knew the Snakes would probably be "dead meat" if they took on the gun trying to protect him while he was busy escaping. Ole Kev had never lost a Snake. He was proud no Snake had taken as much as a single hit protecting him. Foolish to others, possibly, it was an important part of his protective instincts. Kevin Paul Johnson wasn't going to allow anyone to change that score card. The bad guys had broken up their smooth team work and this made Kev mad. Using but a handful of bullets, a crew of three to five bad guys had forced the Cav to run from the valley. Embarrassing to Kev, it was running with its tail tightly tucked between their collective legs. Suddenly, the hot blood began throbbing and pounding through his veins. This surge of pride and emotion gave Kevin Paul Johnson no choice. It was time to even the score. Savagely, he stabbed at the intercom button and spoke in a coldly calm voice. "Here's the hot skinny, guys. I'm really pissed off. We're going to take that SOB out! Now, guys, give me a couple of good ideas." Johnny immediately responded. "I'm with ya boss. That SOB just scared me out of ten years of life. He's got exactly what's coming to him." A third voice, belonging to Pete, issued a low groan of dismay over the intercom. "Dear God, help me. I am going to die with two homicidal maniacs!" A second or two passed without a brilliant idea being tossed into the arena. The mike clicked. A quiet and hesitant voice spoke. "Somehow, I just know I'm going to regret this. What do you guys think about a mini arc light?" Just as Pete had instinctively feared, two enthusiastic voices greeted his hesitant suggestion by sounding their total approval. Muttering something to himself about two homicidal maniacs who were determined to get him killed, Pete grimly went about tightening up his crash harness. One of the most awesome, if not always the most effective, weapons employed in Vietnam was the B-52 "arc light" attack.

The big, old eight-engine B-52, first entered the Air Force inventory in the early fifties. Boeing specifically designed it to deliver nuclear weapons over a vast distance. The Air Force had not designed the majestic old bird for the type of war the political types had dictated for Vietnam. Nevertheless, she could haul an impressive tonnage of conventional bombs. Trying to develop a devastating area weapon, someone thought of modifying some older B-52s. By adding some wing pylons and modifying the bomb bays, the grand old girl could drop something in the neighborhood of thirty, seven-hundred-and-fifty pound bombs. Unseen and unheard at thirty-thousand feet, she could drop all these bombs in a single continuous string. When these conventional bombs struck the dark jungle at night, the flash of them exploding rolled across the ground below. It looked like a welder's electric arc was being struck upon the face of the earth. The unfortunate troops who found themselves at the receiving end of an arc light, usually never knew what hit them. Once, in a beer soaked discussion, the Scout pilots agreed an arc light was almost unfair. Without sound, sight, or other warning, suddenly the earth would heave up and explode. The theory held they would so stun anyone who survived they would be unable to offer any meaningful organized resistance for a long time. Most of the people in the Cav believed that, generally, an arc light only made kindling wood and tore up the earth.

Having seen one from the air, the concentration of fire power nevertheless deeply impressed Kev. In full daylight, he could clearly see the bright welder's arc being struck by the exploding bombs. Sometime, long before Kev joined the Cav, an enterprising Scout got the idea the little Red Birds could copy the big boys. Most likely, after a case or two of beer, the idea of the mini arc light was born. In practice, the lead scout would fly, at twenty to thirty knots, over a bunker complex, small base camp, or other suspected enemy concentration. As they passed over it, they would drop as many fragmentation grenades as possible. Over time, the Cav style mini arc light became well refined. The most important innovation was the placing of a couple of open hooks in the door frames. After their pins were straightened out, the frag grenades would then be suspended upon the hooks by their rings. When the time came to drop them, the hooks allowed the crew members to rake the grenades out like bunches of grapes. Just as a static line opened a parachute, the hook pulled the pins and released the spoons on the grenades. In fact, they came to a point where a good lead bird could put twenty-five to thirty grenades into the area roughly the size of a football field. It wasn't a B-52 strike. No one pretended it was. However, for anyone on the ground, who wasn't well protected, it was just as devastating. Furthermore, it did serve to save the Snakes' rockets which cost one-hundred and twenty-five dollars each.

The well-hidden fifty-one had trapped Kev. He had no Snakes, no rockets, no wingman with a mini-gun, and he was quickly running out of fuel and time. Other bad guys would soon be moving into position to shoot at him as he circled the hill. However, Kev had now unsheathed his fangs. He had not done, nor was he going to do a rational cost analysis of their next move. By this point, Kev was well beyond doing a rational analysis of anything. This does not mean he was caught-up in a berserker's blood lust. Yet, Kev and Johnny's blood was pounding fiercely in their veins. They were going to kill that fifty-one cal. anti-aircraft gun! The whole meaning of life was that straightforward to them. Pete, on the other hand, did not share their lust for the kill. However, he trusted them. Best of all, he knew when Kev's fangs were drawn, they would win. Not only would they win and tell tall tales about it later, when they counted their day as finished they would have put a serious hurt on the bad guys.

One and a half turn around the hill the three of them were set to go. Safety pins had been straightened out on every fragmentation grenade in the little helicopter. Johnny then keyed the intercom first. "All set boss. I've got fifteen hanging on hooks with straight pins and four with pins pulled in my hands." Pete quickly chimed in. "I've got eight on hooks and four in hand, with pins pulled." Kev acknowledged both and added, "Pete set me up with eight on hooks. If nothing else, I do believe we are going to be going for the record on this one, guys."

During the couple of minutes which passed since the fifty-one opened up on them, Kev had eventually gotten their airspeed up to ninety knots. He felt confident this would give him enough airspeed to make their attack and begin their escape. Making a quick mental check, he decided everything was set for them to even the score. "OK, guys. Here's the straight scoop. With just a little luck, they have had great difficulty tracking us by sound only. I'm going to red line the power and then zoom-climb the hill to the crest. I want you guys to be ready for the hairiest helicopter ride of your life. When I start the climb, I am going to pull back hard on the stick. I promise it will feel like she is going all the way over on her back. As we crest the hill, I am planning on facing the opposite direction from which we have been going. Hopefully, that'll cross them up. If they are where I think they are, when I crest the hill and level my wings, we'll be right on top of them. We're going to dump our little basket of eggs right on their heads before they even figure out where we came from. I'll call the drop. Remember; don't drop till you get my command! Everybody set?" Pete clicked his mike button twice in acknowledgment. Johnny responded. "Let's do it. Let's fix this bastard." "Ready? . . . Now!"

Without consciously thinking about it, Kev knew it was time to find out if he was as good as he thought. Trusting his flying instincts and spatial awareness, he went for broke. Holding his breath, Kev yanked the collective stick to the upper stop, pulled the control stick all the way to the back stop, and about half way to the left. Groaning and shuddering, the airspeed quickly began to bleed off and that OH-6 began climbing like an express elevator. Kev had no idea what the instruments were indicating. Looking over his left shoulder, and through the rotor disk, Kev was watching the side of the hill which appeared to be beneath him. He was trying to keep his orientation in relation to the hill. Hearing the low RPM warning in his earphones, Kev eased the upward pressure slightly on the collective stick till the beeper stopped. The forward airspeed bled off to almost nothing. Then, Kev pushed the control stick most of the way forward. Rocketing up the hill, it seemed to those inside her, that the little helicopter was upside down and standing on her tail. The clock stopped and Kev wished he could have been on the outside watching. Hughes Helicopter never designed their little Loach to do the things that Kev had coached her into doing! He was making her fly like she was an F-4 cooking on both afterburners!

At the apex of his zoom climb, about twenty-five feet above the top of the hill, the laws of physics equaled out. The little bird stood still and became weightless for an instant. Kev then stomped in full left pedal, reduced the collective a bit, gave her hard right stick, and pushed the stick to the forward stop. He felt vindicated. His instincts had paid off in spades. An angry young man had turned the tables on the bad guys. The little Red Bird was once again the hunter to be feared. She had become the hawk who scented blood and was about to smash the mouse! For the brief instant, which once or twice in a lifetime seems to last for an eternity, the vengeful hawk was weightlessly suspended above her vulnerable prey. Nose down, Kev had pointed ole 662 directly at the menacing AA site.

A separate part of Kev, who was observing the whole thing, marveled at what was revealed to his eyes. The little bird gave him a panoramic view of the bad guys. Pointing its muzzle about thirty degrees to his right was the fifty-one caliber AA gun. At last, the target was easy to see, no longer was it covered by camouflage. Fifteen foot long tongues of flame were jetting from its muzzle as it vainly spat forth death. Tasting the joy of a clean kill of pure vengeance, Kev was unconcerned. The little Red Bird was not where the bad guys had expected it to be. Suddenly, the clock began rapidly sweeping forward. The little Red Bird started to slowly swoop down upon the abstract figures in NVA uniforms. Somehow disinterested, Kev watched them as they were scurrying here and there seeking cover. Other distant men were cranking furiously at the traverse wheel of the AA gun. In desperation they were trying to bring it to bear upon the swooping hawk. Holding his eagerness carefully in check, and coldly looking at the scene before him, Kev knew they had only one chance to kill that big gun. The game clock had stopped ticking and only this play remained. One play would bring the game to its deadly conclusion. In Kev's mind, it was gamesmanship at its best. Winners take all and no consolation prize for the loser! It was the only way to play the game!

From the edge of his vision, he saw muzzle flashes. They sprouted from several AK-47s and were dotting the area. Shutting them out of his mind, he totally ignored them. Emotionally zeroed in on the kill, Kev bore down on the slow dive. Thumbing the mike button, he loudly hollered. "Now! Now! Now!" Jamming his left leg under the collective stick, he controlled both pedals with his right foot. Simultaneously, he transferred the cyclic stick to his left hand. With his right hand freed, he frantically raked off his eight fragmentation grenades. Everyone was doing his part. Vindicated, Kev had finished the hard part of the flight. Almost as an afterthought, he was adding his little bit to the rain of death showering down upon the AA site. With speed building rapidly, Kev continued his dive down the other side of the hill to the valley floor. Turning and twisting, he began running for his life. Just as the rim of the hill flashed past him, the sweetest symphony his ears had ever heard rewarded his audacious flying. A rolling thunder of many small explosions silenced the booming base beat of the AA gun. It was a special thunder thumped out by more than thirty frag grenades of a Cav style, mini arc light. For the first time in the last five, or less, minutes, Kev allowed himself to breathe. They were part way down the valley doing one-hundred and eighteen knots and all remained quiet. If that AA gun was still operable, it had a clear shot at the fleeing Red Bird. It hadn't shot at them yet. They must have killed it. Relieved and exuberant, Kev keyed the intercom. "I think we pulled it off guys." Just as Kev finished on the intercom, a concerned voice finally got past the blood lust pounding in his ears. "Red Two-Eight, where in the bloody blue blazes, are you?" "Oops! Sorry about that Blue Six. I got a little preoccupied and forgot to keep you informed. We're about half way out of the valley and will be at your location in no more than zero two. The three of us are just fine and we are awaiting the pleasure of serving your needs." With a well-earned, and justified, touch of pride in his voice, Kev added. "Oh, by the way sir. We just killed the fifty-one! If you want to go back in and get it so we can take it home, we're ready to go." "Negative on that, Two-Eight. Big Boss Six decided the valley was a little hotter than he was looking for. He told us to pack up our bags and call it an early day. We'll meet you back at the barn."

Later that evening, at the club, the beer was flowing by the gallon. The Cav pilots were getting a little rowdy as the major sipped a beer at the little bar. Full of life and the spirit of adventure, Kev and Sven invited him to join them for a moment. Joining them at their table, the major asked. "OK Johnson, shoot straight with me. Did you guys really take out that fifty-one?" Sobering slightly, Kev put on his straightest serious face and assured the major Pete and Johnny had taken it out. "I'm just the truck driver, Sir." Sven could take it no longer. "Sir, that's not the story that I heard. Pete and Johnny told me, and I quote, 'That was positively the best (many descriptive and colorful words) piece of flying that they had ever seen.' They should know sir. They've flown with all of us. Who would know better? They were right there when it happened." Those two guys agreed Kev had delivered them perfectly for the mini arc light. Pete added, "That crazy SOB even added eight grenades of his own to the pattern while flying one-handed."

Full of cold beer, excitement, and young life, Sven was completely fired up. Nothing was holding his exuberance back. "Sir, I was thinking." Kev and the major groaned in unison. They found the thought of Sven thinking amusing. Ignoring their unfounded disrespect of his intellect, he continued. "It's not fair that the Air Force pukes get all the great missions. I think that we should become the Army's first 'Wild Weasel' outfit. What the heck, Sir. All the necessary parts are in place. We mere mortal pilots can spend our time unmasking AA batteries. When we find them, we'll have ole Kev along to kill them for us." Laughing and shaking his head, the major responded. "I don't know, Sven. The Air Force guys might just get a little upset if we use inexpensive little Red Birds to do a job that they need Fox 4s to accomplish." Going along with the joke, but also, with a generous helping of beer, a little enamored with the idea of being a Wild Weasel, Kev quickly spoke up. "Sounds like fun to me, Sir. I'll give it a shot, but only on one condition. That is, that we get to use ole Sven here for AA bait." The whole conversation was getting to be too much for the major. Laughing, he excused himself with his own semi-serious comment. "I'm going to go now. If I stay here any longer, you two brainless idiots will talk me into something that we'll all regret when we sober up."

The Final Flight of Curious Yellow

David Hansen

Tomorrow is Veterans' Day – a beautiful weekend lies ahead. The sky is brilliant blue against red sandstone cliffs. The desert air is clean with a light scent of sagebrush. This is an afternoon worth living for.

The cell phone rings – an unfamiliar caller ID.

"Dave, this is Eddie Iacobacci in Florida. You won't believe who just called!"

Whoa. Eddie and I had recently exchanged numbers at the DMZ Dust-off reunion after a gap of 35 years, yet I am surprised he is actually calling.

"You remember the pickup on Hill 950?" he asked.

My pulse rate begins to increase. Of course I remember. No one involved could have forgotten.

"One of the guys we picked up, was a Green Beret named Roger Hill, and, his nephew Bobby Hill has spent three years searching for the crew. He wants to talk to you…TONIGHT!"

Unbelievable! Characters from a distant past life-and-death drama are suddenly reconnecting. What did we each remember?

Dust-off Huey Curious Yellow

Sgt. Roger L. Hill
Special Forces, Hill 950, north of Khe Sanh
June 4, 1971

Front:Roger Hill. Background: SSG. Jon Cavaiani, June 4, 1971

It began at dawn when a Bru* striker anxiously entered my bunker, exclaiming "Trung Se, VC #10... Trung Se, VC #10." I immediately followed him to the northwest corner of our hilltop location. As I peered over the wall, about 20 feet in front of me was a 20-pound Claymore. This sight scared the hell out of me, and it felt like my knees just gave way. I went straight down into the slit trench, pulling the Bru with me, alerting everyone on the wall. After the initial scare, I immediately began moving around the perimeter to survey the situation. I discovered seven Chicom Claymores placed in positions where helicopters would approach the hilltop. They were set to knock down helicopters, because they go off like a giant shotgun.

*The Bru are an ethnic group living in Thailand, Laos, and Vietnam.

Hill 950, looking south toward Khe Sanh

We decided I would go outside the perimeter with three Brus, then try to approach the back of the Claymore, and attempt to capture or kill the North Vietnamese soldiers who had to be somewhere close by the mine. They would be observing us or any helicopters that would come into view, at which time, the mine could be activated. I exited the north-east edge of our perimeter, and was approaching an area behind the mine, when an RPG (B-40 Rocket) was fired, coming from my left rear and exploding on the ground directly in front of me. When it exploded, I was facing south. When the dust cleared, I realized I had been blown approximately 10-15 feet to the north, and was facing in the opposite direction. I was wounded, as were two of the Brus with me, one at the base of his tailbone, and the other in his neck. The only thing we could do was get ourselves back inside the perimeter.

After the first B-40 rocket exploded, the action intensified. SSG Jon Cavaiani (who received the Congressional Medal of Honor for his action on this day) was stationed above me on the perimeter wall, covering us with a .50 cal. machine gun as I gathered the Brus, and scrambled to get back inside the perimeter. Additional B-40 rockets exploded around us. Once inside the compound, we moved down the slit trench on the north side, to a bunker located on the north wall. I went inside the bunker with the wounded Brus, to receive treatment from our indigenous medic. After receiving care, we moved to the slit trench on the north side of the compound, while the entire camp was receiving intense fire from heavy machine guns and 75mm recoilless rifles. The majority of the fire was coming off the top of Elevation 1015, approximately 1000 meters to our east.

East end of Hill 950, the ground attack came here

We were taking direct fire into our compound, our bunkers were being flattened, and the entire eastern end of the camp was almost instantaneously destroyed. The north, south, and west end of the camp became our defensive positions, since we no longer controlled the east end of the compound. After a while, the artillery fire abated because the Communist soldiers had entered our camp on the eastern end, apparently lifting their heavy weapons fire so their infantry could move in. Because of this, a hand grenade battle ensued. Although there was a limited amount of sporadic automatic weapons fire, we proceeded to toss hand grenades over the crest of the hill and at the North Vietnamese as fast as we could; they did the same to us. The Communist soldiers were close, and they couldn't bring their artillery fire any closer. We continued to toss grenades over the north, south, and west walls in an attempt to kill anyone attempting an approach from those directions.

At one point I was in the trench line with the two Brus wounded with me earlier when we received word a Dust-off (medevac) was on its way. We didn't know where it was going to come from or where it was going to put down. We did know we would get as many wounded as possible on the helicopter when it arrived. All I know is I was in a slit trench on the north side of the camp, facing to the east, when I heard the helicopter. As I looked in the sky, the 'Curious Yellow' helicopter was coming over the south-west wall, and it was flaring. Its nose was up in the air, and I could see the whole belly of the helicopter. Just like that, it set down on one of the low, flat top bunkers in the camp.

The sight of the helicopter was like a religious experience for me. It was like coming back from the dead - I can't even describe in words how I felt at the time. I moved toward the helicopter, with the two wounded Brus, and with assistance from other Brus we entered the helicopter on the left side. Very quickly and amid the explosions, the helicopter lifted and rolled right, heading over the cliff on the camp's south side. I remember looking out the left side of the helicopter at the mountain falling away from me and traveling past the trees and rocks.

Dust-off 702 enroute to Hill 950

Specialist Eddie A. Hopper
Crew Chief aboard Dust-off 702
June 4th, 1971

The weather and sky were clear, just about perfect conditions for flying. Within a couple of minutes and a 'clear left' and 'clear right' we were airborne. After a few minutes above highway QL1, we came to the 'Rock Pile.' I then locked and loaded my Thompson, and checked my .38 caliber pistol and my knife. I was thinking of a hoist mission Iacobacci and I had pulled at the Rock Pile not too long before.

After a few more minutes of flight, Hill 1015 came into view, and then Hill 950. After getting a little closer, we went into a holding pattern. I could see smoke coming off the east side of Hill 950. Gunships were on station and after they had made a couple of runs, it was time for us to go in.

Our approach was from the southwest and fast. As we came in along the tree line, it was quiet, too quiet. No one was firing at us!

Everything changed in the blink of an eye; as Dave landed the helicopter, all hell broke loose! Explosions were going off in front and to the east side of the helicopter sending a lot of shrapnel through the air. I moved to my left next to our medic to help get the wounded on board. Specialist Iacobacci was taking shrapnel hits in his "chicken-plate" body armor, and the wounded were being hit as well. Sgt. Shaughnessy got his M60 going just as the F4 Phantom jet with heavy machine guns came in.

Sgt. George Shaughnessy, Volunteer Gunner

After loading as many wounded as we could, our AC, David Hansen, lifted our helicopter and dropped off the side of the cliff. As soon as we departed, both east and west sides of the hill opened fire on us with machine-guns and small arms. Sgt. Shaughnessy, Specialist Iacobacci, and I returned fire. I then checked to my left for our medic and our pilots. Part of my job as Crew Chief was to keep eyes on the helicopter and crew at all times.

Once we were out of range of the small arms fire we needed a place to land, and fast. Both of our pilots were on the controls at the same time. Talk about flying by the seat of your pants! All of the hydraulics were shot out, and white smoke was coming from Curious Yellow. Somehow, our pilots found an old airstrip. The landing was beautiful and just in time, for we had lost all of our fuel as well.

Sgt. Shaughnessy, Specialist Iacobacci, and I got off the helicopter and formed a line to defend our position and our wounded. The Dust-off that came in to pick us up was from the 571st. The Dust-off's Crew Chief's name was Bowmann.

SP5 Edward Iacobacci
Medic aboard Dust-off 702
June 4th, 1971

SP5 Edward Iacobacci, Medic

It was a nice day for flying. There were five crew members on board. We stayed in a holding pattern that seemed too long. We were the first Dust-off to go in.

We were to get the most seriously-wounded out first. When we were loading the injured, I remember looking to the rear of the ship and seeing a line of other choppers. Dave Hansen said we had to go, and I said, "Just one more." There were explosions going off and small arms fire. As the last wounded was on board I yelled, "Let's go!"

As we lifted out, the emergency lights on the center control panel lit up with the alarm going off in the helmet headset. I yelled, "Fly the chopper!" There was no keying the mic, as hands were too busy. As we went over the edge of the firebase, small arms increased, and I told George to fire. As we cleared the area, Dave got control of the craft with the help of the co-pilot. They were both on the controls as it was very difficult to direct the motion of the chopper. George did not know what was going on; he had lost his mic hook-up. I told him we were going down, and I said it may not be a good landing.

Dave and the co-pilot got the chopper to the old air strip at Khe Sanh. I told the injured to hang on; it could be bad. When we landed, I unhooked the co-pilot. Ed Hopper, the Crew Chief, got the injured out while George and I set up security. The only other nearby Dust-off came in and picked us up.

We left the yellow-nose chopper at the air strip. I believe it stayed there for several months. All the injured and the crew were taken to the 18th Surgical Hospital in Quang Tri. About two or three weeks later, the medic and pilot of the Dust-off that picked us up were killed in an LZ not far from Khe Sanh.

WOI Milton Kreger, Pilot; and CW2 David Hansen, Aircraft Commander

CW2 David Hansen, Aircraft Commander
Dust-off 702
June 4, 1971

…we decided to make a top speed run straight at the LZ from the Southwest, coming in about 50 feet below the top of the pinnacle and flaring upward over the wall to lose the forward airspeed. The pandemonium in the LZ was contagious and I couldn't find the exact landing spot. Precious seconds were lost in confusion, and finally I just set the helicopter down on a low bunker top and had the patients thrown in the side door. At the same moment, multiple blasts exploded immediately in front of the helicopter - no doubt about it - we had to get out of there *now*, and not the way originally planned, which would have taken us into the explosions.

I picked the Huey up and dropped it sideways off the edge of the pinnacle in an extreme maneuver we called the 'falling leaf.' Looking straight downward through the side window at green foliage about a thousand feet below, we would fall erratically past rocky crags sheltering NVA soldiers, making it hard for them to lead us with rifle fire. Unfortunately, we were not lucky.

In the midst of this gambit - falling through the air like a pickup truck - we took heavy fire and the emergency panel began to light up. The hydraulics went out and suddenly we couldn't control the position of the ship. We were falling faster and faster toward the ground; it now seemed certain we would crash at high speed, killing everyone.

Somehow the ship leveled out, and as soon as the crisis was over, analytical thinking resumed - the next problem was fuel. At the start of the approach we had just enough to return to Quang Tri, and now the gauges seemed to have dropped markedly. Had the tanks been ruptured? Would we run dry before getting back to the airfield? We couldn't safely land at any of the small firebases between Khe Sahn and Quang Tri without hydraulics, and Steve Woods (Dust-off 509) reported seeing white smoke coming from our aircraft. The only solution was a 'hydraulics off' landing at the abandoned runway at Khe Sahn, even though it was now surrounded by NVA forces.

View of Hill 950 from Khe Sanh

The wind was out of the west, so Kreger and I working together, lined up an approach from the east and brought 'Curious Yellow' down for a running landing, like an airplane, on the rusty, perforated steel plates of the old Khe Sahn runway. With the screeching grind of metal sliding on metal, the aircraft slowed to a stop. Now the problem was how to avoid becoming POWs.

Shaughnessy, who had insisted on coming along as a gunner after listening to the mission request in the radio shack, jumped out and ran to the edge of the runway, kneeling with his M60 machine gun to set up a perimeter. Others joined him. When I opened the door and looked back, there sat Steve Woods' helicopter, along with Joel Dozhier's ship (Dust-off 713) our angels of mercy. They had touched down the same moment we slid to a stop on the steel plates. The crew worked rapidly, moving the patients to Steve and Joel's birds and in only a few minutes we were ready to go. Shaughnessy was the last one aboard, closing out his perimeter. "Its rotor blades were still slowly turning as we lifted off over the top of Curious Yellow."

Dust-off Hueys headed for Khe-Sanh

One Generation Later....

R. W. "Bobby" Hill,
Sgt./ Forensic Sketch Artist
Erie Police Department,
Former 16th MP Brigade (ABN)
November 2006

"I grew up not only as the son of a Vietnam Veteran Green Beret, but also the nephew of a Vietnam Vet Green Beret, and the grandson of an original "Merrill's Marauder". Like every other kid

Bobby Hill displays his artwork on a hand-painted bomber jacket

in a military family, I began hearing "war stories" as a small child, and kept listening to them into my adult life. I became amazed by all the people, the places, and especially by aircraft, mainly the Huey helicopters. My Dad and Uncle Roger both insisted Hueys in Vietnam had saved their hides on several occasions.

I decided to conduct an "official" interview of my Uncle one night. I wanted the actual first-hand account of an incident, which had occurred six months before I was born. All I knew is the story took place on June 4, 1971. It involved a Huey medevac, and my uncle had been wounded and picked up while the base was being overrun by NVA. The interview was slow and deliberate, with every detail explained and every emotion described. He stated the helicopter was named "Mello Yellow" or something to that effect, and I could tell that it was very important to him. After I left that night, I thought, "Man, that helicopter crew is still young if they're alive, and I wonder how hard it would be to find them."

I drove home and decided I would start a secret project to try to locate any of them, and simply say "thank you". I determined which Medevac units were working in the area during that time, and began making phone calls and sending emails. Many Vietnam nurses and soldiers were very helpful, but I still had no luck until June 5th, 2006 when a guy named Phil Marshall emailed me. Phil was with the 237th Med Det (DMZ Dust-off), and said he thought that Huey had been in his unit. I emailed Phil for more info, and my heart raced. A couple of days later, a medic named Wayne "Doc Gordie" Gordon also emailed me and confirmed I had the right unit. I was literally in shock! Not long after that, one of the nurses from Quang Tri, Sandy Peterson, identified the crewmembers, and before long, I had some of their email addresses.

It was all happening quickly. They were all alive, and all within my reach. I wasted no time in making contacts, and making sure they were the ones. They made it clear their bird was called 'Curious Yellow'. It turns out none of them had ever spoken again with anyone they had picked-up in Vietnam. That idea shocked me, and I knew they had to meet my Uncle . . ."

Roger Hill and David Hansen
Erie, Pennsylvania
December 14th, 2006

Roger Hill and David Hansen, 2006

"At about 7:00 p.m. there is a knock on the motel room door. I'm a little anxious about this first meeting. I haven't seen Roger since we unloaded him at the 18th Surgical Hospital in Quang Tri. But as soon as the door opens, Roger and I are smiling and hug each other like old friends. We have a lot to talk about and soon feel very comfortable with each other."

"Roger told me all about his experiences on Hill 950, and filled in a lot of missing details. I told him what it felt like from the left seat of Curious Yellow."

Bobby Hill – April 2007

"Think about this: If the crew of 'Curious Yellow' had not crossed paths with my uncle for a few stressful moments thirty-five years ago, half my family tree would not exist! Yet, they never saw him again, and he was only one of thousands that they had saved, none of which they ever saw again. Furthermore, that UH1-H helicopter was only one of many Medevacs flying on one terrible day in Vietnam. I would like to thank ALL of you for doing a great job, past and present, and I would strongly encourage people to find the people they owe their lives to and thank them. They deserve it."

Excerpt from the Congressional Medal of Honor citation for S/Sgt. Jon Cavaiani:

. . . On the morning of 4 June 1971 the entire camp came under an intense barrage of enemy small arms, automatic weapons, rocket-propelled grenade and mortar fire from a superior size enemy force. S/Sgt. Cavaiani acted with complete disregard for his personal safety as he repeatedly exposed himself to heavy enemy fire in order to move about the camp's perimeter directing the platoon's fire and rallying the platoon in a desperate fight for survival. S/Sgt. Cavaiani also returned heavy suppressive fire upon the assaulting enemy force during this period with a variety of weapons. When the entire platoon was to be evacuated, S/Sgt. Cavaiani unhesitatingly volunteered to remain on the ground and direct the helicopters into the landing zone.

Diary of a Chopper Pilot

February 12th, 1971.

This isn't the stuff I usually write about but it will do for now. Even the atmosphere has changed a lot. Today is one of the worst days I have spent in 'Nam'. We lost two Cobras today. One went in with the crew aboard. The area was real bad.

Heavy stuff all over. So far I have been lucky. I haven't taken a hit. Whether it will hold out or not only time will tell. This is two times maybe three times worse than Cambodia. Laos is in a class all by itself. We haven't lost any LOH (Light Observation Helicopters) crews yet.

This (the Laos action) is something I wanted the U.S to do but they are doing it with ARVN troops. Another thing, I don't want to leave in the middle of this operation, but then again, I do. I feel that when I leave I won't be finishing my job, but it's only a matter of time before I get killed. It's funny, but out here I don't have the worry I had at Phu Bai.

I am very dirty and tired beyond belief. Yet I still perform and survive so that I might go home in April. I have decided to take a well earned R&R to Hong Kong.

February 13th.

No. 390 was shot down today but Pascoe made it back. Our first LOH shut up. I am surprised at myself, especially while in the field. I hope my extension comes through. Well, I am really out of words for now. If I live again to write in this book, I hope to have more to write. Well, good night. It's another night in Khe Sanh.

February 14th.

Valentines Day. Two ships shot up bad, but everyone is okay.

February 16th.

Still alive so far. It's pretty bad out there. Like nothing I have ever seen before. Weather is bad. Cold too. I am feeling well though. Dirty, but all right. My morale is okay. The flying is bad most of the time.

Have been acting platoon leader for two days now.

In about 60 days I will be home.

February 17th.

Nothing new today. No mail. Building bunkers like crazy out here. Must fly tomorrow. Thinking about my future and 60 days to go.

February 18th.

Bad day. Crandall was killed. I was supposed to take his mission. I flew eight hours. I worked the area right behind Crandall when he went down. I couldn't find a thing. That ship was just obliterated off the face of the earth. A weird day.

It was Crandall's first solo as a scout. He was feeling bad because he couldn't find anything on the ground like the rest of us, so he persuaded me to let him take my mission. He wanted to prove something. If he had more experience, he would have known we all have off days.

I told him to be fast, not slow down to mark the targets. But he got slow. I feel real bad. We trained him good.

February 19th.

Flew today into Laos, and took pictures. Nothing much going on. Got shot at bad by the way. Ran into a bunch of people on the (Ho Chi Minh) trail, and they opened up with AKs. No hits. Lucky me.

February 23rd.

I flew into Laos today. I got two kills, and saw a tremendous hooch (enemy hut). I had a lot of fun for a change.

February 24th.

Nothing is going on. Ferris and I are together again. We will have some fun like we did in Cambodia. Laos is different though. The good old days are over. No one really wants to fly out there anymore.

February 25th.

Not much really to write about. I am supposed to look for tanks out on Hill 31. Two LOHs were shot down today. They were out in the area where the Phantom pilots got shot down. One crew made it okay, but the other crew was hurt bad enough to go back to the 'world'. A pilot with a broken arm isn't worth nothing to nobody.

February 26th.

Flew into Laos. Things are looking up and I'm feeling good. I had this crazy dream where I was flying over Hill 31 and they shot me down. I went sideways into the hill. Weird.

February 27th.

Last night was a bummer. I flew to Quang Tri and waited around until dark, then flew to Phu Bai in marginal weather. Man did that shake. I caught vertigo once while enroute.

Well anyway, I woke up after sleeping all night at Phu Bai and then flew to Khe Sanh low level. That's the only way I fly anyway.

When I got there, no one else was around as usual. I know I got the day off. They say they aren't going to use the LOHs anymore until the anti-aircraft guns slow down. In a way I'm glad and in a way, I'm not.

Yesterday I was first standby and my 'Oscar' (observer) was a Special Forces guy. He knows his stuff but I told him it isn't peaches and cream out there. Well, we never got a chance to fly.

Today I told Butch I wanted to take two or three more missions in Laos so I can take some flicks (pictures), and maybe even get some tanks. Who knows? Simpson kind of got concerned about it and said no, but I told him I wouldn't get zapped.

The last time over in Laos, Pascoe hit them with C.S. (tear gas), frags (grenades) and Pete's (Willy Pete i.e., White Phosphorus rockets). I went in and they greeted me with a 21 gun salute.

I just heard that Nixon is going to send in some ground troops to rescue us if we go down. It should have been done long ago, with a lot more G.I.s. The flying will get a little better I think. If I get shot down, at least there will be Americans on the ground.

The whole spirit of the war will go up I think. At least it did when I flew in Cambodia.

Only 50 days left.

February 28th.

Well today is another one of those days where it hits you in the face about what you are doing. Butch got killed today. Only yesterday he was trying to take me off flight status because I was getting short. It's really a drag. He was kind of messed up in some ways, but getting killed makes you realize how good he was.

It's the second scout lost since I've been out here. I just got back from looking at the ship. Blood and guts everywhere, but Wilson still flew it back

I still want to be back out there, though even knowing I'm short. I must be crazy? It's been real hot lately and pilots getting killed doesn't help personalities either. The word's around about my new platoon leader (Butch was the old leader). I will have to break him in. It's weird. Among the scouts they say if you are new you will kill yourself within the first seven missions. So far, this has happened twice.

March 1st.

I just found out I have been wounded. A piece of shrapnel came out of my shoulder, and I didn't even know it was there. So I'm getting a Purple Heart.

"Bear", Ocelot and A Marine

John R. Fox

This story begins in the spring of 1965, at the 3rd Field Hospital, Saigon, Vietnam. It was dark and a voice was calling my name, "John! John!" I was so sleepy! Again, the voice called out "John! John!" It had a familiar sound to it. Slowly, the light turned gray with a large man standing over me. "St. Peter?" No, the shape is familiar now as my eyes began to focus more rapidly. It was Jim Church, my old friend and classmate. He had been assigned to Soc Trang seven months ago. "Jim! What are you doing here?" Suddenly I remembered where I was. "I came to Saigon to pick up a helicopter and heard you were here, and decided to check up on you."

Out of the corner of my eye I spotted this beautiful red-haired nurse (a Major) proceeding towards me. Surely, this must be the one the "Older Guys" referred to as "Old Ion Pants." Sternly, she approached with a tin cup in one hand and a long rubber hose in the other. Handing me the cup she demanded, "You've got 5 minutes to pee and fill it up." Raising the rubber hose she commented, "Or, I'll take it!" Immediate fear struck my heart! Doing an about face, she went striding off.

Jim began to giggle like a high school student, "Tee Hee! Tee Hee!" Panic stricken, I told Jim there was no way I could pee lying down. "Please help me stand up." As soon as my right leg touched the floor, lightning shot up with a fire from Hell; my surgery was due to an accident. Not being an atheist I cried, "Lord have Mercy! Help me pee in this damn cup!" Minutes went by before a small amount began to trickle. "Hurry! Hurry! Iron Pants will be back any minute with that

16 foot long rubber hose!" Half a cup was all I could manage. The pain in my leg was unbearable. Jim helped me back into bed, still giggling.

Here she comes! "Oh No!" The rubber hose was in her hand. Quickly, she picked up the cup, looked in it with a raised eyebrow, and commented, "It's not full, but it will be enough." Thank God, she turned and left with the HUGE rubber hose. Jim Church was laughing out loud saying he had to leave. We would not meet again for another year.

An aide approached with a gurney to take me to a room. Leaving the Recovery room Iron Pants stopped us, informing the aide to get me dressed, and then, get me over to the ER. She explained to me they were short of rooms. I lived in a local Villa where a flight surgeon resided and he agreed to look in on me as I recovered in my room.

I arrived in the ER to await our company driver, retired Vietnam Army Sergeant "Joe" with his ¾ ton truck. Shortly after, a young Warrant Officer was wheeled in still wearing his flight gear and right pants leg cut off. A bright red hole was exposed thru his shinbone. It was his first week in Nam and his first flight. The ER Doctor took one look and told the young pilot the bone was broken and he was going home! He begged the doctor to let him stay and fly again. I knew exactly how he felt. Flying was so important! I would fly again and again.

Joe arrived. Being unable to climb up into the cab of the truck, they put me in back to lie on the wooden seats. The ride thru Saigon traffic to the Villa was sheer terror and pain. Thankfully, I arrived in my room and bed and got more pain pills. My hooch maid, Nuyen Bai, called "Bear" because of her short chubby stature and strong personality, came in. Immediately, she took charge as my nurse, speaking loudly and sternly in pigeon English. I think she could have been a Viet Cong nurse at night, just like my barber turned out to be.

Bear returned shortly with chunks of pineapple heavily spiced with hot cinnamon, demanding "Eat! You Eat. Get well!" while stuffing a hot spiced chunk in my mouth. Finally, peace and calm settled in. I was listening to AFVN Radio and reading a stack of Rex Stout's detective stories. They were all written by Nero Wolfe, wherein the fat man, Stout, would solve all his cases without ever leaving his office and Orchids.

The headboard of my bed was against the wall to the adjoining room where a crazy former Marine roomed by himself. His desk and radio were on the other side of the wall. He would listen to the nauseating local Vietnamese music playing so loudly, I would use my crutch to pound on the wall, trying to get him to turn his radio down. This was one weird guy. He was a former Recondo Marine who decorated his room with a cargo-chute ceiling, bamboo furniture, pictures, and he burned incense candles. He was avoided at all times. No one wanted to fly with him. He also had acquired a parrot that sat on a rung in a cage. He kept it next to his desk so he could feed it and teach it to talk. One day he showed up with an ocelot in a cage, letting it out to roam his room when he was there. Bear and the other hooch maids would then never enter.

The third day began at 0800 with Bear and her charge of hooch maids arriving to gather up uniforms to be washed, and then clean the rooms. After most work was done, all the hooch maids would sit out in the hallway on these very tiny stools with 3 inch legs, to polish boots, gossip and eat snacks. The Villa was protected by V.N. Police (White Mice), but a lot of terror activities had begun to take place in Saigon.

Suddenly, around 1030 Hours a loud explosion occurred in the hallway. We were being attacked or mortared. The thud of fear hit my heart hard again! Bear was squalling out in the hallway amid much commotion by everyone, all in Vietnamese! Immediately, I leapt up with my crutch and AR-15 in hand. Lightning like pain hit me again. Overcoming fear and pain, I made it to the hallway in time to find Bear running around in circles speaking Vietnamese at the top of her lungs, holding up her short-legged stool (she had cut off the legs a few times and it was still too short). This had been a four-legged stool but now was down to three. Great noise and animal cries came from the Marine's room. I saw a chunk of tile missing under his door as I pushed it open. The Marine sat at his desk with pie-pan eyes, holding a .45 pistol pointed in my direction. The parrot was lying flat on his back, talons firmly gripping his perch rung. No, he had not been shot, but died of a heart attack when the .45 fired thru his cage. The ocelot was now racing around the room, three feet above the floor destroying everything in his path.

Full realization of what just happened hit the Marine. He had pulled the slide back on the .45 to clear the chamber. Then he released the magazine in preparation to clean the weapon, not realizing he had just chambered a round. He pulled the trigger to lower the hammer, and was met with a big bang. The round narrowly missed the parrot then hit the floor at the base of the door where Bear had been sitting on her tiny stool. This knocked off one stool leg, and ricocheted up into the wooden hallway entrance door.

This hilarious scene so overcame me and my painful leg that I laid down on the hallway floor holding my stomach from laughing so hard. The Flight Surgeon came running down the hall with his medical bag thinking I had been wounded, but could not understand why I was laughing so hard. Shortly after, the 120th Aviation Company Commander arrived.

After being put back in bed with more hot cinnamon pineapple, I decided it was time to return to the flight line. The Flight Surgeon put me on "light" flight duty. No IP or AC duties. Just sit and shut up. The next day the Marine, ocelot, and parrot disappeared from the Villa.

Next month the US Army was launched into full combat, led by the 173rd Airborne Brigade. I staged out of the Phouc Vinh Special Forces airstrip to begin my many more years of combat and future multiple Vietnam tours. Our lives and America would change.

Return to Table of Contents

Made in the USA
San Bernardino, CA
30 May 2016